Community Penalties

Cambridge Criminal Justice Series

Published in association with the Institute of Criminology, University of Cambridge

Community Penalties
Change and challenges

edited by

Anthony Bottoms
Loraine Gelsthorpe
Sue Rex

WILLAN
PUBLISHING

Published in association with the Institute of Criminology, University of Cambridge by

Willan Publishing
Culmcott House
Mill Street, Uffculme
Cullompton, Devon
EX15 3AT, UK
Tel: +44(0)1884 840337
Fax: +44(0)1884 840251
e-mail: info@willanpublishing.co.uk
website: www.willanpublishing.co.uk

Published simultaneously in the USA and Canada by

Willan Publishing
c/o ISBS, 5824 N.E. Hassalo St,
Portland, Oregon 97213-3644, USA
Tel: +001(0)503 287 3093
Fax: +001(0)503 280 8832
website: www.isbs.com

First published 2001
Reprinted 2002

ISBN 1-903240-49-2 (cased)

British Library Cataloguing-in-Publication Data
A catalogue record for this book is available from the British Library

Printed and bound by T.J. International, Padstow, Cornwall

Contents

List of figures   *vii*

Notes on contributors   *ix*

Preface   *xiii*

**1 Introduction: the contemporary scene for
community penalties**
The Editors   1

2 Community penalties in historical perspective
Mike Nellis   16

**3 Community penalties in the context of contemporary
social change**
Mark Liddle   41

**4 Beyond cognitive-behaviouralism? Reflections on the
effectiveness literature**
Sue Rex   67

5 Compliance and community penalties
Anthony Bottoms   87

6 Making 'What Works' work: challenges in the delivery
of community penalties
Andrew Underdown   117

7 Accountability in the delivery of community penalties:
to whom, for what, and why?
Judith Rumgay   126

8 Accountability: difference and diversity in the delivery
of community penalties
Loraine Gelsthorpe   146

9 Technology and the future of community penalties
George Mair   168

10 Community penalties and social integration: 'community'
as solution and as problem
Peter Raynor   183

11 What future for 'public safety' and 'restorative justice'
in a system of community penalties?
Michael Smith   200

12 Concluding reflections
The Editors   226

Appendix: Key conclusions   241

Index   249

List of figures

Figure 1   An outline of the principal mechanisms
            underpinning compliant behaviour   90

Figure 2   Beetham's dimensions of legitimacy   102

Figure 3   Annual violence rate per thousand domestic
            violence suspects by arrest and stake in
            conformity   105

Figure 4   Giddens's characterisation of environments of
            trust in pre-modern and modern societies   109

Notes on contributors

Anthony Bottoms is Wolfson Professor of Criminology at the University of Cambridge and a Visiting Professor of Criminology at the University of Sheffield. He has a longstanding interest in community penalties, having begun his working career with a brief period as a probation officer. In the late 1980s and early 1990s he carried out empirical research on the effectiveness of intensive intermediate treatment programmes for juvenile offenders, and he has also published on topics such as social inquiry reports and the sociology of punishment.

Loraine Gelsthorpe is a University Senior Lecturer at the Institute of Criminology, and a Fellow of Pembroke College, University of Cambridge. She has carried out a number of empirical research studies since the early 1980s – with particular focus on discretion and discrimination in the conception and delivery of criminal justice. She has published extensively in the field of community penalties, especially in relation to pre-sentence reports and youth justice issues.

Mark Liddle is Head of Research and Evaluation in NACRO's Crime and Social Policy Section (National Association for the Care and Resettlement of Offenders), and Hon. Research Fellow at the Institute of Criminology, University of Cambridge, where he contributes to the MSt./Diploma programme for senior police officers. He has been involved in research and teaching in criminology for some 20 years, and in research and consultancy in crime prevention/community safety specifically since the late 1980s. His previous research has focused on areas including 'nuisance' and anti-social behaviour, community safety strategies, multi-agency crime prevention, and the costs of juvenile offending. He has published on these and other topics, and is currently involved in research on persistent young offenders and young people 'at risk', and in evaluation research including an assessment of the new Detention and Training Order, and of intensive support schemes for inmates in young offender institutions.

George Mair is E. Rex Makin Professor of Criminal Justice at Liverpool John Moores University. Previously he was Principal Research Officer in the Home Office Research and Planning Unit where he was responsible for research into community penalties. Currently he is carrying out an ESRC-funded study of Chief Probation Officers, and directing an evaluation of the Merseyside Arrest Referral Scheme.

Mike Nellis is a Lecturer in Criminal Justice Studies at the University of Birmingham, having previously been the holder of a joint appointment with the University of Sheffield and the South Yorkshire Probation Service, and before that a youth justice worker. He has written widely on aspects of penal policy, particularly on probation training, partnerships with the voluntary sector, the future of the Probation Service, electronic monitoring and the concept of community justice.

Peter Raynor is a Professor in the Centre for Applied Social Studies at the University of Wales, Swansea. A former probation officer, he is currently a member of the West Glamorgan Probation Committee and a member designate of the new South Wales Probation Board, as well as of the Joint Prisons and Probation Accreditation Panel for England and Wales. His research over the last 25 years has included work on offenders who misuse drugs, youth justice, automatic conditional release, pre-sentence reports, through-care and resettlement of short-term prisoners, risk and need assessment, and the effectiveness of probation programmes.

Sue Rex is a Senior Research Associate at the Institute of Criminology, and Fellow of St Edmund's College, University of Cambridge. Following a PhD in which she examined perceptions of probation in a context of just deserts, completed in 1996, she has developed her research interests in the areas of sentencing principles and practice in the supervision of offenders in the community. She currently holds a fellowship with the Economic and Social Research Council to conduct a research programme to develop community penalties in theory and practice.

Judith Rumgay is a Senior Lecturer in the Department of Social Policy, London School of Economics. A former probation officer, her research interests include alcohol- and drug-related offending, the Probation Service, female offenders and voluntary sector involvement in offender rehabilitation. She is the author of *Crime, Punishment and the Drinking Offender* (Macmillan 1998), and *The Addicted Offender: Developments in British Policy and Practice* (Palgrave 2000), as well as articles and chapters in other books. She is currently studying the Griffins Society, a voluntary organisation providing residential services for female offenders, and is undertaking an analysis of inquiries after homicides by mentally disturbed people.

Michael Smith is Associate Professor of Law at the University of Wisconsin and Director of Research for the Law School's Remington Centre for Education, Service and Research in Criminal Justice. Previously he served as Director of the Vera Institute of Justice (1978–1994) and as head of Vera's London office (1974–1977). His research and policy work have been concerned primarily with policing and with the imposition and execution of sentences.

Andrew Underdown is Assistant Chief Probation Officer with Greater Manchester Probation Service and a member of the Prison/Probation Accreditation Panel. He has more than 20 years' experience of implementing and evaluating evidence-based programmes of offender supervision. His particular interests include cognitive training approaches, programmes for substance misuse and Community Service. He was author of an HM Inspectorate of Probation report in 1998 on 'Strategies for Effective Offender Supervision', which has been taken forward in a national What Works strategy for Probation.

Preface

The chapters in this book have been developed from papers and discussions at the 24th Cropwood Round Table Conference, which was held in Cambridge on 28–29 June 2000 to discuss future directions for community penalties. The Cropwood Conferences are made possible by a generous grant to the Institute of Criminology from the Barrow Cadbury Trust. Their purpose is to bring together academics, practitioners and policy makers to discuss specific topical issues relating to criminal justice policy and criminology. Given recent and planned legislative change, it was felt that this was a particularly appropriate moment to convene an informed group for a focused discussion about how community penalties might be developed in the future.

The conference was stimulating and illuminating, as can be judged from the chapters in this volume and the Key Conclusions (see Appendix) which have been produced as a result. We are most grateful to all those who were able to attend and contribute to the occasion. We would also like to thank the staff at New Hall, Cambridge, for providing a pleasant and comfortable venue for the conference.

A number of individuals made considerable efforts to ensure that the conference was successful and enjoyable. Particular thanks are due to Helen Ruddy, the Cropwood secretary until summer 2000, without whose organisational skills and patience the conference would not have been possible. Helen Griffiths has taken over those responsibilities with admirable professionalism since her appointment as Cropwood secretary, and has made a significant contribution to bringing this book to fruition. We also wish to thank Joanne Garner, for providing support and continuity during the transition, and Helen Krarup, who brought oversight and organisational finesse as the Director of the Cropwood programme.

Paul Crosland and Colleen Moore, as rapporteurs, ensured that the sessions at the conference were recorded and transcribed, and produced summaries of the discussions with remarkable speed. Those summaries were immensely helpful as a basis for the Key Conclusions that were published in autumn 2000 (reproduced in the Appendix), as well as for the chapters presented here.

As conference organisers and as editors, we have jointly overseen all the processes involved, from initial conception to final delivery of the manuscript. It is right to record, however, that the lion's share of the organisational work has been shouldered by Sue Rex, who was also principally responsible for developing the Key Conclusions. Sue Rex and Loraine Gelsthorpe wrote the first draft of the Introduction (chapter 1), and Tony Bottoms wrote the first draft of the Concluding Reflections (chapter 12).

A.E.B.
L.R.G.
S.A.R.

Chapter 1

Introduction: the contemporary scene for community penalties

The Editors

Challenging times

The purpose of this book is to discuss possible future directions for 'community penalties'. By these, we mean court-ordered punishments (following the terminology of the Criminal Justice Act 1991), structurally located between custody, on the one hand, and financial or nominal penalties (fines, compensation, discharge), on the other. What distinguishes community penalties from fines and compensation is that they are personally restrictive, involving some active contact with a penal agent; but, unlike custodial sanctions, this contact takes place in a community-based setting. It might take the form of active surveillance of the offender (as in electronic tagging), or participation by the offender in a programme of counselling or treatment (as in probation orders or drug treatment orders) or supervised work or other activities (as in community service orders or attendance centres).

The chapters in this book, and the originating papers and discussion at the Cropwood Conference (see the Preface), mark the fact that this is a particularly important moment for community penalties – and one at which it is especially appropriate to be discussing their possible futures. The reasons for this are multiple. The recent past has seen major transitions in the key rationales for community penalties, from the era of treatment, through periods of 'alternatives to custody' and 'punishment in the community', to a focus on the protection of the public, and culminating most recently in the introduction of what might be seen as a 'new generation' of community orders. These developments have not been confined to England and Wales; they, or some aspects of them, have had an impact in other western jurisdictions (see, for example, the popularity of desert-based sentencing principles and 'the electronic tag', in some north American and northern European jurisdictions).

The overall nature of community penalties has changed significantly over the past quarter of a century, and especially over the last decade. One striking aspect of that change has been a proliferation in the orders available to the courts. Until 1970, the only options in adult courts beyond custody, fines and discharges were the Probation Order and – in a few places – Attendance Centres. Between 1970 and 1990, the Community Service Order, probation with special conditions (requiring attendance at special activities or day centres) and the Suspended Sentence Supervision Order were added. The 1990s saw the introduction of the Combination Order; the Curfew Order with electronic monitoring; the Drug Treatment and Testing Order; and, for juveniles, the Action Plan Order and the Reparation Order (though the last of these is not technically a 'community order' within the terminology of the English legislation). Moreover, in the Criminal Justice and Court Services Act 2000, Parliament has now agreed to create two further community orders – the Exclusion Order and Drug Abstinence Order – as well as renaming some key existing orders (the Probation Order, Community Service Order and Combination Order will become respectively the Community Rehabilitation Order, the Community Punishment Order and the Community Punishment and Rehabilitation Order).

This expansion in the number and variety of community orders has been accompanied by the emergence of a more 'scientific' approach in their actual delivery. The use of technology, in both the assessment and the supervision of offenders, seems certain to become even more firmly embedded in supervisory practices. The last decade has seen a significant advance in research-based understandings about the types of programmes with offenders that offer most in reducing their future offending. Some of this research has strongly influenced probation practice, under the so-called 'What Works' initiative co-ordinated by the Home Office and HM Probation Inspectorate.

Yet, despite these positive developments, and the willingness shown by the government (for example, in the Comprehensive Spending Review 2000) to invest in community penalties, there has been an upward trend in the use of custody since 1993 (for example, among males aged 21 and over convicted of indictable offences, the proportion sentenced to immediate imprisonment rose from 18 per cent in 1993 to 28 per cent in 1999). This is financially expensive, but successive governments – clearly acting on perceptions of public opinion – have been willing to find the necessary resources. Reliance on custody has been prompted – at least partly – by doubts in politicians' and the public's mind about the capacity of community penalties to deliver public protection (or, indeed, punishment). Such doubts have also brought about increased emphasis on the enforcement of community penalties, evidenced for example in the tightening up of arrangements for enforcement in the revised National Standards on Community Supervision (Home Office 2000), and through provisions in the Criminal Justice and Court Services Act 2000 (s.53) which make imprisonment the anticipated standard penalty for a second unjustifiable breach of a requirement of a community order.

This is all at a time of important transformations in the policy and organisational framework for community penalties. Following publication of the Consultation Paper 'Joining Forces to Protect the Public' (Home Office 1998), the government has produced the Correctional Policy Framework (Home Office 1999), for the first time setting out a common policy framework for the work of the two principal services whose task is to provide public protection and to reduce re-offending in respect of identified offenders (i.e. the probation and prison services). The Criminal Justice and Court Services Act 2000 also provides for the establishment of a National Probation Service for England and Wales; at the time of writing the necessary arrangements are being put in place for the creation of a national directorate, and the amalgamation of local probation services to form 42 probation areas coterminous with police force area boundaries.

Against the backdrop of all this change, these are clearly important and challenging times, and we hope that the chapters in this book will stimulate reflection and debate about how community penalties might be developed in the future to rise to those challenges. But, first, this introductory chapter sets the context by summarising the key developments that have impinged on community penalties over the last 25 years. Having sketched the relevant background features, it then seeks to describe the contemporary scene against which participants at the Cropwood Conference were discussing possible future directions for community penalties, and which has informed the preparation of this book.

The 1980s: from providing 'alternatives to custody' to offering 'punishment in the community'

The 'alternatives to custody' approach arose in the 1960s and 1970s from a combination of an empirical crisis surrounding the effectiveness of rehabilitative treatment (closely associated with Martinson 1974, and the now notorious phrase 'Nothing Works'); a resources crisis surrounding the sharp rise in the prison population since the 1950s; and a theoretical crisis arising from alleged injustices resulting from the wide discretion often vouchsafed to treatment agents (Bottoms 1980). Now that rehabilitation had, it seemed, been thoroughly discredited, the key aim of the diversion from custody movement was to offer judges and magistrates options that might avoid the damage and expense of a custodial sentence. The first real manifestation of this approach (in the Criminal Justice Act 1967) was, in fact, to provide for a sentence of imprisonment to be suspended. This was followed soon afterwards by the introduction of a new 'intermediate' sanction, the community service order, in the Criminal Justice Act 1972. A certain amount of confusion was undoubtedly created by the fact that the community service order lacked the explicit status of an 'alternative to custody' that the statutory framework had conferred upon the suspended sentence.

In the event, research suggested that both suspended sentences and community service orders replaced terms of imprisonment only in about half the cases in which they were imposed (see Bottoms 1981; Pease 1985). It was widely accepted that such 'alternatives' led to 'net widening' and 'mesh thinning' (Cohen 1985) – that is, the bringing of more and less serious offenders into the penal net than might otherwise have been the case, and the imposition upon them of more severe sanctions (though for an alternative view see McMahon 1990). Whether or not that was so, 'alternatives to custody' clearly failed to have the desired impact on the prison population, which continued an upward trend (see Bottoms 1987). The government realised that a rethink was necessary: judges and magistrates had to be offered sanctions that were more credible if they were to be persuaded to make less use of custody. To provide a new rationale for community-based sanctions, the government turned to the 'justice model', whose popularity in North America had been prompted by the ideological doubts over the excesses and injustices that had contributed to the downfall of 'treatment'.

Specifically, the government applied the 'desert' model particularly championed by Andrew von Hirsch (see von Hirsch 1993 for a full account). This formed the central plank in the legislative framework for sentencing in the Criminal Justice Act 1991, which sought to apply desert-based principles to the re-named community orders, as well as to custodial sentences. In order to bring community orders within its overall philosophy of proportionality, the 1991 Act defined these personally intrusive measures in terms of restrictions on liberty that should be commensurate with the gravity of the offence, within an overall philosophy of 'punishment in the community'.

The 1991 Act thus enacted a significant departure from the penal-welfare concepts that had predominated in the era of treatment (see Garland 1985) by making the probation order (the archetypal penal-welfare measure) a sentence of the court – a marriage of opposites that was not very successful in practice (see Rex 1998). It also created two new orders, the combination order and the curfew order, intended to be sufficiently credible in terms of their restrictions on liberty to offer 'punishment in the community' for offenders who might otherwise receive a custodial sentence.

Initially successful in reducing reliance on imprisonment, since 1993 the desert framework in the 1991 Act has become increasingly sidelined by growing concerns with public protection and the reduction of risk (Rex 1998). It now remains formally on the statute book, but seems to have only a limited impact on sentencing, and the Home Office's current review of the legal framework for sentencing is likely to lead to its reform (see: http://www.homeoffice.gov.uk/cpd/sou/srfleaft.pdf).

The 1990s: a focus on public protection – the new generation of community orders

The dominant features of community penalties have changed signifi-cantly in the decade since the passage of the 1991 Act. The emphasis on punishment in the community remains, and has intensified, marked by the heightened concerns with enforcement evident in the new National Standards for the Probation Service (see above).[1] Perhaps allied to this, there has been a growing reliance on the use of technology to enforce the requirements of community orders, apparent both in electronic moni-toring in relation to curfew orders and in the new Drug Treatment and Testing Order (created by the Crime and Disorder Act 1998, and piloted locally before its national introduction in 2001). The Criminal Justice and Court Services Act 2000 widens these provisions by enacting new and more general powers relating to electronic monitoring and drug testing in relation to the making and the enforcement of community sentences (ss. 48–52).

Another important trend, exemplified by National Standards, has been a 'management revolution' in the Probation Service. This started in the mid-1980s with the issue of the Statement of National Objectives and Priorities by the Home Office in 1984, and has since gathered pace, with the use of key performance indicators to measure performance by

5

outcomes, and three-year plans for the Probation Service. Managerialism has also been embraced by probation managers as a means of helping them to exercise better control and leadership of 'effective practice' developments in their local services. It has perhaps reached its logical conclusion in the formulation of the Correctional Policy Framework and the establishment of the National Probation Service.

One of the most dramatic changes since the 1980s has been the emphasis on effectiveness, prompted by the revival in the research literature of the idea that some interventions are more effective than others in preventing recidivism (see further below). The simultaneous development of systems (utilising IT) which enable probation services to calculate risk scores, and more recently risk-need scores, has led to a focus on managing and minimising 'risk' in supervising offenders in the community.

A triple concern with punishment, effectiveness and public safety seems to have contributed to a trend towards the 'creative mixing' of different kinds of interventions in offenders' lives (rather than imposing a single type of punishment or treatment). This has been seen, for example, in the enactment and popularity of the combination order, bringing together the requirements to keep in touch with a probation officer and to perform unpaid work. There have also been other important 'mixing' proposals, such as those of the former Conservative administration in its 1995 Green Paper 'Strengthening Punishment in the Community' (Home Office 1995). Such mixing has perhaps – at least in embryonic form – been taken even further by the current Labour administration in its ideas for the so-called 'seamless sentence' containing elements of both custody and community supervision.

One section of the public towards whom a greater sense of accountability has developed recently comprises people who have been victims of crime. A considerable growth in 'victims' movements' has found expression, in the case of community penalties, in an increased interest in direct reparation to the victim and in the adoption of approaches inspired by restorative justice models in Australia, New Zealand and Canada. In England, these developments have been taken furthest in relation to young offenders, recent initiatives in relation to whom are discussed below.

The 'What Works' initiative

Perhaps the current development that has had the greatest impact on probation practice, and which incorporates a number of the strands outlined above (notably, managerialism, technological innovation and the management of risk), has been the emphasis on effective practice. The Effective Practice Initiative, launched in 1998 by the Home Office and HM Probation Inspectorate in conjunction with the main probation organisations, has firmly reinstated rehabilitation on the policy agenda. The Initiative operates within the government's Correctional Policy Framework, which sets out specific aims for all parts of the criminal justice system to contribute to Home Office Aim 4: 'the effective execution of the sentences of the court so as to reduce re-offending and protect the public' (see http://www.homeoffice.gov.uk/cpd/cpu/frlink.htm).

The Effective Practice Initiative is a demonstration that our belief in the ability of the criminal justice system to have a positive impact on offenders' behaviour has come full circle since the pessimism of 'Nothing Works'. In relation to the efficacy of rehabilitative programmes, a major research influence has been 'meta-analysis', which has allowed the findings of a number of different evaluations to be aggregated to achieve statistical significance (see, for example, Lipsey 1992). The application of this technique in reviews of recidivism has shown that rehabilitative programmes can be effective, at least among certain types of offenders. Meta-analytical studies have also provided some guidance as to the broad kinds of programmes that might be effective, but caution is needed in interpreting the claims that can currently be made on the basis of this work. As McIvor observes, 'our understanding ... of what works, with which offenders and under what conditions, in reducing offending behaviour' is 'still embryonic' (1997: 13).

McGuire (1995) was amongst the first to draw from these sorts of studies a set of principles about the assembly of effective programmes, which have now been incorporated in the 'What Works' booklet circulated by the Home Office (1999) to all probation staff. Summarised (and avoiding the worst technicalities of this literature), the key principles articulated by McGuire are:

1. The 'risk' principle

More intensive rehabilitative programmes should be directed at offenders who are more likely to offend (predicted on the basis of statistical tables derived from an analysis of associations between prior history and subsequent rates of conviction in large samples of offenders);

2. Criminogenic needs

Programmes should focus on offenders' problems and aspects of their lives which contribute directly to or are supportive of offending, rather than those that are more distantly related or unrelated to offending;

3. Responsivity

There should be systematic matching between styles of workers and styles of offenders. On balance, the learning styles of most offenders require active, participatory methods of working, rather than a didactic mode on the one hand or a loose, unstructured, 'experiential' mode on the other. The least effective methods have been found to be non-directive counselling and confrontation (as in deterrence-based programmes such as 'scared straight');

4. Community base

McGuire found a marginal advantage in favour of programmes located in the community, perhaps because proximity to individuals' home environments has a greater prospect of facilitating real-life learning;

5. Treatment methods

More effective programmes are broadly-based (multimodal), capable of encompassing the variety of offenders' problems, and use a skills-oriented approach;

6. Programme integrity

It seems a matter of common sense (as with much of the above) that the methods used should relate to the aims of the programme, that adequate resources should be available and that staff should be appropriately trained and supported.

National surveys of probation practice in the mid-1990s showed, however, that these principles were not being universally applied, nor their implementation adequately evaluated (Hedderman and Sugg 1997; Ellis and Underdown 1998). These findings have led directly to the Effective Practice Initiative and the subsequent development of the What Works Strategy.[2] A Joint Prisons/Probation Accreditation Panel has also been appointed, tasked with accrediting programmes against a set of criteria based on, and developing, 'What Works' principles.[3] Starting with the 'Pathfinder' projects, the aim of the accreditation process is to produce a core curriculum of demonstrably effective programmes for offenders, Ministers having set the Probation Service the target of delivering 10,000 offenders through accredited programmes in 2001/2 and 60,000 in 2003/4.[4]

Youth justice in the 1990s

In relation to young offenders, debates in the early years of the 1990s were dominated by the public response to the James Bulger case and fears about persistent young offenders. Few commentators failed to observe an increasing authoritarian and punitive tone, which crossed party political boundaries, accompanied by increases in the use of custody for young offenders (Muncie 1999; Moore 2000).

Throughout their opposition years (1979–1997), the Labour government argued that youth crime and youth justice would be a priority of the next Labour government, and when elected in May 1997 they were quick off the mark to produce changes. The appearance of three consultation papers – *Tackling Youth Crime* (Home Office 1997a), *Tackling Delays in the Youth Justice System* (Home Office 1997b), and *New National and Local Focus on Youth Crime* (Home Office 1997c) – within six months of Labour's election emphasised the government's determination to effect change. The general tenor of these documents was to make proposals 'to improve the effectiveness of the Youth Justice system in preventing, deterring and punishing youth crime' (Home Office 1997a: 2); and here the dual emphasis both on prevention and on punishment/ deterrence echoes New Labour's claims – made when in opposition – that they would be 'tough on crime and tough on the causes of crime'.

The White Paper containing the main framework for fresh legislation was published in November 1997, its title giving a telling clue to what lay within (*No More Excuses: A New Approach to Tackling Youth Crime in England and Wales*) (Home Office 1997d). The White Paper explained:

> An excuse culture has developed within the youth justice system. It excuses itself for its inefficiency, and too often excuses the young offenders before it, implying that they cannot help their behaviour because of their social circumstances. Rarely are they confronted with their behaviour and helped to take more responsibility for their actions.
>
> (Home Office, 1997a: 1)

The Crime and Disorder Act 1998 itself was foreseen as a

'comprehensive and wide-ranging reform programme' (Home Office 1997a: 1), and it is a complex measure, with many of its provisions explicitly aimed not only at young offenders, but at young people more generally. Along with the subsequent Youth Justice and Criminal Evidence Act 1999, the legislation appears both to favour punishment and correction to signal society's disapproval of criminal acts and to deter offending, while at the same time seeking to prevent re-offending through an interventionist, welfare approach reminiscent of some policies of the 1960s and 1970s.

The details of these new youth justice provisions have been addressed elsewhere (see, for example, NACRO 1999; Gelsthorpe and Morris 1999; Fionda 1999; Goldson 1999; Ball 2000). But there are two key youth justice developments which are especially significant in the context of community penalties, and about which it is worth saying more here: namely, the creation of extensive 'partnership' arrangements in the community, and the emphasis on 'restorative justice'.

The 'partnership' arrangements inherent in the new youth justice system are far more comprehensive than any referral schemes between probation services and specialist agencies (statutory and voluntary housing, drugs and alcohol agencies, for example) which have evolved thus far in relation to adults.

The Crime and Disorder Act 1998 includes key measures to ensure the effective functioning of the system at a national level (through, for example, the creation of a national Youth Justice Board to give strategic direction, to set standards for and measure the performance of the youth justice system as a whole. But, at the same time, and more crucially for present purposes, a nation-wide network of YOTs – multi-agency Youth Offending Teams – has been set up. Operating at a local authority level, these bodies bring together probation officers, social workers, police officers, health and education workers. It is envisaged that the Youth Offending Teams, which have statutory authority, will be the primary vehicles through which the aim to prevent offending by children and young people will be delivered. The linked Youth Justice and Criminal Evidence Act 1999 additionally introduces the new primary sentencing disposal of a Referral Order for ten to seventeen year olds pleading guilty and convicted for the first time.[5] This order involves referral of the offender to the local Youth Offender Panel – a forum deliberately removed from the formality of the court, and which victims will be encouraged (although not obliged) to attend. The panel will seek to agree a contract with the young offender, aimed at the prevention of further crime. Significantly, panel members may include representatives from the local community as well as a member of the local Youth Offending Team.

The Crime and Disorder Act 1998 and Youth Justice and Criminal Evidence Act 1999 also contain provisions which indicate the Government's belief in restorative justice principles. These include reparation as part of the contractual package agreed under a Referral Order, and the new Reparation Orders now available to the Youth Court (see, for example, Dignan 1999; Pollard 2000; Morris and Gelsthorpe 2000). This signal theme of 'reparation' aims to bring home to young offenders the experience of their victims and to rehearse notions of responsibility and citizenship so as to ensure social inclusion. The approach adopted here is seemingly rather more normatively–oriented than in some of the other new policies adopted, particularly for adult offenders. Early experience with the Reparation Order suggests some tensions between the development of victim–offender mediation (a delicate process requiring time to bring to adequate fruition) and another of the government's priorities in youth justice, that of reducing delays in the system (see Dignan 1999).

It remains to be seen how far all these fresh initiatives relating to young offenders will impact on crime, but there are certainly plenty of challenges for those criminal justice agency professionals involved with young offenders at the community level. Labour's initiatives, with their interventionist, 'no more excuses' underpinnings, clearly create a platform for potential philosophical clashes between the old and the new in youth justice (see, for example, Gelsthorpe and Morris 1994; Universities of Sheffield and Hull 1999; Goldson 1999). Some features of the initiatives may also chafe against the new Human Rights Act 1998 (there is, for example, by design, no provision for legal representation at Youth Offender Panel meetings). Yet, despite potential problems of this sort, undoubtedly many aspects of the new youth justice developments hold great interest and promise. If the promise is fulfilled, there may be some lessons here for the future of community penalties for adults.

Outline of the book

The book attempts to examine the issues arising from the developments sketched above, and their implications for the future of community penalties. The next two chapters develop the analysis of the current scene by examining recent specific influences upon community penalties. First, in chapter 2, Mike Nellis places community penalties in their historical context, offering a broad review of developments in

England since 1948 and thus providing a valuable backdrop to contemporary debates. In chapter 3, Mark Liddle examines the profound impact of the development of partnership work, and the impact of some aspects of contemporary social change, on the way in which community penalties are conceived of and implemented, suggesting that this kind of analysis can help us to influence the future direction of community penalties in a positive manner.

Attention then turns to the effectiveness debate. In chapter 4, Sue Rex looks beyond the current vogue for cognitive behavioural approaches to other possibilities that the evidence indicates need to be pursued in order to have an impact on recidivism. In discussing 'Compliance and community penalties' in chapter 5, Tony Bottoms applies his wider interest in compliance theory to examine the social mechanisms that might encourage offenders to comply in the short term with the requirements of community orders, and in the longer term with the requirements of the law. In commenting on these chapters, Andew Underdown offers in chapter 6 the perspective of a probation manager who has been at the forefront of the 'evidence-based practice' revolution in the Probation Service.

Chapters 7 and 8 raise questions about accountability, Judith Rumgay first considering to whom accountability is owed, for what and why. She proposes a focus on harm reduction as capable of embracing both relations with partnership agencies and the needs of victims. In chapter 8, Loraine Gelsthorpe argues that accountability towards the offender requires community penalties to be delivered in a way which accommodates social diversity and difference, and that the recognition of diversity is important to the promotion of citizenship, itself an aim to which community penalties might usefully aspire.

Developing the theme of possible future directions for community penalties, in chapter 9 George Mair looks at the growing role of technology in the delivery of community penalties, using electronic monitoring and computerisation as illustrative case studies. Peter Raynor reflects in 'Community penalties and social integration: "Community" as solution and as problem' on various aspects of the 'community' dimension of community penalties, and considers whether community (or restorative) justice might offer a framework for the future. In chapter 11, Michael Smith brings insights from his experiences in the United States to a consideration of the role which community penalties might play within an approach to criminal justice based on 'public safety' (making places and situations feel more secure).

Finally, in chapter 12, the editors survey five 'dimensions' that apply to a consideration of the future of community penalties, reflecting on the chapters in this volume – and on discussions at the Cropwood Conference – in the light of specific events that have occurred since.

Notes

1 National Standards for all community penalties were first introduced in 1992, and revised in 1995 and 2000. The latest version significantly tightens up the arrangements for enforcing community orders, so that offenders are to be taken back to court upon their second (rather than their third) unacceptable absence. Enforcement practice on the ground has been subjected to scrutiny in two national audits (Hedderman and Hearnden 1999, 2000).
2 Circulated under Probation Circular 60/2000.
3 See Probation Circular 40/2000 for First Annual Report of the Accreditation Panel.
4 See What Works Strategy, Probation Circular 60/2000.
5 Unlike the 1998 reforms, this change has not yet been 'rolled out nationally'. It has been piloted in selected areas since April 2000.

References

Ball, C. (2000) 'The Youth Justice and Criminal Evidence Act 1999. Part I: A significant move towards restorative justice, or a recipe for unintended consequences?' *Criminal Law Review* (April), 211–22.

Bottoms, A.E. (1980) 'An Introduction to the Coming Penal Crisis', in A.E. Bottoms and R.H. Preston (eds) *The Coming Penal Crisis: A Criminological and Theological Exploration*. Edinburgh: Scottish Academic Press.

Bottoms, A.E. (1981) 'The Suspended Sentence in England 1967–1987', *British Journal of Criminology*, 21, 1–26.

Bottoms, A.E. (1987) 'Limiting Prison Use in England and Wales', *Howard Journal*, 26, 177–202.

Cohen, S. (1985) *Visions of Social Control: Crime, Punishment and Classification*. Cambridge: Polity Press.

Dignan, J. (1999) 'The Crime and Disorder Act and the prospects for restorative justice', *Criminal Law Review* (January), 48–60.

Ellis, T. and Underdown, A. (1998) *Strategies for Effective Offender Supervision*, Report of the HMIP What Works Project. London: Home Office.

Fionda, J. (1999) 'New Labour, Old Hat: Youth Justice and the Crime and Disorder Act 1998', *Criminal Law Review* (January), 36–47.

Garland, D. (1985) *Punishment and Welfare*. Aldershot: Gower.

Gelsthorpe, L. and Morris, A. (1994) 'Juvenile Justice', in M. Maguire, R. Morgan and R. Reiner (eds.) *The Oxford Handbook of Criminology*. Oxford: Oxford University Press.

Gelsthorpe, L. and Morris, A. (1999) 'Much ado about nothing – a critical comment on key provisions relating to children in the Crime and Disorder Act 1998', *Child and Family Law Quarterly*, 11(3), 209–221.

Goldson, B. (1999) 'Youth (In)Justice: Contemporary Developments in Policy and Practice', in B. Goldson (ed.) *Youth Justice: Contemporary Policy and Practice*. Aldershot: Ashgate.

Hedderman, C. and Hearnden, I. (1999) *Improving Enforcement – The First ACOP Audit*. London: South Bank University.

Hedderman, C. and Hearnden, I. (2000) *Improving Enforcement – The Second ACOP Audit*. London: South Bank University.

Hedderman, C. and Sugg, D. (1997) 'Changing Offenders' Attitudes and Behaviour', *Home Office Research Study No. 171*. London: Home Office.

Home Office (1995) *Strengthening Punishment in the Community*, Cm. 2780. London: HMSO.

Home Office (1997a) *Tackling Youth Crime. A Consultation Paper*. London: Home Office.

Home Office (1997b) *Tackling Delays in the Youth Justice System*, A Consultation Paper. London: Home Office.

Home Office (1997c) *New National and Local Focus on Youth Crime. A Consultation Paper*. London: Home Office.

Home Office (1997d) *No More Excuses: A New Approach to Tackling Youth Crime in England and Wales*, Cmnd, 3809. London: HMSO.

Home Office (1998) *Joining Forces to Protect the Public: Prison–Probation: A Consultation Document*. London: Home Office.

Home Office (1999) *What Works: Reducing Re-offending: Evidence-Based Practice*. London: Home Office Communications Directorate.

Home Office (2000) *National Standards for the Supervision of Offenders in the Community*. London: Home Office.

Lipsey, M. W. (1992) 'Juvenile Delinquency Treatment: A Meta-Analytic Inquiry into the Variability of Effects', in T. Cook, D. Cooper, H. Corday, H. Hartman, L. Hedges, R. Light, T. Louis and F. Mosteller (eds.) *Meta-analysis for Explanation: A Casebook*. New York: Russell Sage Foundation.

Martinson, R. (1974) 'What Works? Questions and Answers about Prison Reforms', *Public Interest*, 35, 22–54.

McGuire, J. (1995) *What Works: Reducing Re-offending*. Chichester: Wiley Press.

McIvor, G. (1997) 'Evaluative Research in Probation: Progress and Prospects', in G. Mair (ed.) *Evaluating the Effectiveness of Community Programmes*. Aldershot: Avebury.

McMahon, M. (1990) ' "Netwidening": Vagaries in the use of a Concept', *British Journal of Criminology*, 30, 121–149.

Moore, S. (2000) 'Child Incarceration and the New Youth Justice', in B. Goldson (ed.) *The New Youth Justice*. Lyme Regis, Dorset: Russell House Publishing.

Morris, A. and Gelsthorpe, L. (2000) 'Something Old, Something Borrowed, Something Blue, but Something New? A comment on the prospects for restorative justice under the Crime and Disorder Act 1998', *Criminal Law Review* (January), 18–30.

Muncie, J. (1999) *Youth and Crime. A Critical Introduction*. London: Sage.

NACRO (1999) *A Brief Outline of the Youth Justice System in England and Wales Incorporating the Crime and Disorder Act 1998*, Briefing Paper. London: National Association for the Care and Resettlement of Offenders.

Pease, K. (1985) 'Community Service Orders', in M. Tonry and N. Morris (eds) *Crime and Justice*. Chicago: University of Chicago Press.

Pollard, C. (2000) 'Victims and the Criminal Justice System: A New Vision', *Criminal Law Review*, (January), 5–17.

Rex, S.A. (1998) 'Applying Desert Principles to Community Sentences: Lessons from two Criminal Justice Acts', *Criminal Law Review*, (June) 361–380.

Universities of Sheffield and Hull (1999) *Second Internal Report: Youth Offending Teams after One Year*. Sheffield: University of Sheffield.

von Hirsch, A. (1993) *Censure and Sanctions*. Oxford: Clarendon Press.

Chapter 2

Community penalties in historical perspective

Mike Nellis

Introduction

The passing of the Criminal Justice and Court Services Act 2000, arguably the most fateful piece of legislation for the Probation Service since 1948, makes this a particularly auspicious moment to review the history of community penalties in England and Wales. A short chapter like this inevitably precludes a comprehensive history of such penalties, but a broad overview of the main developments between 1948 and 1997 – the advent of the New Labour government – is certainly possible. I will conclude with some observations on the changed circumstances in which community penalties are now being created, and also with some thoughts on the value of remembrance. Because the development of community penalties for young and adult offenders has been intertwined, the chapter will encompass both, but will concentrate particularly on the work of the Probation Service.

There are numerous institutional standpoints and theoretical positions from which a history of community penalties could be written, and Mair (1997) is correct to say that, by the sophisticated standards of contemporary penal history, there is as yet no adequate account of community penalties, and certainly no real way of knowing what they actually accomplished in the past. There is a semi-official, but now dated, history of probation (Bochel 1976); there are local histories of particular services (Bissell 1987; Page 1992); there are memoirs by probation officers (Stokes 1950; Todd 1964; Mott 1992) and magistrates (Mullins 1948; Wootton 1982); there is the esteemed McWilliams quartet (1983, 1985, 1986, 1987), a history of senior attendance centres (Mair

1991), a history of intermediate treatment (Nellis 1991a), a reflective celebration of Community Service (Whitfield 1992), and a realist probation novel (Stroud 1961). All of these have doubtless shaped perceptions of the penal past and its relationship – in terms of an implied need for continuity or change – to the present and the future. But, as Connerton (1989) points out, there are usually significant differences between social memory – what a given group of people believe un- reflectively to be their relevant history – and the deliberate acts of historical reconstruction undertaken for whatever reason: to augment or discredit, to 'invent tradition', or to ascertain as objectively as possible the truth and significance of past events (Hobsbawm 1997). It is thus perfectly possible, and indeed quite likely, that ministers, officials, sentencers, probation officers and criminologists will see the post-war history of community penalties differently from one another, and, indeed, might not share the partisan view taken throughout this chapter that the use of community penalties 'is the rational path for most criminals found guilty of most crimes in order to achieve protection, recompense for harm done and a solution that might reduce crime in the future' (Stern 1998: 321).

The concept of community penalties

Over the years, worldwide, the field to which the term 'community penalty' has been applied in England since 1990 – that is, sentences other than fines for dealing with convicted offenders outside prison – has had many different signifiers, each nuanced in subtly different ways. 'Alternative to custody' (or prison), 'non-custodial measures', 'com- munity care programmes', 'community-based alternatives', 'inter- mediate treatment' are the best known in Britain. Sometimes they have been linked to broader penal strategies, variously named diversion, de- institutionalisation, decarceration, or penal reductionism (see Vass 1990 and Rutherford 1986 for further elaboration of these terms). The rationale for dealing with offenders outside prison has rarely been settled for long, and the very vagueness of the terminology used in the past has often helped criminal justice interest groups with competing ambitions to coexist, in a way that more precise terminology would not have done. Non-custodial measures have usually been considered, by most contributors to criminal justice debates, as sentencing *options* within a system that retains the use of custody; more rarely, they have been promoted as *replacements* for custody, either in part (for certain categories of offender), or, by penal 'abolitionists', more comprehensively (see de Haan 1990 for the complexity of abolitionist positions on alternative measures).

In the midst of such conceptual imprecision, a government determined to impose order and coherence on penal policy could easily make a case for greater semantic clarity. In America, the term 'intermediate sanctions' was an attempt to do this (Morris and Tonry 1990). In England, the term 'community penalty', introduced as part of the Home Office's (1988; 1990a; 1990b) 'punishment in the community' initiative, was its near equivalent. Both aimed to clarify the distinctions between financial, community and custodial penalties, graduated in degrees of severity, and, in the English case, the aim was also to portray attendance centres, supervision orders, probation orders, community service, curfew orders with electronic tagging, and combination orders (a mix of probation and community service) as measures in their own right, rather than as something 'less' than – or 'alternative' to – imprisonment. Apparently paradoxically, at the very point (1990–91) at which the Home Office actually wanted probation and community services to function as serious alternatives to custody (i.e. contribute significantly to the reduced use of imprisonment), they proposed dropping the term most usually associated with this intention.[1]

It is unwise (especially from a sentencer's or politician's perspective [Pease 1980]) to exaggerate the importance of the so-called 'rehabilitative ideal' to the development of non-custodial measures in post-war Britain. The various community-based measures were certainly thought of as *beneficial*, as offering offenders 'second' or 'last chances' to make good, as more humane and less stigmatising than imprisonment – but they were not necessarily seen as *therapeutic*. The coining of the term 'community penalty' was rather obviously intended to signify a shift away from overtly rehabilitative concerns – and perhaps of compassion more generally – towards notions of punishment (although a constructive element remained). The new term gave expression to the Home Office's hope that more rigorous and demanding community penalties, together with new, desert-based (Home Office 1990a) restrictions on sentencing powers, would bring about a reduction in the prison population. This hope did not outlast the events of 1993, and in retrospect the 'punishment in the community' initiative, despite its over-rhetorical break with the rehabilitative ideal, can be seen as the apotheosis – the last phase – of post-war penal reductionist thinking. It was not, as some in the Probation Service still want to see it, the primary harbinger of the contemporary penal situation, which differs in very significant ways from the vision which prevailed then. The kind of future that might have resulted from the initiative must now be left to the 'virtual historians' (Ferguson 1997).

The term 'community penalties' was intended to refer to some quite specific sentences, but any history of such penalties cannot properly restrict itself only to the measures that are now signified as such, ignoring the designations used in the past. Fines and compensation, suspended sentences (colloquially if not legally), and disqualification, for example, have traditionally been understood as non-custodial penalties, but they are not, in modern parlance, community penalties. Furthermore, 'community penalties' have not evolved discretely, wholly separate from wider developments in pre-court work or in parole and after-care. Debates about bail and remands in custody are not, strictly speaking, about 'penalties', but similar factors – overcrowded prisons, the limitations of hostel provision, civil libertarian concerns about intrusiveness – have shaped them. Similarly, it has proved difficult to sustain sharp qualitative distinctions between supervising offenders in the community as an alternative to imprisonment, and supervision after imprisonment, on licence; once parole was introduced, for example, questions were inevitably asked as to why probation supervision should be any less rigorous (Advisory Council on the Penal System 1974; para. 43).

The relationship between community penalties and imprisonment is itself complicated. A person found guilty of what in law is an imprisonable offence does not necessarily receive a custodial sentence, and sentencing patterns, in much of the period under discussion, have varied between different parts of the country (Harvey and Pease 1989). Furthermore, what has counted as an 'alternative to custody', has, historically, depended on where the threshold of custody is set – which depends, in complex ways, on economic, political and cultural factors. If the threshold is set low, as it was in Victorian Britain, then even voluntary supervision by a police court missionary counts as a genuine alternative. If the threshold is high (as it progressively became throughout the twentieth century, though it had lowered again by the end) then alternatives have either to become more demanding, or the purpose of community punishment has to be refined. At various times, and sometimes simultaneously, both strategies have been pursued.

Community penalties 1948–1978

A reasonable case can be made for claiming probation as the first community penalty/alternative to custody – although it had distant roots in the much older court practice of 'binding over'. Although first made statutory in 1907, national cover (probation officers attached to all magistrates courts) was not achieved until the early 1930s. The original, three-year probation order was not a sentence (and originally, if completed successfully, it did not even count as a conviction), but an alternative to a sentence, and therefore, strictly speaking, an alternative to punishment, to which the offender had to consent. The relationship formed between supervisor and offender was thought crucial to the latter's reformation; the supervisor's role, famously, was to 'advise, assist and befriend' the probationer.

Had it ever been enacted, the Criminal Justice Bill 1938 (shelved because of the onset of war) would have created a new form of rehabilitative alternative to prison, Howard Houses. Post-war alarm at rising levels of juvenile crime transmuted this proposal, in the Criminal Justice Act 1948, into attendance centres (police-organised deprivation of leisure on Saturdays) and detention centres (military-style 'short sharp, shock' institutions), both originally for boys only. The 1948 Act also established the Probation Service's legal and administrative framework for the next 20 years, and in some respects beyond, as a local service (managed by committees of magistrates, not local government), but guided in policy terms by the Home Office. The probation order itself now became dependent on a conviction; a statutory minimum period of one year was introduced, and a requirement for psychiatric treatment became available, to complement the existing hostel requirement.

Probation had many supporters in the magistracy, but early in the 1950s some influential magistrates began a campaign for a suspended custodial sentence because they felt the probation order itself was insufficiently deterrent – and, more generally, they wished to consolidate and refine the range of the courts' sentencing powers (Hall Williams 1970:272). After much criticism from Home Office advisers (see Advisory Council on the Treatment of Offenders 1957), who did not accept the arguments for toughening probation, suspended sentences were finally introduced in the Criminal Justice Act 1967, seventeen years after they were first proposed. They were not explicitly linked to probation, although suspended sentence supervision orders were created only a few years later by the Criminal Justice Act 1972 – but then little used.

In the mid-to-late 1960s the Probation Service became embroiled in the then Labour government's modernisation strategy. Until then, the Service's work had largely been with offenders – and their families – aged between eight and 21 years. In 1965 it assumed responsibility for 'after-care' and prison welfare (following a report by the Advisory Council on the Treatment of Offenders (1963); and then in 1968 also for parole (a more stringent approach to supervising more serious released prisoners). These changes, which gradually introduced officers to many more adult offenders, were deemed to warrant a name change, to 'The Probation and After-Care Service'. Simultaneously, the Service became embroiled in debates about the future of the juvenile court and the development of local authority services for young offenders (Home Office 1965; 1968). Under the Children and Young Persons Act 1969, these debates culminated in the intended transfer of primary supervisory responsibility for young offenders from probation to the local authority Children's Departments, and the creation of an ill-defined new supervisory measure, 'intermediate treatment', part community-based, part residential, which in the longer term was to have a significant impact on the development of alternatives to custody for juveniles.

The eventual centrepiece of Labour's modernising programme was the attempt to merge small local authority welfare services, including the Children's Department, into larger, multi-functional Social Services Departments (SSDs). Had it not been for the Probation Service's resistance, the support of the magistrates and the then Conservative opposition, together with a chance shortage of parliamentary time before the 1970 election, the Service might well have been absorbed into SSDs, as happened to probation in the equivalent reorganisation in Scotland (Hall 1976). The absorption of the Children's Departments into the new Social Services Departments was one of several reasons why intermediate treatment failed to realise its potential in its early years, and it is not unreasonable to think that probation practice would have been seriously weakened if it too had been caught up in this reorganisation.

As it was, the Service was reasonably well prepared for the report of the Advisory Council on the Penal System (1970), *Non-Custodial and Semi-Custodial Penalties*, which, despite its somewhat narrow focus, generated the most important new 'alternative to custody' since the inception of probation itself. Whilst acknowledging the adversities of imprisonment, the report mostly emphasised the need for sentencers to have a wide, differentiated range of measures at their disposal, arguing in particular that 'new forms of supportive treatment are wanted for recidivists' (Advisory Council on the Penal System 1970: para 196). It concluded that there was 'little scope' for new alternatives for the professional criminal; that it was not 'feasible to devise non-custodial penalties exclusively for female offenders' (*ibid*: para 198), nor for mentally disturbed offenders (without recourse to better health services

21

generally); and it did not even examine alternatives for alcohol- or drug-using offenders, because these were the responsibility of other government bodies.

Nonetheless, *Non-Custodial and Semi-Custodial Penalties* – the Wootton Report – is justly remembered for introducing the community service order (envisaged in part as a replacement for the senior attendance centres – for 17–20 year olds – which had failed to take off in most parts of the country). The Wootton Report also led to the enactment of the deferred sentence (envisaged more as an alternative to probation than to prison) and it considered the further potential of fines, junior attendance centres and probation orders (especially in regard to their use with other penalties) and the as yet untried idea of intermittent custody (recommending weekend imprisonment). Unsurprisingly, given Barbara Wootton's (1959) well-documented scepticism towards therapeutic social work, it was not particularly committed to rehabilitation (at least as the Probation Service understood it), but its favourable view of the potential of disqualification and forfeiture as forms of non-custodial penalty has largely been forgotten. These practices have not subsequently been bracketed with 'conventional' community penalties, although this may be starting to change.

The community service order was piloted in six areas, went national in 1978, and became one of the great success stories in penal reform. It appealed shamelessly to many penal constituencies (Wootton 1982). Its initial growth was, however, paralleled by a significant decline in the use of the probation order, and by the end of the 1970s serious thought was being given as to why this was so, and how the use of probation could be revived. One view, acknowledged by some Service managers, but still controversial with many, was that probation orders needed to be toughened-up to regain credibility with sentencers, and to adequately constrain offenders. The four Day Training Centres – introduced experimentally in the Criminal Justice Act 1972 – were seen by this group to signal a new direction for the Service, but early local reconviction studies cast doubt on their efficacy. Other local probation services (outside the experiment) had nonetheless created their own variants of these centres, and after a brief period in which their legality was questioned, they were made available nationwide – and simply called 'day centres' – by the Criminal Justice Act 1982.

The question of how tough the Probation Service might need to be had been alluded to in *Non-Custodial and Semi-Custodial Penalties*, but was given a more pointed airing in the mid-1970s by another report from the Advisory Council on the Penal System (1974) – the Younger Report. Based on a comprehensive review of the treatment of young adult offenders (17– 21-year olds) over the preceding 60 years, it was destined to have no direct effect on policy whatsoever, neither of its two central recommendations being taken up. But in retrospect, the Younger Report can be seen to have identified trends towards intensive or enhanced probation – and mapped out possible responses to them – that others only recognised much later. The long time frame underpinning the Younger analysis made it particularly sensitive to changed social circumstances, and to the outdatedness of many existing penal procedures. It was mindful of the rising costs of imprisonment and emphasised the need to keep young adult offenders out of custody, but it was equally mindful of rising crime rates, and proposed what it saw as a 'sentencing structure best suited to protect the public and reduce future offences' (*ibid*: para 4).

That said, Younger's key recommendation for a supervision and control order, a tougher version of a probation order (adapted from California), which would not require the offender's consent, and would permit short periods of temporary detention (up to 72 hours for recalcitrant offenders), was a step too far even for the minority in the Probation Service who accepted the Advisory Council's premise that some young adult offenders were now too intransigent for conventional probation. Opponents took comfort from the dissent to the temporary detention proposal by four committee members themselves (Advisory Council on the Penal System 1974: 172–174). The belated government response to the Younger Report (Home Office 1978) used the fact that in the intervening period the IMPACT study (Folkard *et al* 1976) had cast doubt on the likely effectiveness of intensive supervision, so, mostly to the delight of the Probation Service, the proposal was dropped.

The confident belief of so many probation champions in this period that when they rejected arguments to toughen-up community super-vision they necessarily occupied the moral high ground, and thus were engaging in 'progressive' practice, was mistaken. It left the Service ill prepared for the debates that were to come. The Younger Report's idea of temporary detention was indeed excessive, but its underlying belief that the Service had changed too little since the 1920s, and that a culture shift was overdue, should have been more actively engaged within the Service itself. Some individuals, in a variety of different ways, often emphasising the so-called 'decline of the rehabilitative ideal' rather than the Younger Report, did attempt such engagement over the next few years (e.g. Haxby 1978; Bottoms and McWilliams 1979) but the culture of the Service as a whole remained resolutely resistant to new thinking, and committed to a particular conception of 'social work' that hardly seemed adequate to the challenges of real-world criminal behaviour (as evidenced by contemporary ethnographies: see Parker 1974; Cohen 1979).

Community penalties 1978–1997

By 1977, faced with problems of overcrowding, poor industrial relations in prison, and fears of an Attica-style riot, reducing the prison population had become an official aim of penal policy (Home Office 1977). The emphasis was primarily on finding alternatives for drunks, vagrants, inadequates, mentally disordered offenders and persons convicted of prostitution-related offences, and sometimes on less serious property offenders. Various bodies endorsed this approach, including the Advisory Council on the Penal System (1977, 1978), the House of Commons Expenditure Committee (1978; see also Home Office 1980) and the Parliamentary All Party-Penal Affairs Group (1980, 1981). The official May Enquiry (Home Office 1979) into the prison system warned of a prison population of 50,000 by 1990 if nothing was done to forestall it. A consensus emerged that custodial sentences, where unavoidable, should be as short as possible, but that if there were no clear reasons for imposing custody, non-custodial penalties should be used. Nonetheless, a sense of crisis prevailed in the early 1980s, accentuated by the coming to power of a Conservative government in 1979, ostensibly devoid of liberal leanings on penal matters.

Within the academic community doubts of a different kind were emerging about alternatives to custody. Evidence was mounting that the measures which were thought of as alternatives to custody were not consistently used in this way by sentencers. Pease and McWilliams (1980) showed that only about half of community service orders functioned as alternatives, and analyses by Bottoms (1980) similarly suggested that many suspended sentences were given to people who would not have been at risk of immediate custody. Similar findings emerged from several small-scale analyses of juvenile court sentencing, which raised the possibility that premature use of so-called alternatives might increase the likelihood of custody being used at an earlier stage that would otherwise have been the case (Thorpe *et al* 1980). Thus, despite the availability of new alternatives, sentencers were not always using them as policy-makers intended. Numbers of offenders sentenced to immediate custodial sentences had increased from 30,000 in 1973 to 45,000 in 1980 (in part of course because of a rising crime rate). The proportionate use of custody rose over the same period from 11 per cent to 14 per cent. The trend was most marked in relation to juveniles, young male adults and female offenders.

This perceived 'penal crisis' at the end of the 1970s intensified the determination of a number of academic criminologists and penal reformers to increase the use of non-custodial penalties, to find ways of targeting them on the 'right' offender groups. This was particularly true in respect of juvenile justice. The first flush of enthusiasm for 'intermediate treatment' had dissipated and it was clear to a handful of academics, civil servants and practitioners themselves, David Thorpe in particular (Paley and Thorpe 1976) that if the concept was to be rescued it needed to be developed in a more structured and visionary way than was allowed for in the 1969 Act. Outside government, two pressure groups (NACRO 1977; Personal Social Services Council 1978) promoted intermediate treatment as an alternative to both residential care and custody, NACRO linking this to the idea of 'decarceration', and drawing inspiration from the recent closure of the Massachusetts training schools for young offenders (Rutherford 1978). Norman Tutt, a young civil servant, influenced both the NACRO and the PSSC visions, and when he and David Thorpe took up careers at the University of Lancaster in the late 1970s they became formidable promoters of 'decarceration' and structured community alternatives, even as a Conservative government was coming to power on a 'law and order' ticket.

'Short, sharp shock' detention centres for young offenders were the symbolic centrepiece of the Criminal Justice Act 1982, the new government's flagship legislation on crime but, in the course of Parliamentary debate, some useful restrictions on the use of custody were also introduced, influenced by justice model thinking (Bean 1976, von Hirsch 1976). New possibilities for alternatives opened up. Positive and negative requirements (to participate in, or refrain from, specified activities) were introduced into both probation orders and supervision orders (and included a curfew requirement in the latter, though this was to be infrequently used). A 'supervised activity requirement' was introduced for young offenders as an alternative option to the existing intermediate treatment requirements, with magistrates having more control over the content of the programme in the new requirement. This was consistent with the justice model's emphasis on returning decision-making power from the executive (professionals perceived to have too much discretion) to the judiciary (sentencers being perceived as more responsive to public and government concerns). But responses to the new requirements, even the positive ones, were to be very different in the Probation Service and in the local authority social services departments (SSDs).

The Probation Service, basic grade officers more so than managers, and backed by their union (the National Association of Probation Officers [NAPO]), refused to accept additional requirements in probation orders – in particular day-centre requirements – as a legitimate way of reducing prison numbers. One particular attempt to develop an early form of intensive probation, the Kent Close Support Unit, met with considerable resistance (and the centre did eventually close). So strong was commitment among practitioners to the idea of probation as a form of conditional liberty and a means of helping that Bullock and Tildesley (1984), court clerks who researched probation officer attitudes in this period, drew dismaying conclusions about the potential of the Service to work constructively and consistently for the reduced use of imprisonment. The Home Office's (1984c) own attempt to persuade local services to adopt more intensive forms of supervision – the Statement of National Objectives and Priorities (SNOP) – met with mixed-to-poor results; some local services were acquiescent, but most resisted it (Lloyd 1985). Juvenile justice practitioners, on the other hand, much influenced by a model of practice developed at the University of Lancaster (Thorpe *et al* 1980), and driven by 'anti-custodial zeal' (Rutherford 1989), committed themselves wholeheartedly to a strategy of diversion from court, residential care and custody. They jettisoned the conventional language of social work, adopted 'justice model' terminology and emphasised 'systems management' as well as face-to-face work with offenders.

The overall strategy was nonetheless underpinned by the belief that it was in a young offender's best interests (and in the longer term, society's) to be allowed to 'grow out of crime' (Rutherford 1992) with only minimal intervention from formal criminal justice agencies. A minority of probation staff, and many more juvenile court magistrates, championed this approach (which saw 'intermediate treatment centres' flourishing across the country), but juvenile justice practitioners in SSDs and childcare voluntary organisations (see Nellis 1993a) undoubtedly dominated the initiative. The use of care and custody for juveniles was drastically reduced by the end of the 1980s (Allen 1991). This particular outcome of the 1982 Act had never been anticipated by the government, but they eventually took political credit for it, and the Home Office's subsequent strategy for young adult offenders (17–21-year olds) was significantly influenced by the apparent success in the management of juvenile crime (see Home Office 1988, 1990b).

The Probation Service's position became increasingly untenable. By the mid-1980s a number of commentators were encouraging it to emulate the growing success of juvenile justice workers (see generally McGuire and Priestley 1985; Raynor 1985; Rutherford 1986; Pointing

1986). Willis (1986:18), for example, suggested that the time was ripe 'for a major penal initiative to promote non-custodial alternatives' (for adults) believing them, despite evidence of poor targeting, to be 'an elusive but not impossible penal ambition'. He envisaged the Service taking a much more active role, particularly via social enquiry reports, in challenging the use of custody, transforming itself 'into the active champion of alternatives to custody, intent on reducing custodial committals' (*ibid*: 36). Activism of this kind within the Service would thus become 'a prelude to a fundamental re-examination of the purpose and nature of criminal supervision in the community' (*ibid*: 38). Pointing (1986: 2), however, saw the continuing difficulty: many probation officers were still 'uncomfortable about recognising the role of punishment in the criminal justice system, and ... often refuse to accept their role as being based on social control'.

This was the Home Office perception too. After the failure of SNOP to secure change by persuasion, it set about directing the Service to become an agent of 'punishment in the community', 'however discordant with the culture of the Probation Service' (Windlesham 1993: 225) this was going to be. Fiscal pressure to reduce the prison population had been building up within government throughout the 1980s, but the early responses amounted to little more than tinkering (Home Office 1984a). 'Intermittent custody' (weekend detention) (Home Office 1984b; Shaw and Hutchinson 1985) was considered again – the Wootton Report had recommended it – and again discarded. Only after the Conservatives had been elected for a third term in 1987, when Douglas Hurd was already Home Secretary, was a concerted strategy of penal reduction developed. It was largely driven by the official forecasts of a prison population surpassing 60,000,

> possibly reaching 70,000 by the year 2000. ... Ministers and officials were united in their reaction that such a situation would be intolerable and must not be allowed to happen. The aim should be to find ways of reducing numbers, not of increasing them.
>
> (Windlesham 1993: 238–9)

Desperation now bred interest in wholly new measures; electronic monitoring, for example, figured for the first time in official thinking.

A series of well argued official papers (Home Office 1988, 1990a, 1990b) set out the strategy and the Criminal Justice Act 1991 sought to implement it. It promoted longer custodial sentences for more serious offenders, and, for the less serious, non-custodial sentences (now called 'community penalties', and structured by National Standards (Home

27

Office *et al* 1992) to ensure their more uniform application). It was premised on a 'just deserts' philosophy, albeit one which left room for rehabilitative objectives within fixed sentencing frameworks. It insisted nonetheless on a language of punishment, whilst offering the Probation Service a 'centre stage' role in a more integrated criminal justice system. Crucially, though, the Probation Order was to become a sentence, and would no longer be intended to 'advise, assist and befriend'; henceforth its aims were the reduction of crime, the protection of the public and the rehabilitation of the offender. New requirements were introduced relating to drugs and alcohol. A combination order (initially conceived as a multiple element sentence, but ultimately distilled into a mix simply of probation and community service) was introduced as an ostensibly high tariff disposal. Newest of all was a proposal for an electronically monitored curfew order – the curfew requirement of the supervision order, standing alone, having proved difficult to enforce – as both a sentence and as a means of reducing remands to custody. Unit fines, akin to the day fines which the Advisory Council on the Penal System had rejected 20 years earlier, were introduced following a series of successful pilots. It was hoped that such fines, which systematically took account of offenders' means, would make default – and consequent imprisonment – less likely.

Liberal opinion (as expressed by pressure groups and broadsheet newspapers) was in the main supportive of the new Act, because of its overdue emphasis on reducing the prison population. The toughening-up of probation – and the break with tradition which this represented – did not seem too high a price to pay (especially in view of 'the successful revolution in juvenile justice'), and it was not much discussed in media debate on the Act. Many in the Probation Service itself, however, felt that their tradition was being betrayed. Some managers were prepared to countenance community penalties that were 'more demanding that prison' but most basic-grade officers saw the 'centre stage' offer as a poisoned chalice, doubting that tougher community penalties would reduce the prison population, despite evidence that, with care, certain types of alternatives could indeed be properly targeted (Raynor 1988). The Service felt itself to be 'under siege' in this period (May 1991) but its insularity ill-served both offenders and communities: neglect of Carlen's (1990) ideas about the feasibility of non-custodial penalties for women, for example – building on longstanding concern (Field 1963) – was particularly disappointing.

Implementation of the Act took place in 1992. How effective it might have been had it had adequate time to demonstrate its worth will never be known. There were some promising signs. Use of custody had in fact been falling even before enactment, and continued to do so immediately afterwards. Eight experimental 'intensive probation' schemes, which ran between 1990 and 1992 (mostly consisting of enhanced day centre regimes), met with both Home Office and probation officer approval (those working in them, if not always their colleagues) (Mair 1996). But – fatefully – Hurd had left the Home Office even before the Act had been enacted, and his three successors lacked his enthusiasm for the overall strategy and his finesse in dealing with its detractors. A backlash arose among magistrates, judges and police who objected to the Act's restrictions on sentencing and its failure to address 'offending on bail'. Some newspapers branded it 'a criminal's charter' (as they had some previous Criminal Justice Acts) because of its commitment to reducing prison use. The Act's version of the unit fines system (different from the much lauded pilots) produced some unfortunate sentencing anomalies, and the provision was eventually repealed in a hastily drawn-up piece of corrective legislation, the Criminal Justice Act 1993 (which also removed some sentencing restrictions on which the hopes of reduced prison use had, mostly, depended).

Tragedy played a large part in what happened next. A number of high profile crimes by young people aged ten or less, most spectacularly the killing of two-year-old James Bulger, seemed drastically to tilt the mood of the country – sentencers in particular – in a more punitive direction. From that point on (February 1993) the use of custody began to rise from its all-time low (in recent years) of 42,000. So too did the use of tougher community penalties, but less and less on the more serious property offenders which the Act had intended (Raynor 1997). The arrival of Michael Howard as Home Secretary consolidated and enhanced the custodial trend, switching the emphasis, rhetorically and substantively wherever possible, from just deserts sentencing to incapacitation and general deterrence ('prison works'). In the course of this shift, the Probation Service was sidelined, and the offer of a centre-stage role withdrawn just at the point when service managers (if still not all the rank and file) accepted a new conception of the Service's role, based largely on the belief that using cognitive behavioural principles it could intervene more effectively to reduce offending.

Howard's disdain for the Service was demonstrated in a number of ways. Firstly, he tightened-up the first set of National Standards (Home Office *et al* 1992, 1995), reducing officer discretion regarding enforcement still further, as NAPO had always feared he would. Secondly, a new Green Paper, *Strengthening Punishment in the Community* (Home Office 1995) threatened to create a new general purpose community sentence, blurring the distinctions between existing sentences and leaving magistrates free to specify the mix of elements they wanted. The purpose of this new order was to be the reduction of crime and the protection of society; the fact that rehabilitation no longer figured symbolised the marginalisation of the Service and the near-complete break with tradition that was now being countenanced. Nothing came of this Green Paper, however, possibly because the Home Office realised that it gave too much discretion to magistrates (at a time when this was beginning to be questioned), and possibly because magistrates themselves did not like it, and actually preferred more differentiated rather than general purpose sentencing options.

The third of Howard's contributions to the further development of community penalties was to rekindle the use of the electronically-monitored curfew. The 1991 Act had introduced it as a sentence, but this had never been implemented, largely because the three remand experiments in 1989/90 had been inconclusive about the viability of tagging (Mair and Nee 1990). Howard was undeterred. Better technology was now available, and he authorised three (later six) experimental curfew schemes. Probation service resistance to tagging was weakening, but the new sentence had still not been rolled out nationally in May 1997 when, after eighteen years, the Conservative government ceded victory to New Labour. Howard's final contribution, in the Crime (Sentences) Act 1997 (which in general terms was set considerably to increase the use of imprisonment) was uncharacteristic: he introduced, for the first time, after years of inconclusive debate, the use of community penalties (electronically-monitored curfews, community service, attendance centre and, perhaps most significantly, driving disqualifications) as an alternative to prison for fine default. The use of a driving disqualification as a penalty other than in respect of a motoring offence seemed drastic at the time – but it was in fact something that the Advisory Council on the Penal System had recommended in 1970, albeit not specifically as a response to fine default.

What is different now?

In the context of penal policy, the period 1948 to 1993 might legitimately be called 'the age of alternatives'; in the period 1993 to 1997 the first signs that this age might be undergoing significant transformation were becoming apparent. Rather than say too much about the contemporary situation – other chapters in this book will do that – it may be more useful here to identify a number of factors that have obviously changed since the apparent heyday of alternatives.

It is clear, looking back, that the rehabilitative ideal was less important in generating alternatives than might have been thought – attendance centres, suspended sentences and even community service owed little to it. Sentencers' – especially magistrates' – desire for more differentiated sentences, was, on the whole, a more important factor. It is true, for most of the period in question, that the social work ideals of the Probation Service exerted a constraining influence on the shape and ethos of alternatives, and that up until the late 1970s the Service, and its allies among sentencers, had the power to rebuff challenges to them. But it did so at the cost of appearing insular, complacent and anachronistic, and in a period when penal reductionism became steadily more important at government level, the Service, whilst doing good work in its own terms, played its hand very badly, compared to juvenile justice workers. It is against this background that the following factors, derived in part from Bottoms (1995), assume significance.

Firstly, there has been an inevitable loss of innocence in regard to community penalties. At the millennium, it is impossible to speak of them with the same confidence and optimism that prevailed in the 1960s and 1970s. They are no longer, as many of them were then, abstractions on which high hopes could be pinned. Experience has bred a more rounded appraisal of them. There have undoubtedly been successes, some diversion from custody, some diversion from crime (Raynor 1988); there have been expressions of satisfaction from offenders themselves (Bailey 1995). But even the most ardent supporters of community penalties cannot say that they have been spectacularly successful at reforming offenders, or that it is administratively easy to target such penalties and guarantee that they will be used instead of custody. This does not amount to a case against them or against penal reductionism – far from it (Stern 1998; Penal Affairs Consortium 2000) – because, as was noted at the outset, community penalties were so under-evaluated in the past that we have no reliable record of the good that they sometimes did, and can still do. Nonetheless, experience still demands more modest expectations of them.

Secondly, the magistracy – a major promoter of non-custodial measures in post-war England – has declined in influence, in three ways. Firstly, it has less influence as a pressure group; secondly it is no longer a milieu which produces prestigious individual commentators on crime policy; and thirdly its core activity, sentencing, has been increasingly subject to direction by government. Among the most ancient of judicial institutions, 'the bench' has become something of an anomaly in an increasingly centralised system of criminal justice. Attempts in the 1980s, in the name of the justice model, to simultaneously restore powers it had lost to the executive, to be more precise in its demands on offenders, and to eradicate 'justice by geography', have given way to a period in which government itself specifies the purpose of the penalty in precise detail.

Thirdly, perhaps as a consequence of both populism and secularism, there has been a decline in humanitarianism and compassion as adequate and acceptable motives in penal policy; they have come to be associated with sentimentality, with a liberal professional elite, an upper middle class whose members are too insulated from criminal activity to appreciate its impact of 'ordinary' people. Humanity and compassion – by which I mean more than rehabilitative or therapeutic ideals – have always been precarious in criminal justice decision-making, have easily been faked and have, on occasion, masked the development of more subtle control strategies. They nonetheless made it plausible and desirable to individualise sentencing, to encourage toleration of offenders 'in the community', to insist that prison could be harmful and that there might be a 'better way'. Once populist punitiveness prevails, these considerations matter less.

Fourthly, there is greater awareness of crime victims' suffering, more explicit support for victims in the mass media and greater public representation by victims themselves. At the very least, this means that rehabilitation can no longer be looked upon as a principle above all others, even by those who are convinced that it is empirically feasible. Ethically, the needs and interests of victims have come to be seen as having at least equal worth with those of offenders, and all new responses to offenders now need to reflect this. The development of restorative justice as a framework in which the needs and interests of offenders and victims might potentially be balanced possibly points away from the use of imprisonment, towards new forms of community penalties in which offenders are seen to take responsibility, express remorse and make practical or symbolic amends (Wright 1999).

Fifthly, there are incipient signs of renewed interest in disqualification and forfeiture as community penalties, and, significantly, as preventive measures as well. The use of driving bans for non-motoring offences has been introduced, known football hooligans have been banned from travelling in support of their team, and, most dramatically, the possibility of coupling a breach of a community penalty to benefit cuts has recently been introduced. Forfeiture of drug dealers' profits, uncontroversial in itself, may possibly be the precursor of its use in respect of other crimes. Conceptually, the taking away of goods that give status is not far removed from shaming, the removal of someone's good name. All of these measures could be construed as evidence of a revaluation of the punishment–citizenship relationship; citizenship may become conditional upon non-offending, or compliance with community penalties, in a way that (except in regard to imprisonment) was not the case in the past.

The ubiquity of managerialism – an ideology of total, finely calibrated, control – and the increased centralisation which is both its partial cause and usual consequence, may adversely affect the ethics of criminal justice in general. Managerialism's primary emphasis on economy, efficiency and effectiveness tend to supplant other organisational value systems. It fosters a culture of control and an expectation of obedience, emphasising the following of procedures rather than personal discretion and professional autonomy (which may limit the expression of ordinary human qualities such as kindness and empathy). It minionises staff, and objectifies offenders in ways that make it easier to perceive them as 'categories' and 'types', and then manipulate them, as 'risks' rather than as rounded, complex people. The relentless pursuit of efficiency creates a 'time squeeze', and shortens the period in which results – changed attitudes and reduced offending – are expected. The equally relentless pursuit of measurable effectiveness generates an audit culture, an incessant process of monitoring and inspection which may well deplete the resourcefulness and personal commitment that undoubtedly made some community penalties a success in the past.

Lastly, new technology is beginning to have a transformative effect on community penalties. Electronic monitoring ('tagging') in England and Wales originated outside the normal channels of penal innovation (Nellis 1991b) and although, to date, relatively few people have been subjected to it as a penalty, its potential is far-reaching. The Criminal Justice and Court Services Act 2000 envisages the increased use of electronically monitored surveillance in community penalties and post-prison licence supervision; and technological advances promise new variations of electronic monitoring, including 'tracking tagging' (monitoring movement rather than fixed location), whose political appeal has already been registered. Informed observers have shrewdly begun to ask whether electronic surveillance might in time become the dominant means of controlling sentenced offenders in the community, with probation input reduced to an adjunct (Whitfield 2000; Nellis and Lilly 2000).

Conclusions

Modernisation has been the watchword of the New Labour government, and these are undoubtedly detraditionalising times in criminal justice in Britain (Nellis 1999). This is perhaps symbolised most clearly in the readiness of the New Labour government to countenance the merging of the prison and probation services into a single body (Home Office 1998), a proposal which, first time round, met with effective probation and judicial resistance, but which still remains a longer term possibility (Boateng 2000). Resistance to the government's modernisation agenda, across the public sector, is routinely dismissed as signifying the forces of conservatism, as if past achievements never warrant preservation. Politically, neither the strategy nor the resistance is novel:

> The attempt to break definitively with an older social order en-counters a kind of historical deposit and threatens to founder upon it. The more total the aspirations of the new regime the more imperiously will it seek to introduce an era of forced forgetting.
>
> (Connerton 1989:12)

'Forced forgetting' may seem slightly strong in this context, but there is little in official rhetoric which suggests an appreciation of the Service's past, whilst there undoubtedly is an eagerness to 'change the culture', and to recruit employees who will embrace the new agenda. No par-ticular prominence is given to Probation Service history in the curricula for the new probation training programmes; the accent is firmly on the new. The Criminal Justice and Court Services Act has initiated major changes in the structure of the Service, and the well-intentioned probation interest groups who lobbied successfully to retain the name 'probation' won only by a pyrrhic victory, forsaking an opportunity to articulate a new vision, and a new name to match (Nellis 2000). There is little in the newly constituted Service which actually reflects the ethos of the old, despite the efforts of some researchers and practitioners to rework older strategies in new ways, e.g. 'building relationships' as 'pro-social modelling' (Rex and Matravers 1998). Retaining the name 'probation' thus gives a false impression of continuity, and, ironically, given the retentionists' intentions, its increasingly anachronistic flavour may in time make it easier than it would otherwise have been for governments to portray the service as obsolete – so very twentieth-century – and to justify merging it into the Prison Service.

There have been turning points in the history of probation, as in history generally, moments when events could have gone differently. The Service came within a hair's breadth of abolition in 1969; it survived absorption into the social services departments, but the contempor-aneous restructuring of its training arrangements might, in retrospect, be seen to have aligned the Service too closely with social work, and distanced it too much from crime prevention and penal reform (Nellis 1993b). Would the vigour of its commitment to the rehabilitation of offenders as a principle above all others in criminal justice have been as sustainable for so long if a crime victims' movement had developed decades earlier? (Pease 1999). The Service responded naively – when it still had the power to do otherwise – to Haxby's (1978) analysis, and to the Younger Report (Advisory Council on the Penal System 1974); and in the 1980s it reacted very unimaginatively to SNOP and to the 'punishment in the community' initiative. It could have shaped its own future slightly better than it did.

Today, there is little sense of service achievements being built upon, and a far greater sense of traditions, ideals and practices being repudiated because they have seemingly become outmoded in the context of 'actuarial justice' and 'digital rule' (Feeley and Simon 1994; Jones 2000). Traces of a rehabilitative commitment remain in the new discourse of risk management and effective practice (Robinson 1999), but as one means of control among several, no longer a notional end in itself. It would be unwise to anticipate continuity in the forms that community penalties take, let alone a future renaissance of the rehabilitative ideal, on such slender traces as this; astute commentators from quite different generations detect and expect seismic changes in contemporary forms of penality, not necessarily for the best (Radzinowicz 1991; Garland 2000).

In the midst of these changes, someone, somewhere should ensure that the probation contribution to the penal heritage is properly remembered. The orchestration of remembrance may well fall to professional historians, heritage experts and retired probation staff, rather than to serving officers and probation academics/trainers, but their endeavours would be of only limited use if serving officers themselves never learned anything of how their recent predecessors had worked. While the post-war history of community penalties in England and Wales deserves to be remembered simply because it is an honourable and interesting one, it also needs to be remembered because conscious acts of remembrance and reflection – proper analytical history – could remind the contemporary service of its roots and its achievements, its turning points, its lost opportunities, its past ambitions and its still unrealised possibilities. In short, a historically tutored memory may help us to realise that the centralised, highly managerial, and potentially short-lived future into which the Service is being drawn is not the only – or the brightest – future that it might have had.

Notes

1 There was, however, a considered reason for this in Home Office thinking. As I will later show, there was strong evidence that sentences billed specifically as 'alternatives to custody' were used by sentencers not only for those who would otherwise have been sent to prison, but also (and frequently) for others. For the latter group, there was a danger that if they were reconvicted, the second court could simply assume that the first court had intended the initial sentence as, in the strict sense, an 'alternative to custody'; hence, imprisonment might automatically be imposed by the second court, acting on the misapprehension. In Home Office thinking in 1990–91, this was an unintended consequence that should be avoided.

References

Advisory Council on the Penal System (1970) *Non-Custodial and Semi-Custodial Penalties*. London: HMSO.

Advisory Council on the Penal System (1974) *Young Adult Offenders*. London: HMSO.

Advisory Council on the Penal System (1977) *The Length of Prison Sentences*. London: HMSO.

Advisory Council on the Penal System (1978) *Sentences of Imprisonment: A Review of Maximum Penalties*. London: HMSO.

Advisory Council on the Treatment of Offenders (1957) *Alternatives to Short Terms of Imprisonment*. London: HMSO.

Advisory Council on the Treatment of Offenders (1963) *The Organisation of After-Care*. London: HMSO.

Allen, R. (1991) 'Out of Jail: The Reduction in the Use of Custody for Male Juveniles 1981–88', *Howard Journal*, 30 (1), 30–52.

Bailey, R. (1995) 'Helping Offenders as an Element of Justice', in M. Lacey and M. Ward (eds) *Probation: Working for Justice*. London: Whiting and Birch.

Bean, P. (1976) *Rehabilitation and Deviance*. London: Routledge.

Bissell, D. (1987) *Conscience, Courts and Community: A History of the Probation Service in the City of Birmingham*. Birmingham: West Midlands Probation Service.

Boateng, P. (2000) Interview in *Prison Service Journal*, 128, 56–59.

Bochel, D. (1976) *Probation and After-Care: its Development in England and Wales*. Edinburgh: Scottish Academic Press.

Bottoms, A.E. (1980) *The Suspended Sentence after Ten Years*. Leeds: Centre for Applied Social Studies, University of Leeds.

Bottoms, A.E. (1995) 'The Philosophy and Politics of Punishment and Sentencing', in C. Clarkson and R. Morgan (eds) *The Politics of Sentencing Reform*. Oxford: Clarendon Press.

Bottoms, A.E. and McWilliams, W. (1979) 'A Non-Treatment Paradigm for

Probation Practice', *British Journal of Social Work*, 9, 159–202.

Bullock, W.F. and Tildesley, W.M.S. (1984) *Special Requirements in Probation or Supervision Orders: A Local Case Study*. Cambridge: University of Cambridge Institute of Criminology.

Carlen, P. (1990) *Alternatives to Women's Imprisonment*. Milton Keynes: Open University Press.

Cohen, P. (1979) *Knuckle Sandwich*. Harmondsworth: Penguin.

Connerton, P. (1989) *How Societies Remember*. Cambridge: Cambridge University Press.

de Haan, W. (1990) *The Politics of Redress*. London: Unwin Hyman.

Feeley, M. and Simon, J. (1994) 'Actuarial Justice: the Emerging New Criminal Law', in D. Nelken (ed.) *The Futures of Criminology*. London: Sage.

Ferguson, N. (1997) *Virtual History: Alternatives and Counterfactuals*. London: Macmillan.

Field, X. (1963) *Under Lock and Key: A Study of Women in Prison*. London: Max Parrish.

Folkard, S., Smith, D.E. and Smith, D.D. (1976) *IMPACT (Intensive Matched Probation and After-Care Treatment), vol II: The Results of the Experiment*, Home Office Research Study No. 36. London: HMSO.

Garland, D. (2000) 'The Culture of High Crime Societies: Some Preconditions of Recent "Law and Order" Policies', *British Journal of Criminology*, 40, 347–375.

Hall, P. (1976) *Reforming the Welfare: The Politics of Change in Personal Social Services*. London: Heinemann.

Hall Williams, J.E. (1970) *The English Penal System in Transition*. London: Butterworths.

Harvey, L. and Pease, K. (1989) 'Variations in Punishment in England and Wales', in D. Evans and D. Herbert (eds) *The Geography of Crime*. London: Routledge.

Haxby, D. (1978) *Probation: A Changing Service*. London: Constable.

Hobsbawm, E. (1997) *On History*. London: Weidenfeld and Nicholson.

Home Office (1965) *The Child, the Family and the Young Offender*, Cmnd. 2742. London: HMSO.

Home Office (1968) *Children in Trouble*, Cmnd. 3601. London: HMSO.

Home Office (1977) *A Review of Criminal Justice Policy 1976*. London: HMSO.

Home Office (1978) *Youth Custody and Supervision: A New Sentence*, Cmnd 7406. London: HMSO.

Home Office (1979) *Report of the Committee of Inquiry into the United Kingdom Prison Services*, Cmnd. 7673. London: HMSO.

Home Office (1980) *The Reduction of Pressure on the Prison System: Observations on the Fifteenth Report from the Expenditure Committee*, Cmnd. 7948. London: HMSO.

Home Office (1983) *Report of Her Majesty's Chief Inspector of Prisons*. London: HMSO.

Home Office (1984a) *Criminal Justice: A Working Paper*. London: Home Office.

Home Office (1984b) *Intermittent Custody*, Cmnd. 9281. London: HMSO.

Home Office (1984c) *Statement of National Objectives and Priorities for the Probation Service*. London: Home Office.

Home Office (1988) *Punishment, Custody and the Community*, Cmnd. 424. London: HMSO.

Home Office (1990a) *Crime, Justice and Protecting the Public*, Cmnd. 965. London: HMSO.

Home Office (1990b) *Supervision and Punishment in the Community: A Framework for Action*, Cmnd. 966. London: HMSO.

Home Office (1995) *Strengthening Punishment in the Community: A Consultation Document*, Cmnd. 2780. London: Home Office.

Home Office (1998) *Joining Forces: The Prisons-Probation Review*. London: Home Office.

Home Office, Department of Health and Welsh Office (1992) *National Standards for the Supervision of Offenders in the Community*. London: Home Office.

Home Office, Department of Health and Welsh Office (1995) *National Standards for the Supervision of Offenders in the Community* (revised). London: Home Office.

House of Commons (1978) *Fifteenth Report from the Expenditure Committee, Session 1977–78: The Reduction of Pressure on the Prison System*. London: HMSO.

Jones, R. (2000) 'Digital Rule: punishment, control and technology', *Punishment and Society*, 2 (1), 5–22.

Lloyd, C. (1985) *Responses to SNOP*. Cambridge: University of Cambridge Institute of Criminology.

McGuire, J. and Priestley, P. (1985) *Offending Behaviour: Skills and Stratagems for Going Straight*. London: Batsford.

McWilliams, W. (1983) 'The Mission to the English Police Courts 1876–1936', *Howard Journal of Penology and Crime Prevention*, 22, 129–147.

McWilliams, W. (1985) 'The Mission Transformed: Professionalisation of Probation between the wars', *Howard Journal of Criminal Justice*, 24, 257–274.

McWilliams, W. (1986) 'The English Probation System and the Diagnostic Ideal', *Howard Journal of Criminal Justice*, 25, 241–260.

McWilliams, W. (1987) 'Probation, Pragmatism and Policy', *Howard Journal of Criminal Justice*, 26, 97–121.

Mair, G. (1991) *Part-time Punishment: The Origins and Development of Senior Attendance Centres*. London: HMSO.

Mair, G. (1996) 'Intensive Probation', in G. McIvor (ed.) *Working with Offenders*. London: Jessica Kingsley.

Mair, G. (1997) 'Community Penalties and Probation', in M. Maguire, R. Morgan and R. Reiner (eds) *The Oxford Handbook of Criminology* (second edition). Oxford: Clarendon Press.

Mair, G. and Nee, C. (1990) *Electronic Monitoring: The Trials and Their Results*, Home Office Research Study No. 120. London: HMSO.

May, T. (1991) 'Under Siege: Probation in a Changing Environment', in R. Reiner and M. Cross (eds) *Beyond Law and Order: Criminal Justice Policy and Politics in the 1990s*. Basingstoke: MacMillan.

Morris, N. and Tonry, M. (1990) *Between Prison and Probation: Intermediate Punishments in a Rational Sentencing System*. Oxford: Oxford University Press.

Mott, J.R. (1992) *Probation, Prison and Parole: the True Story of the Work of a Probation Officer*. Lewes: Temple House Books.

Mullins, C. (1948) *Fifteen Years Hard Labour*. London: Gollancz.

NACRO (1977) *Children and Young Persons in Custody*. London: NACRO.

Nellis, M. (1991a) Intermediate Treatment and Juvenile Justice in England and Wales 1960–1985. Unpublished Ph.D thesis, University of Cambridge.

Nellis, M. (1991b) 'The Electronic Monitoring of Offenders in England and Wales: Recent Developments and Future Prospects', *British Journal of Criminology*, 31, 165–85.

Nellis, M. (1993a) 'Juvenile Justice and the Voluntary Sector', in R. Matthews (ed.) *Privatising Criminal Justice.* London: Sage.

Nellis M. (1993b) 'Criminology, Crime Prevention and the Future of Probation Training', in K. Bottomley, T. Fowles and R. Reiner (eds) *Criminal Justice: Theory and Practice*. British Criminology Conference 1991 selected papers, vol. 2. London: British Society of Criminology/ISTD.

Nellis, M. (1999) 'Towards the Field of Corrections: Modernising the Probation Service in the 1990s', *Social Policy and Administration*, 33 (3), 302–323.

Nellis, M. (2000) 'Renaming Probation', *Probation Journal*, 47 (1), 39–44.

Nellis, M. and Lilly, J.R. (2000) 'Accepting the Tag: Probation Officers and Home Detention Curfew', *Vista*, 6 (1), 68–80.

Page, M. (1992) *Crimefighters of London: A History of the Origins and Development of the London Probation Service 1876–1965*. London: Inner London Probation Service.

Paley, J. and Thorpe, D. (1976) *Children: Handle with Care*. Leicester: National Youth Bureau.

Parker, H. (1974) *View from the Boys*. London: David and Charles.

Parliamentary All-Party Penal Affairs Group (1980) *Too Many Prisoners*. Chichester: Barry Rose.

Parliamentary All-Party Penal Affairs Group (1981) *Still Too Many Prisoners*. Chichester: Barry Rose.

Pease, K. (1980) 'The Future of the Community Treatment of Offenders in Britain', in A.E. Bottoms and R.H. Preston (eds) *The Coming Penal Crisis: A Criminological and Theological Exploration.* Edinburgh: Scottish Academic Press.

Pease, K. (1999) 'The Probation Career of Al Truism', *Howard Journal of Criminal Justice*, 38 (1), 2–16.

Pease, K. and McWilliams, W. (ed.) (1980) *Community Service by Order*. Edinburgh: Scottish Academic Press.

Penal Affairs Consortium (2000) *A Manifesto for Penal Reform*. London: Penal Affairs Consortium.

Personal Social Services Council (1978) *A Future for Intermediate Treatment*. London: Personal Social Services Council.

Pointing, J. (ed.) (1986) *Alternatives to Custody*. Oxford: Blackwell.

Radzinowicz, L. (1991) 'Penal Regressions', *Cambridge Law Journal*, 50, 422–444.

Raynor, P. (1985) *Social Work, Justice and Control*. London: Blackwell.

Raynor, P. (1988) *Probation as an Alternative to Custody*. Aldershot: Avebury.

Raynor, P. (1997) 'Reading Probation Statistics: A Critical Comment', *Vista*, 3 (3), 181–185.

Rex, S. and Matravers, A. (eds) (1998) *Pro-Social Modelling and Legitimacy – The Clarke Hall Day Conference*. Cambridge: University of Cambridge, Institute of Criminology.

Robinson, G. (1999) 'Risk Management and Rehabilitation in the Probation Service', *Howard Journal of Criminal Justice*, 38, 421–433.

Rutherford, A. (1978) 'Decarceration of Young Offenders in Massachusetts', in N. Tutt (ed.) *Alternative Strategies for Coping with Crime*. Oxford: Basil Blackwell.

Rutherford, A. (1986) *Prisons and the Process of Justice*. Oxford: Oxford University Press.

Rutherford, A. (1989) 'The Mood and Temper of Penal Policy: Curious Happenings in England during the 1980s', *Youth and Policy*, 27, 27–31.

Rutherford, A. (1992) *Growing Out of Crime: The New Era*. Winchester: Waterside Press.

Shaw, R. and Hutchinson, M. (1985) *Periodic Restriction of Liberty*. Cropwood Conference Series 17. Cambridge: University of Cambridge, Institute of Criminology.

Stern, V. (1998) *A Sin against the Future: Imprisonment in the World*. Harmondsworth: Penguin.

Stokes, S. (1950) *Court Circular: Experiences of a London Probation Officer*. London: Michael Joseph.

Stroud, J. (1961) *Touch and Go*. London: Longmans.

Thorpe, D., Smith, D., Green, C. and Paley, J. (1980) *Out of Care: The Community Support of Juvenile Offenders*. London: George Allen and Unwin.

Todd, M. (1964) *Ever Such a Nice Lady*. London: Gollancz.

Vass, A.A. (1990) *Alternatives to Prison*. London: Sage.

von Hirsch, A. (1976) *Doing Justice*. New York: Hill and Wang.

Whitfield, D. (ed.) (1992) *Twenty Years of Community Service*. Winchester: Waterside Press.

Whitfield, D. (2000) 'What Next – The Magic Bracelet?', *Criminal Justice Matters*, 39, 24–25.

Willis, A. (1986) 'Alternatives to imprisonment: an elusive paradise?', in J. Pointing (ed.) *Alternatives to Custody*. Oxford: Blackwell.

Windlesham, Lord (1993) *Responses to Crime, Volume 2: Penal Policy in the Making*. Oxford: Clarendon Press.

Wootton, B. (1959) *Social Science and Social Pathology*. London: George Allen and Unwin.

Wootton, B. (1982) *Crime and the Penal System*. London: George Allen and Unwin.

Wright, M. (1999) *Restoring Respect for Justice*. Winchester: Waterside Press.

Chapter 3

Community penalties in the context of contemporary social change

Mark Liddle

Introduction

While historical accounts of community penalties and their evolution suggest that issues concerning the purpose and appropriateness of community penalties have often generated heated debate, a range of broader developments have lent these issues a particular salience very recently. At the time of writing, community penalties are changing rapidly in terms of the way in which they are being implemented, 'managed' and evaluated by relevant criminal justice agencies and professionals, but the way in which such penalties are conceived of and justified, is also seeing some significant shifts.

Such changes are seldom straightforward, and full discussion of their causes and background cannot be undertaken in a short paper, but a number of factors having a key impact on the current terrain of debate and activity around community penalties are worth highlighting specifically. Some of these will be returned to in separate sections, below.

First, it is clear that significant changes in communities and local social structures themselves are having an impact on the conception and development of community penalties, although it is obligatory to note when making such claims, that phrases such as 'the community' have their own particular difficulties. This general claim will be elaborated in more detail in section three.

Second, an impressive (and apparently accelerating) growth in new technology is having a fundamental impact on the way in which community penalties are currently being implemented and planned. I mention this particular factor only to dispense with it, as George Mair's chapter in this book (chapter 9) deals specifically with issues concerning these technological developments and their implications for community penalties.

Third, community penalties and the debate surrounding them are closely linked to the ascendancy of crime prevention/'community safety' ideas (which have become increasingly broad and inter-con-nected – or 'joined-up' – of late), and of the continuing development of new forms of partnership or multi-agency working. These two developments (dealt with in sections one and two, respectively) have together had a profound impact on agencies such as the Probation Service (and on current plans for re-organisation), and on the way in which 'community interventions' are discussed and implemented more generally.

After a brief discussion of these key factors and some of their implications, some comments on the future direction of community penalties are offered. It is concluded that a deeper understanding of contemporary social change can not only shed light on factors which help to shape public and government thinking about community penalties, but can also help us to influence this 'direction' in a positive manner.

1 Crime prevention, community safety, and 'joined-up' thinking about offending

Even a brief examination of developments in the 'local governance of crime' over the last two decades makes it clear that there have been fundamental changes, not only in the way in which offending is perceived and experienced by the public, but in the approaches taken by governments (and the criminal justice agencies which they ostensibly direct) to address it. From the development of crime prevention as a discipline, to the spread of broader notions of 'community safety' (which sought to contextualise offending and redefine responsibility for addressing it), to more recent moves toward 'joined-up thinking' about offending in an even broader context of multi-faceted phenomena such as 'social exclusion', the last two decades have arguably transformed the field quite radically (or are set to do so).

Although conceptions of crime prevention have been around in one form or another for a very long time, the range of crime prevention activity, both in Britain and internationally, has by all accounts increased dramatically over the last two decades. As Pease (1994) and others have noted, all theories of crime operate with some notion of crime prevention, implicit or otherwise, but the 1980s and 1990s have seen crime prevention develop into a more specifically focused and integrated field of activity, with its own conceptual frameworks, methodologies, and increasingly, its own manifestations in public policy and funding sources. These developments have also generated a broad and diverse literature, within which 'histories of crime prevention' are now increasingly common. Given that a number of comprehensive historical overviews of crime prevention and its growth have already been offered elsewhere,[1] remarks here will be limited to presentation of some of the key developments in Britain which supply a context for the following discussion.

References to the importance of crime prevention can be found in a wide variety of government and other publications dating as far back as the last century, but a number of developments in the late 1970s and early 1980s served to give crime prevention a new kind of prominence in Britain, and to set the scene for further growth and diversification during the latter half of the 1980s and into the 1990s. Situational crime prevention had already gained popularity during the 1970s, but following a number of influential conferences in the early 1980s, and also in the wake of the 1981 urban riots (which both opened the door to new discussions of 'community policing', and raised questions about the capacity of the police to address problems of crime and social order on their own), crime prevention began both to diversify, and to become more established institutionally. In the latter regard, the Home Office created a separate Crime Prevention Unit in 1983, and the government's previous Standing Committee on Crime Prevention was re-cast as a Standing Conference, under the chairmanship of a Home Office minister. Also in 1983, work began on an inter-departmental circular on crime prevention, which was finally released in the following year (Home Office *et al* 1984); although the focus of that circular was also largely situational, it attached considerable importance to multi-agency work, and it invited greater participation from agencies outside the police in addressing crime problems.

The circular also invited the Probation Service to become involved in new 'co-ordinated approaches' to crime prevention, and it was followed by the Home Office's 'SNOP' document ('Statement of National Objectives and Priorities', 1984), which urged the Service to range more widely than individual work with offenders. Initial response from the Probation Service to these developments seems to have been mixed, and although documents published by ACOP (the Association of Chief Officers of Probation) at the time suggested that crime prevention ideas were regarded as being broadly consistent with current and future work of the Service, rank and file members seemed more suspicious (see, e.g., National Association of Probation Officers 1984).

A number of other important events followed over the next few years, including the launch of the Home Office's *Crack Crime* campaign in 1987, and in 1988, the launch of the Safer Cities Programme, the publication by the Home Office of the *Costs of Crime* report, and the creation of Crime Concern. In 1989 the Home Office published its report on *The Fear of Crime* (the Grade Report, Home Office 1989), produced by a working party set up to examine public concern about crime and its impact, and also during the late 1980s more generally, local authorities such as Southwark, Hammersmith and Fulham, and Birmingham had begun to create 'community safety' posts or units, whose purpose was both to promote local authority involvement in crime prevention/community safety, and to develop and enhance relations with other agencies and groups.

Also around the turn of the decade, a series of government papers (Home Office 1988; 1990a, 1990b) paved the way for a more specific regime of 'community punishments'. It was noted in the Green Paper that 'Imprisonment is not the most effective punishment for most crime. Custody should be reserved as punishment for very serious offences', although it was also added that 'punishment in the community should be more economical in public resources' (Home Office 1988:2). Indeed, prison over-crowding and Treasury pressures are often referred to in discussions of this phase of the history of community penalties[2] although some of the 'appeals to community' that can be found in government publications during the period are consistent with some of those already referred to above.

Local authority involvement in crime prevention and community safety activity expanded markedly during the first half of the 1990s, spurred on to some extent by the release of major reports by the Association of District Councils (1990) and the Association of Metropolitan Authorities (1990), and by the release of the inter-departmental Circular 44/90 (Home Office *et al* 1990), and the 'partnership booklet' (Home Office 1990c). The latter two documents updated the previous circular 8/84, and offered descriptions of 'good practice' models from around the country, and were quickly followed by the release of the Morgan Report in August 1991 (Home Office 1991), a document which was to have a major impact in the field. The report focused on a wide range of issues concerning the local delivery of crime prevention and community safety work, but it became best known for its endorsement of a broad definition of 'community safety' itself, and for its recommendation that local authority involvement in such work be recognised and reinforced in a new statutory framework.

The popularity that the term 'community safety' had already started to gain by the late 1980s was certainly enhanced by the release of the Morgan Report in 1991, and the small number of definitions which could be found in the literature prior to that time grew steadily after the report's release. Although these definitions obviously vary in terms of their scope and/or emphasis, they tend to place a similar stress on the importance both of partnerships and community involvement, and to focus on issues which range more widely than traditional crime categories. Whereas 'crime prevention' and 'crime reduction' have usually been understood in terms of efforts to address circumstances which cause crime or criminal events, community safety definitions invariably contain some of the wider references publicised in the Morgan definition:

> The term 'crime prevention' is often narrowly interpreted and this reinforces the view that it is solely the responsibility of the police. On the other hand, the term 'community safety', is open to wider interpretation and could encourage greater participation from all sections of the community in the fight against crime … . We see community safety as having both social and situational aspects, as being concerned with people, as well as with attempting to reduce particular types of crime and the fear of crime. Community safety should be seen as the legitimate concern of all in the local community.
>
> (1991: 13)

Such references to community involvement, multi-agency working, and to wider issues such as 'fear of crime' continue to be reflected in more recent definitions, such as that offered in a 1996 survey report on local authority involvement in community safety:

> Community safety is the concept of community-based action to inhibit and remedy the causes and consequences of criminal, intimidatory and other related anti-social behaviour. Its purpose is to secure sustainable reductions in crime and fear of crime in local communities. Its approach is based on the formation of multi-agency partnerships between the public, private and voluntary sectors to formulate and introduce community-based measures against crime.
>
> (Local Authority Associations and Local Government Management Board 1996)[3]

The important thing to note about such definitions as they relate to community penalties specifically, is not only that they seek to draw tighter connections between primary, secondary, and tertiary crime prevention (where the latter is usually understood as involving interventions to reduce re-offending), but that they give special prominence to 'community-based measures' to address crime in the broadest sense. Increasingly, 'the community' is referred to in such definitions not only as being an important site for interventions to address crime or re-offending, but as a 'partner' whose involvement is crucial to the effectiveness of such interventions.

By the time of the local government community safety survey referred to above, nine out of ten local authorities surveyed in England and Wales indicated that they recognised community safety as a policy area, and over half claimed to have community safety strategies, published policy statements, or aims and objectives. Almost two-fifths of authorities had dedicated community safety officers to address both strategic/policy issues and service delivery. These findings provided a marked contrast with those of earlier surveys such as that referred to in the Association of Metropolitan Authorities 1990 report, which suggested relatively low levels of reported crime prevention/community safety activity, but they also indicated the extent to which community safety had come to be regarded by local authorities as an area requiring a *strategic* response.

The Probation Service had by the mid-1990s also gone much further in 'mainstreaming' crime prevention/community safety ideas, and by the time of the release of the *Three Year Plan for the Probation Service 1993–96* (Home Office 1993d), the goal of 'reducing and preventing crime and the fear of crime by working in partnership with others' was given priority as the first operational goal of the service. Some individual services around the country had also developed their own 'community safety strategies' by this time, although some uncertainty about the Probation Service's role in such work was still evident in research conducted during the 1990s (e.g. Liddle and Gelsthorpe 1994b: 19–21).[4]

Crime prevention and community safety also began to assume more importance within central government funded initiatives during the 1990s, including those concerned with economic or urban regeneration. Crime prevention and community safety were incorporated into the bidding criteria for initiatives such as City Challenge, for example, and this recognition was reinforced by the creation of the new Single Regeneration Budget (SRB) in 1994.

As 'community safety' definitions such as that endorsed in the Morgan Report began to gain popularity during the early 1990s, issues concerning public insecurity or 'fear of crime' also continued to attract more attention, and more routinely to inform surveys of city centre users or residents in local areas. Reducing fear of crime was of course one of the three key objectives of the national Safer Cities programme (launched just prior to the release of the Grade Report, Home Office 1989), but similar objectives also began to appear more frequently within the bidding priorities of spending initiatives such as City Challenge and the Single Regeneration Budget, and within 'mission statements' produced by a wide range of organisations and multi-agency groups having a crime prevention or community safety focus. At national level, reducing fear of crime was highlighted as a key aim of the Crime Prevention Agency when it was launched in 1995, for example, and within the growing pool of more local community safety strategies which had begun to evolve at the turn of the decade, the importance of fear of crime as an issue began to be asserted with increasing regularity.

A related development during the same period was the policy attention which issues such as 'neighbour nuisance' and 'anti-social behaviour' began to attract, in the wake of both intense media interest, and increasingly vocal complaints from residents in particular housing areas. This increased attention has in the last few years led some local authorities to draft 'nuisance policies', or to create special inter-departmental working groups with a remit to consider the local authority response to anti-social behaviour, nuisance, or 'incivilities'. Wider-ranging groups such as the Local Authority Working Group on Anti-Social Behaviour have also been formed, and have been active both in publicising some of the particular problems faced by housing authorities in England and Wales, and in lobbying central government for extra powers to address them. Organisations such as the Chartered Institute of Housing issued papers and good practice reports on the subject of 'nuisance', although many of the issues addressed in such publications are now often subsumed in wider ranging community safety strategies; the sub-title of the statement issued by the local authority associations at the launch of their survey reflects the latter trend, for example: 'Preventing crime, fear of crime and anti-social behaviour in our communities'.[5]

Controversy about nuisance problems and anti-social behaviour also saw the term 'community safety' acquire more punitive overtones than its earlier usage reflected. 'Community safety orders' were proposed by the government in September 1997 (Home Office 1997), for example, as a means for targeting individuals or groups involved in criminal or anti-social behaviour which 'causes harassment to a community'. Similar measures have been proposed in response to public concern about 'aggressive beggars', 'squeegee merchants' and other forms of anti-social behaviour, and also in the context of debates around zero tolerance policing, a notion which itself featured prominently in conference agendas during 1996–97.

A more punitive side to 'public concerns' of this kind also materialised intermittently during the mid-1990s in response to some much publicised cases where offenders on community sentences were perceived to have been 'rewarded' by being sent on holiday. Public displeasure about such cases led the then Home Secretary to remark (in advance of the release of the consultation document *Strengthening Punishment in the Community*, Home Office 1995): 'These measures will mean an end to the approach which offers holidays for offenders ... . Out go holidays and in come tightly controlled community sentences.'[6]

Some of the most significant developments in the field have occurred since the general election in May 1997, and a whole range of crime prevention/community safety and offending-related activity in Britain has intensified noticeably since that time. Although the previous Conservative government had not accepted some of the key recommendations offered in the Morgan Report, the incoming administration had already announced an intention to review the existing statutory framework for community safety, and to implement changes to this framework which would clarify and extend the role of local authorities in planning and delivering community safety work. Following the release of a series of consultation papers dealing with this and a range of other issues, such changes were incorporated into the 1998 Crime and Disorder Act, which places joint responsibility on local authorities and the police, to develop and implement community safety work in partnership with other local agencies and groups, including the Probation Service. The new Act requires not only that local partners focus more clearly on the implications of their own practice on crime and disorder, but that local strategies be designed to address such problems, in consultation with local communities and within a suitable framework for monitoring and evaluation (interestingly, the Act does not employ the term 'community safety', but is instead framed in terms of 'crime and disorder' reduction). New legal tools were also provided to local partnerships for addressing such problems, including anti-social behaviour orders (civil orders which can be imposed by the court onto named individuals whose behaviour causes significant stress to others).

More recently still, the government's current focus on social exclusion and on the development of comprehensive strategies for 'neighbourhood renewal' has placed offending and efforts to reduce it at the heart of a range of inter-connected policy initiatives. This kind of 'mainstreaming' of crime and disorder reduction has been described by some in terms of a 'criminalisation of social policy', but it illustrates the extent to which 'joined-up thinking' about issues such as crime and disorder has impacted on areas of activity which tended to be much more compartmentalised in previous decades.

2 The rise of 'partnerships'/multi-agency approaches

Alongside the above developments, there has been a clear growth in the popularity of 'partnerships' and multi-agency approaches more generally. Although these approaches (or prescriptions to adopt them) were already familiar some time ago in a number of fields of practice – such as work to address child abuse, or juvenile offending – 'partnerships' have acquired a special prominence in a wide range of areas over the last 15 years or so, perhaps especially within the field of economic regeneration. Concerning the latter, the trend toward utilising 'public–private' partnerships to address local economic development has generated a broad literature, within which questions concerning accountability and new forms of 'local governance' have attracted a great deal of comment. Evidence concerning the trends themselves is also quite impressive; the extent to which partnership arrangements now cover this area of work is reflected in a recent estimate, for example, that some £46.6 billion of public money (nearly one-third of total public spending) is overseen by unelected 'quangos' (Hutchinson 1994), involving partnerships between local government and private sector interests. The proliferation of partnership arrangements more generally in some large urban areas has been quite pronounced, and has extended well beyond economic regeneration work and into a diverse range of fields including drugs, health, racial harassment, and domestic violence.

At the same time, local government has become increasingly fragmented, and trends toward such things as competitive tendering and devolved management during the 1990s tended to accelerate this process (Clarke and Stewart 1994). Hambleton (1991) has estimated that over 50 Acts of Parliament which had the effect of eroding or further regulating local authority activity were passed between 1979 and 1991, for example, and this general development has clearly provided a context for recent trends toward partnership working.

This focus on partnership working has also had a significant impact on particular funding regimes; clear description of multi-agency structures for planning and implementing programmes is now a prerequisite for securing funds under initiatives such as the Single Regeneration

Budget, for example, and it is also a necessary component of successful bids for many European funding sources.

Given that notions of partnership enjoy this kind of prominence, some writers have found it striking that this development seems to have occurred in the absence of much critical comment until quite recently. Focusing on the notion of 'community partnerships' in a regeneration context (and reinforcing the point made earlier about the increasing stress on 'community involvement' in much partnership work), McArthur (1995) has noted, for example:

> There is a theoretical framework developing around community partnerships, but with a few exceptions, the tone of much of the commentary from both researchers and policy makers has been optimistic and relatively unsceptical. [Since] most community partnerships are still in progress and have not yet been fully evaluated, the lack of critical consideration is surprising.
>
> (1995: 64)

Similar remarks have been offered from within the crime prevention field specifically; it was famously noted in the Morgan Report, for example, that 'the case for the partnership approach stands virtually unchallenged but also hardly tested' (Home Office 1991: 14), and although there has been an increasing interest within the field during the 1990s in research into multi-agency approaches to crime and related problems, these approaches have continued to be recommended in the absence of much evidence concerning their functioning or effectiveness. In short, although the potential benefits of partnership working in terms of improved co-ordination, more efficient use of resources, and so on are often referred to both in the growing accumulation of community safety strategies, and in government reports and circulars such as those referred to in the above section, the movement toward multi-agency crime prevention has clearly not been a 'research-driven' development, and in much of the literature, the value of partnership approaches seems to be regarded as being self-evident.

A body of research on particular aspects of partnerships and their functioning has grown steadily alongside the developments referred to above, however, and a critical literature on these developments has also broadened since the Morgan Working Group's reference to the un-challenged and untested nature of partnership working. Some useful summaries of relevant research relating specifically to multi-agency crime prevention have already been offered elsewhere,[7] but it is worth noting here that although the popularity of partnership working does not seem to have been adversely affected by it, the available research has highlighted both the complex and contested nature of partnerships, and some of the ideological and political currents which seem to have informed the concept and its evolution. While much of this research has tended to focus on the activities of single initiatives or on a small number of specific multi-agency groups, some recent academic work has also adopted a broader and perhaps more critical theoretical focus on multi-agency crime prevention and its development, and (to anticipate some of the remarks in the following section) has usefully attempted to draw links between such developments and other (e.g. sociological or global) factors.

3 Why these changes, and why now? – theorising recent developments

The main developments outlined above – i.e. the rise of crime prevention as an area of policy and research interest, and the increased popularity of partnership working – are clearly related, although they have each generated a body of literature, and are often considered separately within it. The breadth and pace of these developments also raises some obvious questions about causation, and a number of criminologists and others have been led to consider historical or theoretical explanations for what is referred to above as the rise of 'multi-agency crime and disorder reduction'. Full discussion of these explanations is beyond the scope of this paper, but it is worth summarising some of the key strands.

Concerning partnership working specifically for the moment, it is sometimes pointed out that multi-agency working is simply more efficient and effective than work undertaken by agencies independently and in isolation from one another, and that recent trends are simply the result of a 'pendulum swing' away from previous undue specialisation. Common sense examples are then sometimes provided, one of which is well illustrated by John Mudd's 'rat problem'. As Mudd (an American commentator), puts it:

> If a rat is found in an apartment, it is a housing inspection responsibility; if it runs into a restaurant, the health department has jurisdiction; if it goes outside and dies in an alley, public works takes over. More complex undertakings compound the confusion.
>
> (Mudd 1984: 8)

He argues that this kind of 'confusion' is a direct result of systems of management, which have placed great importance on specialisation and institutional autonomy. Part of his point is just that when we consider particular social problems, the boundaries across different services are, in an important sense, artificial. The problem in this case is rats, but depending on what rats do and on how you look at what rats do, there will be disagreements about which agencies are responsible for doing something about them.

It is arguable that many crimes and offending-related issues are of this kind; nuisance problems on difficult housing estates, for example, are often inter-connected and overlapping. If the problems include noise, then residents might call the Environmental Services department, who will record it, and maybe even come out to investigate and take action under the EPA. If the noise is caused by young people hanging around on the streets however, or if the noise is associated with criminality or other anti-social behaviour, then different agencies might have jurisdiction as well. In any case, single agency responses might be quite ineffective here, and there is a kind of obviousness to this conclusion. Similar accounts could be given about efforts to address single 'risk factors' where an offender is multiply vulnerable to subsequent offending, for example, or about interventions to address a specific aspect of deprivation on a housing estate without contextualising it.

A key question obviously concerns the *timing* of these developments, however, and explanations such as the above tell us little about why 'partnership working' has become so popular so quickly.

It is often noted in this regard that recent changes in crime control strategies have been motivated primarily by rising crime rates which the state has seemed unable to stem. While there are numerous and well-documented problems associated with measuring changes in crime rates over time, it is now widely accepted that much of the increase reflected in recorded crime statistics over the last 50 years or so (not just in the UK, but across the western world) is probably real. Since hitherto existing arrangements for crime control have apparently been unable to arrest this steady growth, it is sometimes argued, there has been an obvious necessity for new approaches, and crime prevention partnerships have been one inevitable result of this search for alternatives to traditional crime control models. The remarks of a police participant in a community-based crime prevention project focused on in Adam Crawford's (1997) recent research into community safety partnerships, exemplify this kind of perspective: 'We've just got to do something new. The crime rate is getting out of control and we don't know what else to do' (in Crawford 1997: 64).

Recognising that the apparent inability of traditional crime control strategies to contain rising crime cannot on its own explain the *form* that alternative models have taken, others have focused instead on broader factors which have impacted on structures of governance across a wide range of areas including crime and criminal justice. Processes of globalisation and localisation have often been referred to in this context, especially in discussions about the rise of partnership approaches more generally. On the one hand, it is pointed out that technological advances and the internationalisation of capital have tended to erode state power at a global level, since national states are more often simply bypassed in the conduct of business/commerce whose direction is determined by decisions made at a multi-national corporate level. On the other hand, global economic changes have also made it more difficult for national governments to retain sufficient flexibility and responsiveness to co-ordinate economic activity and service delivery at *local* level, as mass production has declined in importance, and as the location of economic activity itself has become less constrained by geographical con-siderations such as the presence of raw materials. These changes have impacted on both levels of government and also on relationships between local and central government; as Prior suggests:

> Change in the nature of local government's role within the socio-economic system of capitalist democracy is driven by the demands of the increasing global mobility of capital. The global economy, as it moves out of the 'fordist' era, requires a high degree of local specificity in providing conditions for production and repro-duction. National governments lack sufficiently sensitive policy levers to enable them to create such conditions, opening up a space for local economic action, which locally based interests can fill. This, it is argued, points to a growing significance of the local state in the development of new forms of relationship between the spheres of economic and political activity.
>
> (1996: 94)

These tendencies toward globalisation and localisation have com-bined to force changes not only in the way that the state functions – by generating a shift away from direct service provision toward policy formation and the co-ordination of services delivered by others, for example, or from a 'rowing' function to a 'steering' one, as Osborne and Gaebler (1992) describe it – but also in the structures through which the state acts. Concerning the latter, although there is an evolving debate about the extent to which the state has been 'hollowed out' or made leaner by the processes referred to, it does seem clear that the growth of partnership arrangements is strongly linked to these tendencies toward the 'two-ended' erosion of state power, and that partnerships are one way in which governments have sought to maintain their influence over spheres of activity which they were previously able to dominate much more directly. These arguments are perhaps especially relevant to the growth of 'quangos' during the 1990s, many of which were focused on the co-ordination or delivery of economic regeneration programmes at local level.

The increased popularity of partnership working has also been linked in the literature to the growth of managerialism, and to the focus on efficiency, effectiveness and economy (the so-called 'three "Es" ') which characterise the managerialist ethos. The spread of managerialism within the public sector has led not only to an increasing focus on the performance of individual agencies (as reflected in relevant 'output measures' and 'performance indicators') and to an increasing stress on the importance of 'strategic management', but also to an increasing focus on the importance of improved co-ordination, especially 'inter-agency co-ordination'. Managerialist perspectives are particularly well-suited to identifying system inefficiencies, in regard to which better co-ordination is often recommended as something of an antidote; where service delivery involves a range of agencies that are highly specialised and relatively autonomous, a lack of co-ordination can blunt overall system effectiveness, as such things as inconsistent agency policies, duplication or overlaps in service, and imprecisely targeted resources remain unidentified. Hence, inter-agency co-ordination is a means by which policies can be harmonised, and impediments to efficient service delivery addressed.

Managerialist perspectives within the criminal justice field specifically have been described by Young (1986, 1988) and others as being related to the rise of an 'administrative criminology', within which theoretical questions about causation assume very little importance, and where crime is regarded as something which needs to be managed rather than understood or eradicated. Some writers have further argued that the current popularity of multi-agency crime prevention is partly a result of the way in which 'the state' responds to this inability of traditional crime control strategies to reduce crime, by becoming more active at the level of ideology, and by re-describing crime problems and responsibility for them. Hence, the increasingly common references in official documents since the early 1980s, to the effect that neither the police nor governments can 'tackle crime' on their own – addressing crime problems is a 'task for all of us'. This process has been referred to by Garland as 'responsibilisation', and is described as being accompanied both by efforts to forge new crime control alliances between state agencies and other 'partners' and by the growth of new areas of expertise around co-ordination and multi-agency working; as Garland puts it:

> The practical problems involved in this new role are now the subject of dozens of government research publications which detail the obstacles to multi-agency working, the resistance it is liable to encounter, and the best means of manipulating diverse interests into crime control alliances ... A need for new experts in 'co-ordination' and 'inter-agency working' has been discovered, heralding the development of a strange new 'specialism' which will be defined by its interstitial role and its interdisciplinary skills. At the same time, a new form of knowledge is being assembled which will support and extend this strategy in the same way that positivist criminology once supported strategies of rehabilitation and individual correction. And, like that earlier knowledge of the criminal individual, which grew up quietly in the routines of institutional practice, this new knowledge is developing in out of the way reports and research studies which receive little public attention or scrutiny.
>
> (Garland 1996: 455)

Garland also claims that in the British context, the state is anything but 'hollowed out' in terms of its retention of power over criminal justice matters, although as noted above, such views are contested (see, for example, Bottoms 1996; Cope *et al* 1995).

In any case, while accounts of this sort obviously have something to contribute to an understanding of particular developments such as changes in relations between central and local government, or connections between 'inter-agency co-ordination' and managerialist conceptions of criminal justice, they have clear limitations when it comes to offering an overall explanation for the 'rise of multi-agency community safety', and also when it comes to describing what the motors of such change could be. Why, for example, does increasing public concern about such things as anti-social behaviour, fear of crime, disorder, and so on seem to have developed at the same time that managerialist and/or strategic responses (which highlight the importance of partnership working and co-ordination) have become more popular?

Some key contributions from recent social theory

Recent contributions by Bottoms and Wiles (1995, 1996) are among the most promising for addressing such questions. Drawing on recent social theory – most notably, on Giddens' analysis of late modernity – Bottoms and Wiles manage to link together some of the broad trends outlined above, in a way which helps us to understand not only why there seems to have been an increase in concern about crime and personal safety in the recent past, but why the range of proposed measures to address such problems (inter-agency co-operation, community safety strategies, and so on) have taken the form that they have.

As Giddens (1990) argues at some length, economic and technological changes have had a profound impact on everyday life in local communities, and on the way in which we experience time and place; these changes are wide-ranging and complex, but have together had the effect of 'dis-embedding' social relations from local neighbourhoods. Whereas in the past, an individual's 'environment of trust' was rooted in the local community, kinship relations, and tradition, the modern environment of trust is linked to personal relationships, abstract systems, and what he calls 'future-oriented, counter-factual thought' (instead of tradition, as a mode for connecting past and present). Rapid technological change, especially over the last 30 years, has greatly accelerated this general shift, and has also accelerated what he calls the 'emptying out of time and space'. New technology *and* changes in the world economy have simply made 'place' less important or relevant, and have eroded the basis on which tradition 'made sense of' or linked past and present.

As 'environments of trust' have shifted in the wake of these changes, so too have 'environments of *risk*', where risk is understood in terms of threats to one's 'ontological security'. Human beings have an essential need to maintain their own psychological integrity and keep anxiety at bay, and they do this most effectively in circumstances of familiarity and everyday routine. The predictability of everyday routine is also an important prerequisite to individual security, since predictability obviously makes the maintenance of security easier. But the key point to make here, and one which is effectively drawn out by Bottoms and Wiles in their discussion of crime prevention, is that the need to maintain ontological security is the driving force behind these twin developments; it is behind rising concerns about crime, anti-social behaviour, and so on, because the range of things which individuals find threatening or upsetting has shifted in the wake of those processes which characterise late modern society, and it is behind the increasing popularity of such things as 'inter-agency co-ordination' because the shift in bases of trust has also been a shift *toward* increased trust in abstract systems.

Claims of this kind obviously need further elaboration and defence, but the general account has some clear advantages in allowing us to understand the rise of multi-agency community safety. Although the increased popularity of conceptions of community safety over 'crime prevention' is itself a complex development, it is probably rooted at least partly in the fact that public concerns or anxieties are themselves so diffuse and wide-ranging; it has increasingly been recognised that they range more widely than conventional crime categories, even though public concern about conventional crime is also very real. Hence, there have been moves to recognise the importance of 'anti-social behaviour', 'incivilities' and 'nuisance', which, although they may not always be criminal in nature, can and do cause high levels of public concern and insecurity in particular circumstances. The research evidence concerning such things also suggests that feelings of insecurity do not bear a straightforward relationship to conventional crime categories (Hale 1996); in a recent survey of nuisance and crime undertaken by NACRO, for example, respondents who reported high levels of insecurity did not necessarily report having been directly victimised themselves, although they tended to perceive their housing estates as being alien, forbidding, and beyond their control (Liddle and Feloy 1997; Liddle *et al* 1997).

Similar arguments could be made concerning the roots of 'populist punitiveness'; just as feelings of insecurity appear to have risen (although not consistently or uniformly), levels of tolerance for perceived incivility ('squeegee merchants', aggressive beggars and the like) have shifted – perhaps they are always shifting, but recent developments again suggest that recent changes are different.

The account also has the advantage of allowing such things as the much referred to gap between the fear of crime and the 'real probabilities' of criminal victimisation to be understood, since it allows us to see that such fears are in fact more diffuse than a focus on crime would suggest, and they are therefore not straightforwardly amenable to reduction in the wake of education campaigns which aim to allow people to re-align their fears in the face of more accurate statistics. That women usually report higher levels of fear than men do in public surveys, for example, can be understood in terms of the fact that women's more subordinate position within the structure of power leaves them more vulnerable to threats to individual security, and as feminist researchers have argued for some time, such 'threats' take place routinely, albeit on a continuum, from sexual harassment and intimidation, to actual sexual or other violence.

It also has the advantage of allowing us to understand why some of the more effective community development initiatives which aim to reduce crime and anti-social behaviour can also have fear-reduction potential – they have such potential because they effectively 're-embed' local social relations, and modify residents' everyday routines in a way which allows for easier maintenance of ontological security. More generally, such an account might also make the increasing 'appeals to community' described by Crawford (1997) and others more understandable; the dis-embedding and other mechanisms associated with late modernity impact on local community relations in ways that erode social capital. Local community life does not in these circumstances supply what it used to, an observation that is consistent not only with the views of some elderly people that 'local villages aren't what they used to be', for example, but with views that there is 'something wrong with communities' which needs to be addressed, and with views that things like community development and community empowerment are self-evidently good things.

Connections between community safety and 'private public space' also seem more understandable in terms of such a theory; the private sector has arguably come closer to understanding some of these issues than governments have, and has become quite successful in applying such understanding in particular contexts to maximise profits. Shopping malls, for example, can be highly similar transnationally, in terms of their structure and ambience, and these similarities are by no means accidental; they are themselves a product of accumulated learning at the level of multi-national corporations, the result of regular attention to those features which potential customers find pleasing, attractive, and safe. Although driven by the need to generate profit, the designers and managers of such facilities have understood that subjective perceptions of this kind are not only highly relevant to individual behaviour and everyday routines (and it is of course precisely these things that businesses wish to alter or influence to their own advantage), but that such perceptions are subtle and multiply determined. In a word, they are not simply about crime or concern about direct victimisation (although these things can obviously be relevant); they are linked to a concern about the maintenance of individual integrity and security, and these things are in turn easiest to maintain in circumstances of routinization and familiarity.

4 Community penalties in a late modern context

It was argued in the previous section that the key motors driving some of these changes are rooted primarily in shifting bases of trust and security in late modern society. If such an account is plausible, then the implications can also seem quite radical, since shifts in what we find threatening are themselves in a sense rooted in shifts in the social order itself. By the same token, efforts to address social problems 'in the community' are really about creating new forms of social order.

As far as the recommended 'solutions' to offending problems are concerned, an increasing trust in abstract systems is clearly consistent with responses which stress co-ordination, targets, performance indicators, and other managerialist concepts, and responses of this kind do seem to have become increasingly common in the criminal justice field more generally – where social problems persist, more and better managerialism (and 'strategic thinking') is required; when initiatives or agency activities appear to be inefficient, more finely specified targets and outputs are the recommended antidote, and so on.

At the same time, increasing trust in abstract systems arguably gives higher prominence to bodies of professional knowledge about 'what works and why' – managerialist approaches in this sense require that the effectiveness of interventions in terms of their key objectives, e.g. the reduction of crime or re-offending – be 'evidence-based'. Hence, the recent focus in a wide range of government documentation, for example, on effectiveness and cost-benefit analysis, and the more general deployment of a practical and research-based discourse, which makes regular appeals to risk factors or criminogenic need.

The recent consultation paper *Joining Forces to Protect the Public* (Home Office 1998) provides a useful example of how some of these strands can infuse key policy statements (which in turn have a major influence on the way in which community penalties are designed, implemented and justified):

> Our probation services already make a great contribution, but this can be greatly increased if we enable them to work in a larger, national framework of aims, objectives and accountability so that their work is better targeted and focused, and their efforts more effectively supported. A system of punishment which is effective, credible and commands public confidence requires both community and custodial sentences to work, and to work well together. This means better integration between newly organised probation services and a more effective prison service placing a clearer

59

emphasis on constructive regimes and the day on which the prisoner will return to society for resettlement.

Both services must also be better at working and sharing information with the other agencies which are making a vital contribution to the achievement of their aims. In particular, a close collaborative and effective relationship must be maintained with the police on public protection issues.

A modern approach means taking advantage of modern systems and opportunities – both in respect of information systems, and new technology like electronic monitoring. And we need modern ways of taking advantage quickly of evidence derived from evaluations of 'What Works' so that both services can benefit in harmony with each other ....

To deliver its goals the service needs to be more accountable and better organised to develop its work in close co-operation and partnership with central government, the prison service, the police, mental health services, health authorities, local authorities, the CPS, victim support groups, TECs, and a range of voluntary sector groups and others. It must be organised to reflect the modern focus of its core business and the purpose of these partnerships: the protection of the public from predictably dangerous offenders under supervision in the community; and from those who pose a more general risk of re-offending.

Documentation concerning the new Detention and Training Order contains similar references to the need for evidence-based practice and demonstrable reductions in re-offending, for effective partnerships with other agencies and with communities, and, related to the latter, for tighter linkages between programmes of intervention and individual criminogenic need.

A key difficulty concerning the two changes referred to above, however – i.e. changes in the way in which crime problems are experienced and defined, on the one hand, and in the forms that solutions are perceived to take, on the other – is that they do not necessarily 'fit' together in a straightforward manner. If the focus on managerial, technological approaches to essentially social problems loses sight of the more deep-seated subjective determinants of current definitions of problems around crime and offending, it could produce a range of further difficulties without at the same time producing satis-factory results. One key 'satisfactory' outcome for a community penalty would involve the successful re-insertion (or maintenance) of an offender in his or her local community without further offending, for example, but what it is that makes community penalties 'work' in this sense might not be accessible through an exclusive focus on risk factors, or on the range of outputs and outcomes that are currently being specified in relevant documentation concerning such sentences and their implementation and evaluation. Some understanding of the dynamics of local communities (and of interventions which can 're-embed' local social relations more generally) are precisely what can be derived from recent social theory, however, and the sort of 'context' sketched out above is therefore of some importance to current developments in community penalties.

We have yet to see what some of these developments will lead to, but some of the most recent work being conducted by criminal justice agencies 'in partnership' across the country, does highlight the way in which broad policy aims that are about 'being tough on crime and tough on the causes of crime', for example, can turn out in practice to be dominated almost exclusively by management concerns – concerns to get the figures down, to produce the outputs, to generate better reconviction rates, and so on.

If anything, the inevitable tensions between supervision, support and surveillance also seem more acute in some of this recent work than they have been in the past, and the terrain of community penalties is likely to remain fraught with ambivalence, although such tensions in a sense allow practitioners and others an opening to history.

And finally, it is clearly possible that the sort of managerialist approaches referred to earlier will stand a better chance of producing interventions which can address factors that actually *are* related to an offender's likelihood of re-offending, and having a positive impact on such factors can obviously be justified both on humanitarian and 'cost' grounds. A managerialist, research-based discourse is also arguably far more preferable than the sort of populist punitive discourse mentioned in section one, which quite often tends to generate interventions (or even longer-term legislation or policy initiatives) that in research terms might intensify offending problems, and in humanitarian terms might be regarded as being excessive or unjust. Perhaps a key point here is also that 'justice' itself does not feature prominently in managerialist approaches to reducing offending, even though they might produce more benign outcomes than some of their 'law and order' competitors.

Notes

1 A useful and detailed account can be found in Gilling (1994, 1997) and Crawford's (1997) recent work also contains a historical overview of developments within the field, along with a discussion of the rise both of partnership approaches, and of 'appeals to community' in crime prevention work.

2 Although it is sometimes noted that there are few 'histories' that focus specifically on the evolution of community penalties (Mair 1997: 1198); see also Nellis in this volume.

3 These key themes were further elaborated by the Local Authority Associations at the launch of the survey results:

> Community safety presents a new and challenging agenda to central and local government. The conventional criminal justice system only touches the tip of an iceberg of crime and offending in our society. Local initiatives based on prevention rather than cure, that marshal all the resources and services of the local community in the defence of its own safety and quality of life, are the best and most cost-effective way forward if crime and fear are to be defeated.
>
> (Local Authority Associations and Local
> Government Management Board 1996)

4 For a useful early discussion of probation service involvement in crime prevention see Geraghty (1991).

5 A focus on issues of nuisance and anti-social behaviour was also incorporated into the Audit Commission's recent examination of local authority involvement in community safety work (Audit Commission 1999). For a brief discussion of such problems and examples of 'good practice' in addressing them, see Chartered Institute of Housing (1995), *Neighbour Nuisance: Ending the Nightmare.*

6 Bottoms has used the term 'populist punitiveness' (Bottoms 1995: 18) to refer to connections of this kind between punitive public attitudes toward offenders and swift (and punitive) governmental responses. Unfortunately, this history of community penalties seems to reflect the fairly constant presence of such linkages.

7 For a recent overview of some of this research see Hughes (1996); other summaries can be found in Crawford (1997), and Gilling (1997). Some early research focusing on multi-agency working at implementation level is reported in Hope and Murphy (1983), and reports emanating from the 1980s ESTC research into multi-agency crime prevention are also much referred to (Blagg *et al* 1988; Sampson *et al* 1988; Sampson *et al* 1991). For research focusing specifically on the Home Office Five Towns Initiative, see Liddle and Bottoms (1991, 1994) and on relevant aspects of Safer Cities work see Tilley (1992) and Sutton (1996). Liddle and Gelsthorpe (1994a, 1994b, 1994c)

have reported on research undertaken on multi-agency crime prevention in a range of areas in England and Wales; other research focusing on similar initiatives, or broader discussions of the research literature can be found in Crawford (1994, 1995), Crawford and Jones (1996), and Gilling (1994).

References

Association of District Councils (1990) *Promoting Safer Communities: A District Council Perspective*. London: Association of District Councils.

Association of Metropolitan Authorities (1990) *Crime Reduction: A Framework for the Nineties*. London: Association of Metropolitan Authorities.

Audit Commission (1999) *Safety in Numbers: Promoting Community Safety*. London: Audit Commission.

Blagg, H., Pearson, G., Sampson, A., Smith, D. and Stubbs, P. (1988) 'Inter-agency co-operation: rhetoric and reality', in T. Hope and M. Shaw (eds) *Communities and Crime Reduction*. London: HMSO.

Bottoms, A.E. (1995) 'The Philosophy and Politics of Punishment and Sentencing', in C. Clarkson and R. Morgan (eds) *The Politics of Sentencing Reform*. Oxford: Clarendon Press.

Bottoms, A.E. and Wiles, P. (1995) 'Crime and insecurity in the city', in C. Fijnaut, J. Goethals, T. Peters and L. Walgrave (eds) *Changes in Society, Crime and Criminal Justice in Europe – Vol. 1, Crime and Insecurity in the City*. The Hague: Kluwer.

Bottoms, A.E. and Wiles, P. (1996) 'Understanding crime prevention in late modern societies', in T. Bennett (ed.) *Preventing Crime and Disorder: Targeting Strategies and Responsibilities*. Cambridge: Institute of Criminology, University of Cambridge, Cropwood Conference Series.

Broad, B. (1991) *Punishment under Pressure*. London: Jessica Kingsley.

Chartered Institute of Housing (1995) *Neighbour Nuisance: Ending the Nightmare*. Good Practice Briefing Issue, No.3, December 1995. Coventry: Chartered Institute of Housing, Good Practice Unit.

Clarke, M. and Stewart, J. (1994) 'The local authority and the new community governance', *Local Government Studies*, 20 (2), 163–176.

Cope, S., Leishman, F. and Starie, P. (1995) 'Hollowing-out and hiving-off: reinventing policing in Britain', in J. Lovenduski and J. Stanyer (eds) *Contemporary Political Studies Vol. 2, 1995*. Belfast: Political Studies Association.

Crawford, A. (1993) *Crime Prevention and the Multi-Agency Approach: A Study of the Attitudes and Experiences of Police and Probation Officers*. Hertfordshire: University of Hertfordshire.

Crawford, A. (1994) 'The partnership approach to community crime prevention: corporatism at the local level?', *Social and Legal Studies*, 3, 497–519.

Crawford, A. (1995) 'Appeals to community and crime prevention', *Crime, Law and Social Change*, 22, 97–126.

Crawford, A. (1997) *The Local Governance of Crime: Appeals to Community and Partnerships*. Oxford: Clarendon Press.

Garland, D. (1996) 'The limits of the sovereign state: strategies of crime control in contemporary society', *British Journal of Criminology*, 36 (4), 445–471.

Gerachty, J. (1991) *Probation Practice in Crime Prevention*. Crime Prevention Unit Papers. London: Home Office.

Gibbs, A. (1998) *Probation Partnerships: A Study of Roles, Relationships and Meanings*. Oxford: Probation Studies Unit, University of Oxford.

Giddens, A. (1990) *The Consequences of Modernity*. Cambridge: Polity Press.

Gilling, D. (1994) 'Multi-agency crime prevention: some barriers to collaboration', *The Howard Journal*, 33 (3), 246–257.

Gilling, D. (1997) *Crime Prevention: Theory, Policy and Politics*. London: UCL Press.

Hale, C. (1996) 'Fear of crime: a review of the literature', *International Review of Victimology*, 4, 79–150.

Hambleton, R. (1991) 'The regeneration of US and British cities', *Local Government Studies*, 17 (5), 53–65.

Hine, J., Holdaway, S., Wiles, P., Davidson, N., Dignan, J., Hammersley, R. and Marsh, P. (1999) Youth justice Pilots Evaluation, Interim Report on Youth Offending Teams.

Home Office (1988) *Punishment, Custody and the Community*. CM 424. London: Home Office.

Home Office (1989) *Home Office Standing Conference. Report on Fear of Crime*. London: Home Office.

Home Office (1990) *Partnership in Crime Prevention*. London: Home Office.

Home Office (1990a) *Crime, Justice and Protecting the Public*. London: HMSO.

Home Office (1990b) *Supervision and Punishment in the Community*. London: HMSO.

Home Office (1990c) *Partnership in Dealing with Offenders in the Community. A Decision Document*. London: HMSO.

Home Office (1991) *Safer Communities: The Local Delivery of Crime Prevention through the Partnership Approach* (the 'Morgan Report'). London: Home Office.

Home Office (1992) *Partnership in Dealing with Offenders in the Community*. London: Home Office.

Home Office (1993a) *PC No. 6/1993: Probation Services and the Management of Voluntary Sector Organisations*. London: HMSO.

Home Office (1993b) *CPO 23/1993: Probation Service Partnership Policy; Submission of Partnership Plans 1993–1994*. London: Home Office.

Home Office (1993c) *PC No. 17/1993: Partnership in Dealing with Offenders in the Community: Submission of Partnership Plans 1994–1997*. London: Home Office.

Home Office (1993d) *Three Year Plan for the Probation Service 1993–1996*. London: Home Office.

Home Office (1995) *Strengthening Punishment in the Community. A Consultation Document*. London: Home Office.

Home Office (1996) *Probation Services Working in Partnership: Increasing Impact and Value for Money*. London: Home Office.

Home Office (1997) *Community Safety Order: A Consultation Paper*, September 1997. London: Home Office.

Home Office (1998) *Joining Forces to Protect the Public. Prisons–Probation: A Consultation Document*. London: Home Office.

Home Office, Department of Education and Science, Department of Employment, Department of the Environment, Department of Health, Department of Social Security, Department of Trade and Industry, Department of Transport and the Welsh Office (1990) *Crime Prevention: The Success of the Partnership Approach* (Home Office circular 44/1990). London: Home Office.

Home Office, Department of Education and Science, Department of Environment, Department of Health and Social Security and the Welsh Office (1984) *Crime Prevention* (Home Office Circular 8/1984). London: Home Office.

HM Inspectorate of Probation (1996) *Probation Services Working in Partnership: Increasing Impact and Value for Money* (Report of a Thematic Inspection). London: Home Office.

Hope, T. and Murphy, D.J.I. (1983) 'Problems of implementing crime prevention: the experience of a demonstration project', *The Howard Journal*, 22, 38–50.

Hughes, G. (1996) 'Strategies of multi-agency crime prevention and community safety in contemporary Britain', *Studies on Crime and Crime Prevention*, 5 (2), 221–244.

Hutchinson, J. (1994) 'The practice of partnership in local economic development', *Local Government Studies*, 20 (3), 335–344.

Liddle, A. M. (1999) *Monitoring and Evaluation Probation Partnership Work – Key Findings and Implications from a National Research Project*. Report submitted to the Home Office (being prepared for publication in 2001).

Liddle, A.M. (2001) *Implementing Strategic Approaches to Community Safety – Key Lessons from a Case Study in Birmingham* (forthcoming). Home Office.

Liddle, A.M. and Bottoms, A.E. (1991) *Implementing Circular 8/84: A Retrospective Assessment of the Five Towns Crime Prevention Initiative*. Research report submitted to the Home Office by the Institute of Criminology, University of Cambridge (unpublished; copy lodged in the Radzinowicz Library at the Institute of Criminology, University of Cambridge).

Liddle, A.M. and Bottoms, A.E. (1994) *The Five Towns Initiative: Key Findings and Implications from a Retrospective Research Analysis*. Cambridge: Institute of Criminology, University of Cambridge.

Liddle, A.M. and Feloy, M. (1997) *Nuisance Problems in Brixton – Describing Local Experience, Designing Effective Solutions*. London: NACRO.

Liddle, A.M. and Gelsthorpe, L.R. (1994a) *Inter-Agency Crime Prevention: Organising Local Delivery*. Home Office Crime Prevention Unit, Paper 52. London: Home Office.

Liddle, A.M. and Gelsthorpe, L.R. (1994b) *Crime Prevention and Inter-Agency Co-operation.* Home Office Crime Prevention Unit, Paper 53. London: Home Office.

Liddle, A.M. and Gelsthorpe, L.R. (1994c) *Inter-Agency Crime Prevention: Further Issues*. Supplementary Paper to Home Office Crime Prevention Unit, Papers 52 and 53. London: Home Office.

Liddle, A.M., Warburton, F. and Feloy, M. (1997) *Nuisance and Crime Problems in Brixton – Research Summary*. London: NACRO.

Local Authority Associations and Local Government Management Board (1996) *Survey of Community Safety Activities in Local Government in England and Wales*. Luton: Local Government Management Board.

McArthur, A. (1995) 'The active involvement of local residents in strategic community partnerships', *Policy and Politics*, 23 (1), 61–71.

Mair, G. (1997) 'A Brief History of the Probation Service', in M. Maguire, R. Morgan and R. Reiner (eds) *The Oxford Handbook of Criminology*. Oxford: Clarendon Press.

Mudd, J. (1984) *Neighborhood Services*. New Haven: Yale University Press.

National Association of Probation Officers (1984) *Draft Policy Statement: Crime Prevention and Reduction Strategies*. London: NAPO.

Osborne, D. and Gaebler, T. (1992) *Reinventing Government: How the Entrepreneurial Spirit is Transforming the Public Sector*. Reading, Massachusetts: Addison-Wesley.

Pease, K. (1994) 'Crime Prevention', in M. Maguire, R. Morgan and R. Reiner (eds) *The Oxford Handbook of Criminology*. Oxford: Clarendon Press.

Prior, D. ' "Working the Network": local authority strategies in the reticulated local state', *Local Government Studies*, 22 (2) Summer, 92–104.

Sampson, A., Smith, D., Pearson, G., Blagg, H. and Stubbs, P. (1991) 'Gender issues in inter-agency relations: police, probation and social services', in P. Abbott and C. Wallace (eds) *Gender, Power and Sexuality*. Basingstoke: Macmillan.

Sampson, A., Stubbs, P., Smith, D., Pearson, G. and Blagg, H. (1988) 'Crime, localities and the multi-agency approach', *British Journal of Criminology*, 28, 478–493.

Sutton, M. (1996) *Implementing Crime Prevention Schemes in a Multi-Agency Setting: Aspects of Process in the Safer Cities Programme*. Home Office Research Study 160. London: Home Office.

Tilley, N. (1992) *Safer Cities and Community Safety Strategies*. Home Office Crime Prevention Unit, Paper 38. London: Home Office.

Young, J. (1986) 'The failure of criminology: the need for radical realism', in R. Matthews and J. Young (eds) *Confronting Crime*. London: Sage.

Young, J. (1988) 'Radical criminology in Britain: the emergence of a competing paradigm', *British Journal of Criminology*, 28, 159–183.

Chapter 4

Beyond cognitive-behaviouralism? Reflections on the effectiveness literature

Sue Rex

Introduction

My aim in this chapter is to discuss what might be needed to help people stop offending beyond cognitive-behavioural programmes. Recognising the value of teaching cognitive skills, I nonetheless raise questions about the effective implementation and evaluation of these approaches (and their applicability to female offenders). For rehabilitative programmes to be effective, I argue, there is at least an equally pressing need to pay attention to offenders' social environments, and the normative processes that support non-offending choices. In the final section of the chapter, I move on to a discussion of the rehabilitative potential of Community Service, which offers what might be seen as a somewhat 'sideways' approach to tackling offending behaviour.

Teaching cognitive skills: the supporting conditions

A great deal has changed in academic and policy views about the efficacy of rehabilitative programmes since the pessimism of the 'Nothing Works' era. Meta-analytical studies have yielded a set of principles about how effective programmes should be assembled, which have gained considerable currency in a remarkable short period of time. Originally drawn together by James McGuire (1995), these principles have now been incorporated in the 'What Works' booklet circulated by the Home Office (1999a) to all probation staff. The principles have been set out in the Introduction, and do not need to be rehearsed here.

Perhaps one of the most influential of the 'What Works' findings is the reported efficacy of methods drawn from cognitive-behavioural sources. Its consequence has been a heavy reliance on teaching cognitive skills in the range of strategies now being developed for dealing with offenders under the Crime Reduction Programme. In anticipation of the national roll-out of the core curriculum of accredited probation programmes, Probation Circular 64/1999 (Home Office 1999b) asked probation services to select the predominantly cognitive-behavioural general offending programmes that they intend to run in their areas. These included 'Reasoning and Rehabilitation' and 'Enhanced Thinking Skills' as well as the renamed McGuire 'Think First' programme, which was accredited by the Joint Prisons Probation Accreditation Panel in April 2000, and is due for national roll-out in 2000/01 (see What Works Strategy for the Probation Service attached to Probation Circular 60/ 2000 [Home Office 2000b]).

Indeed, the rationale underlying cognitive-behavioural programmes (that developing offenders' reasoning skills may accelerate the 'maturing' process by which they abandon crime) fits in with what the criminal careers research tells us about the impulsivity and poor abstract reasoning characteristic of persistent offenders (see Farrington 1997). It is hardly surprising, therefore, that these approaches had already found favour with probation services, though they seemed not always to have been well applied. In their national survey of probation services, Hedderman and Sugg (1997) found little systematic monitoring or evaluation of these kinds of techniques; and that staff felt they lacked understanding of the broader psychological theories and practices which underpin cognitive-behavioural therapy. Perhaps in consequence, Ellis and Underdown (1998) found a greater emphasis on cognition than on practising changed behaviour in such programmes.

The widespread use of cognitive-behavioural approaches in probation services by the mid-1990s demonstrates that the reinstatement of rehabilitation on the policy agenda owes a considerable amount – not just to Canadian research – but also to developments in UK practice in the face of official 'Nothing Works' pessimism, as described by Vanstone (2000). What we should have learnt from that experience, according to Vanstone, is the danger that poor implementation may erode positive effects, not least because enthusiasm for the group programme leads to the neglect of the supporting work that needs to be conducted outside the group. Of the Straight Thinking on Probation (STOP) programme in Mid-Glamorgan (reported fully in Raynor and Vanstone 1997), Vanstone concludes that 'the resultant lack of reinforcement of learning may well have contributed to the deterioration in positive impact on offending rates' found by the evaluation (Vanstone 2000: 179).

The Home Office is now seeking to overcome these shortcomings by strengthening the implementation and evaluation of cognitive-behavioural techniques through the work of the Joint Prisons Probation Accreditation Panel. The criteria that guide the Accreditation Panel are intended to ensure that offenders are prepared for programmes, and that learning is reinforced afterwards (see Version 28/4/00 of the Community Programme Accreditation Criteria circulated under Probation Circular 40/2000; Home Office 2000a). These criteria place considerable emphasis on case management, to ensure that programmes are integrated into the overall objectives of supervision. As well as preparatory exercises beforehand, there is an expectation that case managers will undertake reinforcement and relapse prevention with participating offenders afterwards. To enable this to take place, effective arrangements for liaison, handover and communication are to be put in place. It is perhaps too obvious to point out that specifying the requirement and even the arrangements in the manual is not the same as ensuring delivery on the ground. This may not be because the offender fails to turn up. It may be due to competing priorities and pressures for programme staff and case managers. How do we make sure that this preparation and reinforcement really happens? If it does not, will that invalidate an offender's attendance on a programme?

In the long term, we will not do probation staff managing and implementing these programmes any favours if we disregard the inconclusive nature of the evidence on which effective practice principles are actually based. Until the Pathfinder programmes have been fully evaluated, it probably remains the case that 'our understanding [...] of what works, with which offenders and under what conditions, in reducing offending behaviour' is 'still embryonic' (McIvor 1997: 13). Discussing the limitations of the findings so far produced by meta-analysis, Palmer (1995) argues that the focus needs to shift from *whether* something works to *why* it works. Different combinations of programme components and non-programmatic features, such as staff characteristics, and staff/offender interactions, should be evaluated to produce 'a broader and more realistic description and understanding of correctional intervention' than is encapsulated in sweeping assertions such as 'counselling does not work' or 'behavioural approaches work' (Palmer 1995: 114–5).

Difficulties of implementation and evaluation aside, cognitive-behavioural programmes have been criticised for ignoring social factors and being insensitive to the needs of women and ethnic minorities. As Vanstone (2000) argues, such criticisms may be more fairly directed at those who implement such programmes rather than their original authors. Ross and Ross themselves declare that 'cognition is not enough' (Ross and Ross 1995: 8). Yet, there is a real danger that if such messages are not conveyed loudly and clearly enough to practitioners, the potential gains of cognitive-behavioural programmes may be lost. In the next section, I will discuss the factors in offenders' social environments to which research directs attention. First, though, a note of caution about women offenders.

The applicability of cognitive-behavioural techniques to women is a question on which there is as yet very little evidence, but considerable debate. A meta-analysis of programmes predominantly or entirely directed at female offenders reported by Dowden and Andrews (1999) concluded that the principles of risk, need and responsivity (addressed through social learning and cognitive-behavioural techniques) were associated with reductions in offending. Interestingly, the strongest predictors of treatment success proved to be interpersonal criminogenic need targets, especially family process variables, rather than personal criminogenic targets such as anti-social cognition and skills deficit. However, as the authors acknowledge, the evidence on which their conclusions are based is sparse, and more work is needed. Given women's different needs, circumstances and risks compared with men,[1] the application to women of programmes that have been shown to work with male offenders may be a flawed strategy. Certainly, the Correctional Service of Canada has held back from applying the accreditation process to programmes for women offenders until the evaluation of these programmes has been further developed.[2]

Wider conditions: the social environment

The emphasis on cognitive skills programmes, because of the availability of evidence about their efficacy, has led to some neglect of environmental factors. However, a considerable weight of evidence has accumulated pointing to the need to take account of the social environments in which offenders are taking decisions and acting upon them in designing effective rehabilitative programmes. The failure of the STOP programme to sustain its initial achievements into the second year prompted Raynor and Vanstone to reflect that 'work on the thinking and behaviour of people who are at a high risk of further offending [needs to be] complemented by attempts to assist them with the problems that they encounter in their everyday lives in the community' (Raynor and Vanstone 1997: 39). Looking at women released from custody, Kendall (1998) cites a number of studies identifying social factors – peer pressure, job discrimination and the availability of drugs and alcohol – which subverted programme effectiveness. The point is reinforced by May's (1999) study of the role of social factors in explaining reconviction following a community sentence, which found that drugs misuse was strongly related to reconviction and a relationship between unemployment plus unstable accommodation and reconviction.

The importance of social environment emerges also from the somewhat different perspective of criminal careers research, and what it tells us about the difficulties encountered by offenders in desisting from offending. As Shover (1996) observes, the fact that 'criminal career' research shows that a large proportion of offenders do eventually abandon crime does not mean that this is accomplished cleanly or abruptly. We have yet to develop a clear understanding of the processes by which desistance is achieved, though this is becoming an area of greater research interest. Farrall and Bowling (1999) argue that studies of desistance have been limited by focusing too much either on human agency (decision-making) or social structure (employment and family). Although social development and individual choice are both important, neither alone fully explains why people stop offending.[3] What is needed is an approach capable of examining the inter-play between an individual's decisions and actions and the social situation in which they are taken.

Burnett (1994) illuminates why prisoners' desire to 'go straight' was stronger than their belief that they would succeed in doing so, and why, even then, they failed to live up to their own expectations. She found that, following release, 'persisters' were less likely than 'desisters' to have employment, satisfactory accommodation and stable relationships (though, for both groups, employment was often for short-lived periods and frequently unofficial). They were more likely to be using hard drugs and to have criminal associations. Attitudes towards crime also seemed important, different motivational patterns being associated with desistance and persistence. However, equivocation was a significant feature of responses to direct questioning about re-offending, offenders often prevaricating between criminal behaviour or desistance from it and keeping their options open. In these circumstances, the absence of a job or shortage of cash might easily push them back into crime. Burnett also identified transitional positions, in which ex-prisoners were temporarily abstaining, committing less serious or risky offences or anticipating a reduction and eventual abandonment of crime. The literature reveals a similar ambivalence in attitudes towards desisting from the use of drugs, and similar difficulties for ex-addicts trying to move away from the social world surrounding their drug-taking (Biernacki 1986; Measham *et al* 1998).

Though Burnett's study related to ex-prisoners, I have found probationers to be similarly conscious of the precarious nature of their decisions to stop offending (see Rex 1999). As one young woman commented, 'even now, I'm not saying that I'm not tempted to go back into crime because I am … If you've got no money, you think "oh, shoplifting's easy".' An older man described his increased perception of the risks involved as prompting him to slow down a criminal career, which he assessed his prospects of ending as poor: 'I should be settling into something else really, but it's finding something. There's not much going for people who are clean let alone people with a criminal record.' In the light of findings such as these, the social situations in which offenders find themselves seem central to their ability to deal with the personal and social problems that contribute to their offending.

Against this background, risk/needs tools such as OASys (see Probation Circular 88/1999; Home Office 1999c) are at least aimed at identifying the wider social and personal 'factors' underlying an individual's offending, so that their impact on the risk of re-offending can be calculated. Depending on the quality of such assessments, and the information on which they rely, they have the potential to take us considerably closer to an understanding of the relationship between social factors and reconviction than was possible in May's (1999) study.[4] Of course, we should be wary of regarding as entirely scientific and objective actuarial predictions produced by clinical judgements that are ultimately subjective (see Hannah-Moffat's [1999] discussion of the use of the Offender Intake Assessment process in relation to Canadian women prisoners).

It is one thing to identify and assess the personal and social problems that may have contributed to someone's offending, and make them more likely to offend in the future. It is quite another to identify how that individual can be helped to surmount formidable social obstacles, such as a lack of employable skills or the resources to overcome addiction. Concluding that what counts in prisoners' resettlement is the social environment to which they return (the support of family and friends, and a situation that fosters law-abiding attitudes and behaviour), Haines (1990) argues that after-care services for released prisoners should focus on maintaining and strengthening the community networks that can be more successful in meeting employment and accommodation needs than efforts by social work agencies. For probation services to tackle these areas surely requires active collaboration with other community-based agencies, a point that takes us beyond the scope of this particular chapter, but is relevant to discussion in others.

Unfortunately, research by Maguire *et al* (1998) suggests that a focus on the Probation Service's main aim of reducing offending may discourage probation areas from undertaking what might be viewed primarily as welfare work. In the somewhat different context of the provision of voluntary after-care for released prisoners, this study shows that preoccupation with 'offending behaviour' may lead to a neglect of other important areas of criminogenic risk and need. It must be all the more tempting to dismiss these as beyond the remit of probation work when the underlying problems seem intractable and the solutions inaccessible to frontline probation staff.

Using authority to encourage socially responsible behaviour

The desistance literature indicates that, in addition to improvements in cognitive skills and life circumstances, 'normative' processes play a part in people's movement away from crime. Graham and Bowling's life-history interviews showed that 'events and experiences associated with desistance exert their effect through bringing about changes in an individual's identity, outlook and sense of maturity and responsibility' (Graham and Bowling 1995: 82). According to Graham and Bowling, offenders do not simply stop offending because they acquire partners, children, employment and economic independence, but because they make a fresh start, find some direction or meaning in life, or learn that ultimately crime does not pay. A common thread running through the personal accounts of 'Going Straight' collected by Devlin and Turney (1999) is of people getting out of crime because they acquire 'something to lose', whether a home, partner, family, self-respect or personal achievement. Again, similar themes emerge in the literature on moving away from drug addiction (Biernacki 1986).

The questions relevant to the present discussion is how those changes in self-identity come about, and whether practitioners supervising offenders in the community can contribute to the underlying processes. 'Pro-social modelling' has now gained currency in British probation practice, following the raising of its profile by HMIP's Effective Practice Guide as 'a necessary input for effective programme delivery' (HMIP 1998: 49–50). That staff should adopt an appropriate ('pro-social') style of delivery counts amongst the accreditation criteria for prison and community programmes. However, there is as yet little British evidence on what constitutes 'pro-social modelling', and what its effects might be.

It is Christopher Trotter's research in Australia that is known for providing the most thorough exploration of pro-social modelling (Trotter 1993, 1996, 1999). According to Trotter, pro-social modelling,

> involves the practice of offering praise and reward for ... pro-social expressions and actions ... [Also] the probation officer becomes a positive role model acting to reinforce pro-social or non-criminal behaviour.
>
> (Trotter 1993)

In other words, the offender is given a definite lead (hence 'modelling' rather than non-directive counselling), and this is done in a constructive and positive way, rather than through negative threats (hence, 'pro-social' rather than deterrence). Entwined in these practices are elements of reinforcement through encouragement and reward, and modelling through positively exemplifying the desired behaviour.

Trotter's study found that the breach and reconviction rates of offenders supervised by Community Corrections Officers (CCOs) assessed (on the basis of questionnaires completed by probationers and an analysis of case files) as using 'pro-social' methods were significantly lower than similar groups of offenders. He also claimed a strong statistical relationship between pro-social modelling and lower rates of recidivism, which was sustained over a four-year follow-up period (Trotter 1996), though it is not entirely clear how pro-social modelling was disentangled from other elements of problem-solving and reflective listening (see Raynor 1998).

Although its impact has yet to be specifically tested, 'pro-social modelling' is not an entirely new concept to probation practice (indeed, elements have been found in social work practice more generally ever since the 'supportive-directive' typology originally developed by Mayer and Timms 1970). Collectively, British research specifically on probation suggests that probationers want supervision to be a 'purposeful' experience, and appreciate probation officers' showing respect and concern for them. Significantly, they seem more ready to accept a certain amount of encouragement and direction from supervisors who do so – though practitioners may not always realise that this is the case.[5] It should be stressed that pro-social modelling is not an alternative to programmatic work with offenders, but a set of underpinning attitudes and behaviour that are part of effective delivery, elements of which have featured in cognitive-behavioural group work programmes (see Gendreau 1996). Raynor (1998) describes elements of pro-social modelling in the STOP programme (very closely based on the Canadian R&R programmes on which other British cognitive-behavioural programmes are also modelled), and summarises results that appeared to show that these elements led to some learning in social behaviour. (Incidentally, the Crime Pics results from that evaluation support the argument in the last section that people's social environments as well as their attitudes need to be improved if reductions in offending are to be achieved).[6]

Because it concerns the manner in which offenders are supervised or programmes undertaken with them, pro-social modelling clearly encompasses a broad set of practices that can be used in a wide range of circumstances. Unfortunately, this flexibility carries the concomitant difficulty of identifying what concrete supervisory practices the approach actually involves, and what makes it distinctive. Even then, although the idea might be admirable in theory, sustaining the intricate practices required to deliver pro-social modelling may be quite difficult. In Trotter's work with Australian CCOs, the aim was for participants to understand the broad concept of pro-social modelling and collectively to develop techniques for reinforcing pro-social behaviour and presenting themselves as pro-social models. The kinds of techniques practitioners were described as identifying (being punctual and reliable; being polite and friendly; and being honest and open) may not seem particularly novel to British probation officers, lending credence to the claim often made by practitioners that they 'are doing it anyway'. More recently, Trotter (1999) has used case scenarios to illustrate the use of pro-social modelling in different settings, arguing that research shows that the use of the approach can be strengthened through training and awareness. He has also emphasised the need for practitioners to focus on positives and to be open and explicit about their role and the goals they are pursuing, to ensure that pro-social modelling is distinguished from 'moralising' and remains sensitive to differences of gender, race and culture (a question raised in chapter 8 of this volume).

Between October 1997 and October 1999, the Institute of Criminology, University of Cambridge, participated in a pilot project with Cambridgeshire Probation Service aimed at incorporating principles of pro-social modelling (and legitimacy) in probation (and community service) practice and assessing the impact (see Bottoms and Rex 1998). Unfortunately, staff movement, and other implementation difficulties, together with incomplete data, meant that findings were inconclusive.[7] However, the project did provide some opportunities for practitioners to develop their understanding of the concept of pro-social modelling and how it might translate into specific practices. Some of that learning took place in a preparatory two-day workshop in which probation officers who had volunteered to participate developed ideas for applying pro-social modelling and legitimacy to their practice.

Subsequent interviews revealed some under-development of the principles in practice. One example was in encouraging pro-social behaviour through the use of rewards, where there was a heavy emphasis in the workshop on the simple acknowledgement of progress. Other opportunities to reward probationers were identified in addition to positive feedback: early termination; reduction in frequency of appointments; setting time aside to address particular problems; home visits; and advocacy. It was recognised that such steps needed to be seen as 'rewards' by probationers at the receiving end; not all would welcome reductions in the frequency of appointments. These probation officers would have agreed with Trotter (1999) about the need to be clear that what was being given was a reward, in response to specific action(s) by the probationer. In discussing their practice afterwards, however, it was positive feedback and praise that project probation officers seemed most able to provide; they perceived limitations in what else they could offer probationers, and in the scope for identifying positive achievements in some people's lives.

The Cambridgeshire pilot project also encompassed principles of legitimacy – seen as complementing pro-social modelling (see Bottoms and Rex 1998). In chapter 5, Anthony Bottoms explores the evidence that legitimate modes of authority can generate both short-term compliance with the requirements of the order and longer-term compliance with the law (Tyler 1990; Paternoster *et al* 1997). In the context of the Cambridgeshire pilot, the way in which they used their authority was seen as one way in which probation officers exemplified what kinds of behaviour they were seeking to encourage in the people they supervised. As such, it was seen to enhance the 'modelling' aspect of pro-social modelling, and as helping to explain why a practitioner using this approach might hope to exert a positive influence on offenders.

Once again, a useful aspect of the Cambridgeshire pilot was the opportunity given to project probation officers to translate the principles into specific practices that could be incorporated in supervision. This is how the components of legitimacy were elaborated by probation officers participating in the preparatory workshop (though, once again, subsequent interviews indicated some under-development of the principles in practice):[8]

- **Representation** (*giving the person an opportunity to play a part in the making of important decisions*): ensuring that the probationer has an opportunity to state their point of view or tell their side of the story, and giving proper consideration to their viewpoint so that they have an opportunity to take part in the making of decisions. An important aspect of negotiation, applying not only to dealings between the supervisor and the probationer, but also to the probationer's dealings with other authorities, services and agencies.

- **Consistency** (*treating like cases alike*): treating people the same as others and over time, e.g. making sure their expectations are realistic, so that they do not feel 'let down'.

- **Impartiality** (*suppressing personal bias when acting professionally*): not allowing personal biases or feelings to influence your decisions and actions, so that you do not treat people in a particular way because of their personal characteristics (e.g. ethnicity, sex, age).

- **Accuracy** (*displaying competence to make high quality decisions*): demonstrating one's ability to make high quality decisions by being open about the nature of an issue or problem and using valid/reliable information to address it.

- **Correctability** (*reviewing decisions where necessary*): being prepared to change a decision that later proves to be unfair or incorrect.

- **Ethicality** (*treating people with respect and dignity*): showing probationers that they are valued members of society.

Examining a 'sideways' approach – Community Service

Despite the rehabilitative aspirations of the Wootton Committee whose recommendations led to its introduction,[9] the classic image of Community Service has been one of a 'fine' on time (which offers incidental reparation to the community). That is now beginning to change, partly thanks to hints from three different research studies that Community Service may be effective in reducing offending,[10] and in 2000 Community Service was included in the Pathfinder probation programmes funded under the Crime Reduction Programme.[11]

The differences between predicted and actual rates of reconviction following Community Service found by Lloyd *et al* (1995), Raynor and Vanstone (1997) and May (1999) are slight, and in no sense conclusive, since they might be accounted for by some factor in the prior experience of the groups sentenced to CS excluded from the prediction models (May's was alone in including some social factors). Cumulatively, however, they do suggest that something might be happening that merits closer attention. For May, the fact that 'the low reconviction rate for [community service] could not be explained by the criminal history and available social factors of offenders [suggests] that the sentence itself may have had a positive effect on reconviction' (May 1999: x). The Pathfinder CS projects provide an opportunity to examine the nature of that positive effect, a question on which the research so far has been somewhat limited. Below, I touch on two studies that have looked at the links between Community Service and recidivism.

Uncovering a positive effect compared with short periods of custody, Killias and Ribeaud (2000) used quantitative data to investigate what it was about Community Service that might produce lower rates of re-arrest and reconviction. A strong statistical relationship was found between having served prison rather than community work and regarding the sentence as 'unfair', but no clear relationship emerged between the latter and recidivism. Those sentenced to prison were found to have fared no worse than those serving community work in terms of their employment or relationships (probably because they were serving very short periods in custody). Following Paternoster *et al* (1997), the authors speculate that 'reductions in recidivism may depend less on improving job and other life perspectives, and more on helping offenders to view their conviction and sentence as a result of their own behaviour and not of a judge's … fault' (Killias and Ribeaud 2000: 53).[12] They draw from this the inference that judges and other criminal justice personnel should make more effort to explain to defendants the rationale for decisions, so that they feel they have been treated fairly.

Killias and Ribeaud (2000) were not in a position to examine the *processes* involved in Community Service, which might help to elucidate the connection between being sentenced to community work and lower rates of recidivism. It seems conceivable, as originally envisaged by the Wootton Committee, that offenders might be less likely to be reconvicted following Community Service, not just because they see the sentence as more 'fair' than custody, but also because they undergo 'constructive' experiences in undertaking community work. This possibility is suggested by McIvor (1992), whose study of Community Service in Scotland found that people who viewed their experience of Community Service as useful (or 'rewarding') in a number of respects had higher rates of compliance and lower rates of recidivism.

McIvor (1998) suggests that that the most 'rewarding' Community Service placements 'might best be characterised as re-integrative and as entailing a degree of reciprocity or exchange' (page 55). Specifically:

> In many instances, it seems, contact with the beneficiaries gave offenders an insight into other people, and an increased insight into themselves; the acquisition of skills had instilled in them greater confidence and self-esteem; and the experience of completing their Community Service Orders place them in a position where they could enjoy reciprocal relationships – gaining the trust, confidence and appreciation of other people and having the opportunity to give something back to them.
>
> (McIvor 1998: 55–56)[13]

Incidentally, drawn from the offender's perspective, this seems to model features of the 'direct exchange relationship' between communities and probation/parole agencies identified by Dickey and Smith (1999) as an important constituent of community justice. In this regard, Community Service was cited as providing an opportunity simultaneously to punish and restore and as providing 'openings for more complex co-operation between community corrections agencies and the public they depend on for authority and resources' (Dickey and Smith 1999: 24).

Returning to the individual offender, McIvor has suggested that 'Community Service placements may provide an important vehicle through which an informal yet potentially powerful process of pro-social modelling may occur' (McIvor 1998: 56). That was in a paper given at the Clarke Hall Day Conference launching the Cambridgeshire pilot on pro-social modelling and legitimacy, which encompassed community service as well as probation practice (the rationale being that these principles might be of use to any criminal justice personnel delivering community penalties). Although a pilot study, involving a small number of CS supervisors and around 50 offenders supervised by them, the initial findings are encouraging (summarised by Rex and Crosland 1999).[14] They indicate that this might be a promising approach for Community Service, a possibility that the inclusion of pro-social modelling as a significant feature of the Pathfinder CS projects offers an opportunity to investigate more systematically.[15]

Indeed, the Pathfinder projects provide an opportunity to explore the rehabilitative potential of Community Service at a number of levels.[16] Apart from pro-social modelling, other key strands are: accrediting offenders' employable skills; allocating offenders to placements that might meet their criminogenic needs; and integrating the CS element into the planning of a Combination Order. One can discern here the application of What Works principles to CS, for example that programmes should target criminogenic needs and that they should teach skills that will help people avoid offending (employment skills as well as cognitive and interpersonal skills), discussed more fully in Rex (2000). The emphasis on employability, and on providing routes to further training and employment, also seems to be aimed at improving offenders' positions in the social environments contributing to their offending/non-offending choices.[17] What is particularly interesting about the Community Service projects is the fact that, unlike probation programmes, the focus is not directly on 'offending behaviour'. The evidence referred to above indicates that the practical setting in which CS occurs, and the nature of the contacts into which it brings offenders, might well offer learning experiences at least as powerful as an approach that directly tackles offending.

Conclusions

The reinstatement of rehabilitation on the policy agenda poses important challenges to those agencies responsible for the delivery of community penalties (presently, chiefly the Probation Service). The delivery of effective programmes requires careful attention to the conditions supporting their implementation, and to the evaluation of what works for whom in what circumstances. Yet programmatic work must not eclipse the social environments in which offenders are placed, which play a crucial role in their ability to make – and to sustain – decisions not to offend. Nor should opportunities be lost for practitioners to promote, and build upon, the normative development that seems to help motivate people to move away from crime. Unfortunately, work on these wider 'environmental' factors may seem daunting, and difficult to reconcile with a focus on offending behaviour. Here, Community Service provides an interesting case study, which might offer opportunities to develop offenders' skills as well as to have some positive impact on their social situation and to contribute to the kind of changed outlook that appears to accompany a cessation of offending.

Notes

1 An overview of the relevant literature is provided by Loraine Gelsthorpe in chapter 8, 'Accountability: difference and diversity in the delivery of community penalties'.

2 See Minutes of Consultation on Possible Accreditation for Women Offender Programs, 6–7 January 1999, The Correctional Service of Canada.

3 Sampson and Laub's (1993) re-analysis of the Gluecks' longitudinal data on 500 persistent delinquents and 500 non-delinquents in Boston concluded that the formation of 'adult social bonds' (essentially, a stable job and a strong marriage) is associated with a reversal in delinquency. Other studies have suggested that the impact of social development on delinquency is more complex and ambiguous, perhaps, as West (1982) suggests, 'because of the tendency of delinquents to marry females who are themselves socially delinquent' (page 104). Studying self-reported offending amongst 14–25 year olds, Graham and Bowling (1995) found that passing the landmarks to adulthood identified in the human development literature (acquiring partners, children, employment and economic independence) were associated with desistance from offending for women, but not for young men. What mattered for the latter was avoiding criminal associations and the use of hard drugs and heavy drinking. For Clarke and Cornish (1985), desistance is a matter of rational choice, a position for which Cusson and Pissonneault (1986), and Cromwell *et al* (1991) provide empirical illustration of desisters' 'decision' to give up crime following a 're-evaluation' of the costs and benefits. According to Farrall and Bowling (1999), the mistake such writers make is to see social factors as helping rather than constraining decision-making or influencing the offender in unacknowledged ways, and in assuming that respondents themselves were fully aware of what happened without appreciating that the interviews may have prompted some post-hoc rationalisation.

4 Of 55 probation services that May asked for information recorded on the social problems of offenders sentenced in 1993, only six were able to provide sufficiently comprehensive data for analysis. Even then, differences in definitions and recording practices severely restricted the analysis that could be undertaken.

5 See Rex (1999), citing Ditton and Ford's (1994) conclusion that a recidivist at the turning-point might need active encouragement and Sainsbury *et al*'s (1982) finding that probation officers massively underestimated the importance of their encouragement to probationers.

6 Whereas people with attitudes strongly favourable to crime (as measured by Crime Pics) were reconvicted whether their self-perceived problems increased or decreased, those whose attitudes were less strongly favourable to crime were reconvicted if their self-perceived problems remained severe but seemed to cope better if they saw their problems as becoming less severe (see Raynor 1998).

7 Only three project probation officers upon whom the evaluation could be based had been involved from the outset and had attended all the training (four of the original recruits were transferred to other posts, and another five probation officers joined the project having received a personal briefing) – this illustrates the difficulties (and dangers) of implementing a project with a selected group of staff. In interviews, participants sometimes saw the practice of ideas as quite elusive, and pointed to external pressures and countervailing trends which impeded the use or impact of pro-social modelling (see Rex and Crosland 2000).

8 One example concerned representation. In the workshop, there was some emphasis on helping probationers express their views more constructively in their dealings with other agencies; however, in describing their practice in subsequent interviews, probation officers focused on their own negotiations with other agencies on probationers' behalf.

9 What attracted the Committee was 'the opportunity which [CS] could give for constructive activity in the form of personal service to the community and the possibility of a changed outlook on the part of the offender' (Advisory Council on the Penal System 1970: 13).

10 In Lloyd *et al* (1995), the reconviction rate for CSOs was, uniquely, three per cent lower than the rate predicted on the basis of offenders' sex, age and previous criminal histories. In Raynor and Vanstone's (1997) STOP research, the CSO control group was after 24 months – again uniquely – three per cent below the predicted reconviction rate. In Chris May's (1999) study of reconviction following community sentences, CSOs were, once again, alone in being two per cent below the predicted reconviction rate. When pre-sentence social factors (principally drug problems and employment) were added to the baseline prediction model used by May, offenders in CSO were still statistically significantly below the predicted reconviction rate (though, in absolute terms, only by one percentage point).

11 The selection of CS projects for Pathfinder status under the Crime Reduction Programme was announced in Probation Circular 35/1999.

12 Although, as Killias and Ribeaud (2000) acknowledge, their findings did not really qualify them to comment on the impact of employment or other prospects.

13 What is being described here seems to bear some relation to the development of 'self-efficacy' – see Bandura (1997), who distinguished it from self-esteem, which concerns judgements of self-worth whereas perceived self-efficacy concerns judgements of personal capability.

14 Briefly, offenders supervised predominantly by project CS supervisors were more likely than offenders supervised predominantly outside the project to report experiences consistent with pro-social modelling and legitimacy. They were also far more likely to select positive statements about their experience of community service (i.e. that they were pleased with a job well done, were glad to have done something for the community and were pleased with what they had learnt). As well as gaining better work rating (possibly as a 'reward' by their 'pro-social' CS supervisors), offenders supervised within the project

were less likely than other offenders to have unacceptable absences or to have been breached.

15 For example, the use of pro-social modelling is being supported by the auditing of CS placements for features identified by McIvor (1992, 1998) as 'rewarding' – contact with beneficiaries; work obviously useful to beneficiary; opportunities to acquire practical and interpersonal skills.

16 Probation Circular 35/1999 summarises the key components of the CRP-CS projects. The evaluation is being undertaken by the Institute of Criminology, University of Cambridge (Loraine Gelsthorpe and Sue Rex) in conjunction with the Probation Studies Unit, University of Oxford, a final report being due in March 2002.

17 Supported by the allowance in paragraph D14 of the 2000 National Standards for ten per cent of C's hours to be used for basic literacy training and the provision of qualifications.

References

Advisory Council on the Penal System (1970) *Non-Custodial and Semi-Custodial Penalties*. London: HMSO.

Bandura, A (1997) *Self-Efficacy: The Exercise of Control*. New York: Freeman & Co.

Biernacki, P. (1986) *Pathways From Heroin Addiction: Recovery Without Treatment*. Philadelphia: Temple University Press.

Bottoms, A.E. and Rex, S.A. (1998) 'Pro-social Modelling and Legitimacy: Their Potential Contribution to Effective Practice', in S. Rex and A. Matravers (eds) *Pro-Social Modelling and Legitimacy: The Clarke Hall Day Conference*. Cambridge: Institute of Criminology, University of Cambridge.

Burnett, R. (1994) 'The Odds of Going Straight: Offenders' Own Predictions', in *Sentencing, Quality and Risk: Proceedings of the 10th Annual Conference on Research and Information in the Probation Service*, University of Loughborough. Birmingham: Midlands Probation Training Consortium.

Clarke, R.V. and Cornish, D.B. (1985) 'Modelling Offenders' Decisions: A Framework for Research and Policy', in M. Tonry and N. Morris (eds) *Crime and Justice: An Annual Review of Research, Vol. VI*. London: University of Chicago Press.

Cromwell, P.F., Olson, J.N. and Wester Avery, D'A. (1991) *Breaking and Entering: An Ethnographic Analysis of Burglary*. London: Sage.

Cusson, M. and Pissonneault, P. (1986) 'The Decision to Give up Crime', in D.B. Cornish and R.V. Clarke (eds) *The Reasoning Criminal: Rational Choice Perspectives on Offending*. New York: Springer-Verlag.

Devlin, A. and Turney, B. (1999) *Going Straight: After Crime and Punishment*. Winchester: Waterside Press.

Dickey, W.J. and Smith, M.E. (1999) *Rethinking Probation: Community Supervision, Community Safety*. Washington: Office of Justice.

Ditton, J. and Ford, R. (1994) *The Reality of Probation: A Formal Ethnography of*

Process and Practice. Aldershot: Avebury.

Dowden, C. and Andrews, D.A. (1999) 'What Works for Female Offenders: A Meta-analytic Review', *Crime and Delinquency*, 45 (4), 438–452.

Ellis, T. and Underdown, A. (1998) *Strategies for Effective Offender Supervision*, Report of the HMIP What Works Project. London: Home Office.

Farrall, S. and Bowling, B. (1999) 'Structuration, Human Development and Desistance from Crime', *British Journal of Criminology*, 39, 252–267.

Farrington, D.P. (1997) 'Human Development and Criminal Careers', in M. Maguire, R. Morgan and R. Reiner (eds) *Oxford Handbook of Criminology*, 2nd Ed. Oxford: Clarendon Press.

Gendreau, P. (1996) 'Offender Rehabilitation: What we Know and What Needs to be Done', *Criminal Justice and Behavior*, 23, 144–161.

Graham, J. and Bowling, B. (1995) 'Young People and Crime', *Home Office Research Study No. 145*. London: Home Office.

Haines, K. (1990) *After-Care Services for Released Prisoners: A Review of the Literature*. Cambridge: University of Cambridge, Institute of Criminology.

Hannah-Moffat (1999) 'Moral Agent or Actuarial Subject: Risk and Canadian Women's Imprisonment', *Theoretical Criminology*, 3 (1), 71–94.

Hedderman, C. and Sugg, D. (1997) 'Changing Offenders' Attitudes and Behaviour', *Home Office Research Study No. 171*. London: Home Office.

HMIP (1998) *Evidence-Based Practice: A Guide to Effective Practice*. London: Home Office.

Home Office (1999a) *What Works: Reducing Re-offending: Evidence-Based Practice*. London: Home Office Communications Directorate.

Home Office (1999b) Probation Circular 64/1999, *What Works – Effective Practice Initiative: the Core Curriculum*. London: Home Office.

Home Office (1999c) Probation Circular 88/1999, *What Works: update on the Joint Prison/Probation Assessment (OASys) Project*. London: Home Office.

Home Office (2000a) Probation Circular 40/2000, *What Works: Joint Prison Probation Accreditation Panel – Update*. London: Home Office.

Home Office (2000b) Probation Circular 60/2000, *What Works Strategy for the Probation Service*. London: Home Office.

Home Office (2000c) *National Standards for the Supervision of Offenders in the Community*. London: Home Office.

Kendall, K. (1998) 'Evaluations of Programs for Female Offenders', in R. Zaplin (ed.) *Female Offenders: Critical Perspectives and Effective Interventions*. Baltimore, Maryland: Aspen Publishers.

Killias, Aebi M. and Ribeaud, D. (2000) 'Does Community Service Rehabilitate Better than Short-term Imprisonment? Results of a Controlled Experiment', *Howard Journal*, 39 (1), 40–57.

Lloyd, C., Mair, G. and Hough, M. (1995) 'Explaining Reconviction Rates: A Critical Analysis', *Home Office Research Study No. 136*. London: Home Office.

Maguire, M., Raynor, P., Vanstone, M. and Kynchy, J. (1998) 'Voluntary After-Care', *Home Office Research Findings No. 73*. London: Home Office.

May, C. (1999) 'Explaining Reconviction Following a Community Sentence: The

Role of Social Factors', *Home Office Research Study No. 192*. London: Home Office.

Mayer, J.E. and Timms, N. (1970) *The Client Speaks*. London: Routledge and Kegan Paul.

Measham, F., Parker, H. and Aldridge, J. (1998) *Starting, Switching, Slowing and Stopping*, Report for the Drugs Prevention Initiative Integrated Programme (DPI Paper No. 21). London: Home Office.

McGuire, J. (1995) *What Works: Reducing Re-offending*. Chichester: Wiley Press.

McIvor, G. (1992) *Sentenced to Serve*. Aldershot: Avebury.

McIvor, G. (1997) 'Evaluative Research in Probation: Progress and Prospects', in G. Mair (ed.) *Evaluating the Effectiveness of Community Programmes*. Aldershot: Avebury.

McIvor, G. (1998) 'Pro-Social Modelling and Legitimacy: Lessons from a Study of Community Service', in S. Rex and A. Matravers (eds.) *Pro-Social Modelling and Legitimacy: The Clarke Hall Day Conference*. Cambridge: Institute of Criminology, University of Cambridge.

Palmer, T. (1995) 'Programmatic and Nonprogrammatic Aspects of Successful Intervention: New Directions for Research', *Crime and Delinquency*, 41, 100–131.

Paternoster, R., Bachman, R., Brame, R. and Sherman, L.W. (1997) 'Do Fair Procedures Matter? The Effect of Procedural Justice on Spouse Assault', *Law Society Review*, 31, 163–204.

Raynor, P. (1998) 'Pro-social approaches and Legitimacy: Implications from Research in Mid-Glamorgan and Elsewhere', in S. Rex and A. Matravers (eds) *Pro-Social Modelling and Legitimacy: The Clarke Hall Day Conference*. Cambridge: University of Cambridge, Institute of Criminology.

Raynor, P. and Vanstone, M. (1997) *Straight Thinking on Probation (STOP): The Mid-Glamorgan Experiment* (Probation Studies Unit Report No. 4). Oxford: University of Oxford, Centre for Criminological Research.

Rex, S.A. (1999) 'Desistance From Offending: Experiences of Probation', *Howard Journal*, 38, 366–383.

Rex, S.A. (2000) *Applying Accreditation Criteria to Community Service*, paper prepared for advice by Joint Prison and Probation Accreditation Panel.

Rex, S.A. and Crosland, P.E. (1999) *Project on Pro-social Modelling and Legitimacy: Findings from Community Service*, Report to Cambridgeshire Probation Service. Cambridge: University of Cambridge, Institute of Criminology.

Rex, S.A. and Crosland, P.E. (2000) *Project on Pro-social Modelling and Legitimacy: Findings from Probation Order Supervision, Report to Cambridgeshire Probation Service*. Cambridge: University of Cambridge, Institute of Criminology.

Ross, R.R. and Ross, R.D. (1995) *Thinking Straight: The Reasoning and Rehabilitation Programme for Delinquency Prevention and Offender Rehabilitation*. Ottawa: Air Training and Publication.

Sainsbury, E., Nixon, S. and Phillips, D. (1982) *Social Work in Focus*. London: Routledge & Kegan Paul.

Sampson, R.J. and Laub, J.H. (1993) *Crime in the Making: Pathways and Turning Points Through Life*. Cambridge, MA.: Harvard University Press.

Shover, N. (1996) *Great Pretenders: Pursuits and Careers of Persistent Thieves.* Oxford: Westview Press.

Trotter, C. (1993) *The Supervision of Offenders: What Works.* Sydney: Victoria Office of Corrections.

Trotter, C. (1996) 'The Impact of Different Supervision Practices in Community Corrections: Causes for Optimism', *Australian and New Zealand Journal of Criminology*, 29, 29–46.

Trotter, C. (1999) *Working with Involuntary Clients: A Guide to Practice.* London: Sage.

Tyler, T.R. (1990) *Why People Obey the Law.* New Haven, CT: Yale UP.

Vanstone, M. (2000) 'Cognitive-Behavioural Work with Offenders in the UK: A History of Influential Endeavour', *Howard Journal*, 39 (2), 171–183.

West, D.J. (1982) *Delinquency: Its Roots, Careers and Prospects.* London: Heinemann.

Chapter 5

Compliance and community penalties

Anthony Bottoms

The main purpose of this chapter is to attempt to provide some enrichment of the debates about the effectiveness of community penalties. I shall seek to achieve this by placing such debates within a broader theoretical framework, namely that of theories of compliance.

The chapter is divided into five sections. The first argues that a concern with the effectiveness of community penalties inevitably entails some engagement with theories of compliance, and it distinguishes between short-term and long-term compliance. The next section provides a brief overview of the main social and psychological processes that might be involved when an individual complies with legal rules in a given situation. Community penalties are wherever possible used as examples in this discussion. There is then, thirdly, some further conceptual exploration of the notion of 'compliance', with special reference to questions of subjectivity, legitimacy and possible interaction effects. The fourth section briefly explores aspects of social change in Britain in the last fifty years, and argues that these changes have inevitably affected the ways in which community penalties are enforced. It follows from this that the topic of compliance with community penalties needs to be thought about differently now than it was in the past. Finally, it is suggested in the conclusion that a main implication of this analysis is that our thinking about the effectiveness of community penalties needs to become more holistic.

The scope of this chapter is thus deliberately broad and exploratory, and I aim to open up a way of thinking rather than to reach any definitive conclusions. I shall have partially succeeded in my aim if this analysis is thought to shed interesting light on the issue of how and why offenders comply with community penalties; I shall have fully succeeded if the discussion is thought to be relevant to policy and practice debates about the effectiveness of community penalties.

Effectiveness and compliance

In what circumstances are community sentences effective? A variety of possible answers can be given to this important question. Some of these might be as follows:

A A community sentence is effective if it results in no further offending by the offender within a specified time period. [Simple non-re-offending]

B A community sentence is effective if it results in no further offending by the offender within a specified time period, and it is probable (using appropriate statistical comparisons) that had he been given a different penalty (e.g. a nominal penalty such as a conditional discharge) he would have been more likely to re-offend. [Comparative non-re-offending]

C A community sentence is effective if the offender completes it with no breach of the formal requirements of the order: for example, an offender given community service attends regularly at community service work sessions, and works hard and diligently during those sessions. [Successful completion of order]

D A community sentence is at least partially effective if certain intermediate treatment goals are achieved: for example, an offender whose criminality has been closely linked to heavy drinking significantly reduces his alcohol consumption after attending a prescribed treatment programme for heavy drinkers. [Intermediate treatment goals]

These possible definitions of 'effectiveness' are, of course, very familiar to anyone working in the field of community penalties. I have nevertheless spelt them out rather fully here, in order to emphasise three key points. First, if one is interested in any of the above types of effectiveness, one is necessarily and inevitably interested in the subject of *compliant behaviour*. That compliance might be legally compliant behaviour (as in A, B and C above), or compliance with expectations of a treatment programme (as in D above); but either way, effectiveness and compliance are, in the field of community penalties, topics that are inextricably linked. Despite this, there has not been much systematic exploration of the nature and characteristics of compliant behaviour in the literature on the effectiveness of community penalties.

Secondly, although the examples given at A, B and C are all concerned with legal compliance, they are nevertheless of two different kinds. Example C concerns *compliance with the specific legal requirements of the community penalty,* and might in shorthand usefully be described as 'short-term requirement compliance'. Examples A and B are concerned with the ultimately more fundamental issue of the offender's *compliance with the criminal law*, and can in shorthand be called 'longer-term legal compliance'. Clearly, the Probation Service, and others involved with the delivery of community penalties, are (or should be) inescapably involved in trying to maximise both 'short-term requirement compliance' and 'longer-term legal compliance'.

The third key point is that it is by no means foolish or fanciful to suggest that a particular offender might, when one considers the various kinds of effectiveness set out above, be compliant for different reasons in different contexts. For example, perhaps an offender with a drink problem has recently been placed on probation, but while on bail awaiting trial he has met and fallen in love with a woman who has now urged him to give up drinking almost completely. In such circumstances it could be the strong attachment to his new partner, coupled with the specific techniques he learns on the alcohol programme, that cause him to be compliant with the intermediate treatment goal of reduced alcohol consumption (see D above); at the same time, however, his more general compliance with the terms of the probation order (see C above) might principally derive from fear of the legal consequences if he does not do so (i.e. deterrent-based compliance).

Compliance, then, turns out to be inextricably linked to the effectiveness of community penalties, but also a more complex idea than is apparent at first sight. The complexity of compliance as a concept suggests that we need some kind of map or guide to this terrain, setting out the main different mechanisms of compliance, and how these might in principle be related to one another. I shall attempt to provide such a guide in the next section.

A basic framework for understanding compliance

In one or two recent papers (see, for example, Bottoms 1999: 250ff), I have begun to sketch a basic framework for the understanding of compliant behaviour. Figure 1 is an adaptation of these previous attempts, and I shall here set out some of the main features of the framework offered.[1]

As may be seen, four main kinds of compliant behaviour are distinguished in Figure 1. These are:

- *instrumental/prudential compliance* (based on self-interested calculation)

- *normative compliance* (based on a felt moral obligation, commitment or attachment)

- *constraint-based compliance* (derived from some form of constraint or coercion), and

- *compliance based on habit or routine.*

This fourfold framework is derived from theories of social order, which have been similarly categorised (see especially Cohen 1968: ch. 2); social order and individual compliance are concepts that are necessarily connected, although of course not identical.[2]

We must now look in a little more detail at each of these four kinds of compliance, using examples wherever possible from the field of community penalties.

Figure 1 An outline of the principal mechanisms underpinning compliant behaviour

---

A Instrumental/prudential compliance
    (a) Incentives
    (b) Disincentives

B Normative compliance
    (a) Acceptance of/belief in norm
    (b) Attachment leading to compliance
    (c) Legitimacy

C Constraint-based compliance
    (1) Physical restrictions or requirements on individual leading
       to compliance
       (a) Natural
       (b) Imposed
    (2) Restrictions on access to target
    (3) Structural constraints

D Compliance based on habit or routine

From an *instrumental or prudential perspective*, two simple reasons for compliance may operate – incentives and disincentives. Disincentives are of course commonly built into the legal frameworks of community penalties, through provisions for punishment when the requirements of the order are not fulfilled by the offender. Simple incentives have also long existed in English community penalties (especially in the 'early termination for good progress' in the probation order), and some community sanctions for offenders are now developing more complex incentives structures (e.g. the drug courts in the US: see for example Harrell 1999; Nelson 2000).

Normative compliance may be of three main sub-types. The first is a conscious belief in or moral acceptance of the norm in question (for example, a norm against the deliberate killing of a human being). We initially derive most of our normative beliefs, of course, from socialisation (in families, schools, churches or wherever). Very often, this socialisation produces a *mental disposition* which may result in a *habitual* compliance with law (see further below). But, in a concrete situation, the habitual behaviour arising from the disposition may be consciously called to mind, reflected upon, and morally reaffirmed by the individual, and it may then reasonably be described as a *normative belief* – as, of course, may beliefs developed through more conscious processes of moral reasoning.

Fortunately for the health of our society, very few if any individuals have no such normative beliefs. This is of potential importance for a probation officer (or other person supervising an offender serving a community penalty), inasmuch as if an offender does indeed have some normative beliefs, then it must in principle be possible, by moral reasoning, to cause him to consider extending those beliefs in a way that might increase future short-term or long-term compliance. (An improvement in long-term compliance might, for example, be attempted by causing the offender to reflect on the distress he has caused to the victim of his crime, perhaps after a face-to-face meeting with the victim.)

The other two sub-types of normative compliance do not derive from conscious acceptance of the norm itself. Rather, their source lies in certain key social relationships that link the compliant individual to other individuals or social groups (including, perhaps, those who hold power in the society in question). Normative compliance through the social bond created by emotive attachment to an individual, or a small group such as the family, was long ago identified as an element in delinquency prevention in Travis Hirschi's (1969) control theory. The mechanism involved here – as is shown by the example given in the previous section of the offender with the drink problem – is that the meaningfulness of the relationship to the individual acts so as to modify his/her normative frameworks in the direction of compliance (e.g. 'She wants me to stop drinking because she loves me, and she says the drinking will harm our relationship: I'd better try and change'). As Sue Rex points out in chapter 4, there is evidence in the research literature on criminal careers to suggest that forming emotively important links with non-criminal individuals is not infrequently associated with desistance from crimes, though the relevant literature is not wholly clearcut (for a particularly important source, see Sampson and Laub 1993).

Legitimacy, the third sub-type of normative compliance, is similar to attachment in that the compliance derives from the individual's perceived social bonds, linking him/her to others in society; but it differs from attachment inasmuch as those others are specifically *those in formal authority*, and the linkage does not have to be of a personal kind. Compliance through legitimacy, then, is compliance with a rule (or social expectation) on normative grounds, precisely because it has been promulgated by a person or body with legitimate authority, acting in a proper way to exercise that authority. Hence, some citizens might obey the speed limit on a motorway not because they are normatively committed to that particular rule (they might prefer a much higher limit) but because the speed limit has been set by the appropriate legal authorities within a democratic state, to which state the citizens feel a sense of allegiance.[3] I shall discuss legitimacy more fully in the next main section of this chapter, with specific reference to its role in community penalties.

The third main kind of compliance is *constraint-based compliance*, which like normative compliance has three sub-types. The first of these sub-types is constraint-based compliance deriving from the physical characteristics and limitations of the human body. We all need sleep, and when we are asleep we cannot burgle; similarly, when we are busy watching a football match, because we cannot be in two places at once we cannot shoplift (this is Hirschi's [1969] 'involvement'). These are the *natural* limitations of the human body that aid compliant behaviour; to them may be added the possibility of various *imposed* physical restrictions on the body, the most obvious example in a criminological context being when the individual is locked away in a prison or a police cell. But we should also note that imposed constraint-based measures focussing on the offender's physicality can take more subtle forms than cellular confinement, as in the familiar tactic of the classroom teacher who requires X and Y, persistent troublemakers, to stop sitting together in class.

It could be said that a central political problem for community penalties is that, by their nature, they inevitably find it more difficult to deliver imposed constraint-based physical restrictions on an individual than does the prison. (It is, I believe, more helpful to analyse the problem in this manner than through the language of 'toughness'.) But that does not mean that the physical constraints of community penalties are always negligible, a point that is surely becoming increasingly obvious in a context of increasing electronic surveillance, plus the ability to monitor bodily substances by devices such as drug testing or the breathalyser. To this one should add the important point that, in penalties delivered in a community context, it is actually far easier than it is in prisons to think constructively about how the physical restrictions of the penalty might be linked with other aspects of an offender's life (particularly the habitual and the normative aspects of his life), in integrated 'penalty packages' that might try to produce compliance based on a creative mixture of habitual, normative, instrumental and constraint-based mechanisms. This emphasis on how the various modes of compliance set out in Figure 1 might, in the real world, interact with one another, is a point that I shall be developing in the next section, and I will also return to it in the conclusion.

The other two sub-types of constraint-based compliance can, in the present context, be dealt with very briefly. One is compliance based on restrictions on one's access to the possible target of non-compliance, and it raises the familiar 'opportunity' motif that is central to the rationale of situational crime prevention (see generally Clarke 1995). The other sub-type I have called 'structural constraint'; it occurs essentially when someone is cowed into submission by the coercion inherent in a power-based relationship, even where they are not explicitly concerned about potential penalties for non-compliance (hence, the compliance is not instrumental), and there is also no normative consensus. This is not a kind of compliance that is likely to be of much importance in the field of the administration of community penalties. It is, however, a type of compliance that intra-family offenders such as child sex abusers are wont to try to impose upon their victims, hence it is certainly not devoid of criminological interest.

We come finally, then, to the fourth main type of compliance, *compliance based upon habit or routine*. This is the kind of compliance that most obviously occurs unthinkingly (though some of the other kinds previously listed might sometimes also be unthinking). I have suggested that such unthinking compliance occurs either through 'routine' or through 'habit', and it is perhaps worth distinguishing these two mechanisms.

Consider, then, parental compliance with the law requiring that children between certain ages should receive compulsory education. On the average morning in school term-time, in the average household with school-age children, there is no debate about whether to comply with this law. There is simply the semi-organised bustle of breakfast, packing a school bag, 'have you got your sandwiches?', 'Mum, have you got that note for the PE teacher?', and so forth. Unthinking routine prevails, and compliance rates are very high. This is not a unique example – the wearing of front-seat seat-belts could be analysed very similarly (interestingly, back-seat belt-wearing seems to be different).

These are *routines* that are integrally involved in the production of compliance. More psychologically, individuals often also develop *mental dispositions*, which may take the form of settled inclinations to comply with certain laws: these are appropriately called, in colloquial speech, *habits of mind*. Why do females commit much less crime than males, even in high crime areas? The answer to this question remains surprisingly unclear, and controversial, but some at least would wish to argue that a 'settled mental disposition' (however acquired) has merit as an explanation. Richard Wollheim (1984: 54) interestingly and helpfully tries to characterise the nature of mental dispositions:

> mental dispositions … are persistent phenomena, which manifest themselves intermittently. They do not occur, nor are they events. They are mutable. Dispositions have histories, which are made up of events, and these histories are varied … [S]ome are innate, some arise in the mind, and some are acquired … some remain constant, and some change …

As Wollheim's quotation makes clear, habits of mind (or dispositions) can change. If they can be altered in a more compliant direction, then such changes seem particularly likely to have lasting effects. This, essentially, is the kind of change that cognitive-behavioural programmes seek to achieve: an *altered way of thinking* (disposition) of the offender, that is linked (in a two-way process) to *altered behavioural routines*.

How are habits and routines originally developed? Obviously, through complex social processes that will certainly have included a *normative* component, and also to some degree a *coercive* element based on social power.[4] In that sense, compliance based on habit or routine is not independent, in its origins, from some of the other mechanisms previously discussed. It is nevertheless helpful, in my view, to include it as a distinct form of compliance (as in Figure 1), because once the habit or routine has been established, it becomes a mechanism of compliance in its own right, separate from the processes that initially produced it.

This concludes the sketch of what I would suggest are the principal mechanisms underpinning compliant behaviour. Before leaving this conceptual overview, however, it might be important to re-emphasise a point made briefly in the previous section; namely that, for a particular individual, compliance is very often a complex mixture of these various mechanisms, operating in different ways in different contexts. Readers of this chapter might perhaps gain some insight into this point by reflecting upon their own compliant behaviour at various different stages in their lifespan; or in different aspects of their activities – as drivers, taxpayers, employees, etc. – at a particular stage of life. Almost all of us, I would suggest, have at some stage complied with laws (or with strong social expectations) for all or most of the various reasons set out in Figure 1. The fact that this is so is perhaps simultaneously an encouraging reaffirmation of the potential value of a schema of this kind, and an illustration of how theoretically and empirically complex the field of compliance actually is. That last point is further strengthened when we recognise that even recidivist offenders do not offend all the time: they move between compliance and offending at different times and in different contexts, in a complicated kaleidoscope of activities, including – sometimes – relatively sustained 'crime free gaps' (see for example West 1963: ch. 5).

Finally, I think it would be interesting to attempt to relate the above discussion more directly to the field of community penalties, in two ways. The first is to reconsider, in the light of the schema shown in Figure 1, some results from an evaluation of community penalties undertaken thirty years ago. The second application of Figure 1 is more contemporary, and will seek to show how some of the present Government's strategies in the field of community penalties relate to the various different mechanisms of compliance identified above.

Ian Sinclair (1971) examined data from 46 regimes in so-called 'approved probation hostels' for male offenders aged between 15–21 years in England and Wales in the period 1954–1963. The offenders studied had all been sentenced to probation orders, usually for two or three years, but with a requirement that the first year be spent as a resident in a probation hostel. Sinclair found that 'failure rates' during the year in the hostel, varied markedly by hostel regime, from 14 per cent to 78 per cent – a very wide variation in rates, judged by the normal standards of offender treatment studies.[5] These rate differences by hostel were only partially accounted for by differences in the previous criminal and social history of the residents. Much more important in explaining the varying failure rates, Sinclair found, was the style of the small number of staff in each hostel: successful hostels had staff who combined emotional warmth (kindness and understanding of the boys' problems) with a set of clear rules (of a non-permissive character, administered consistently). Sinclair himself drew attention to the similarity between these results and what was known from the general research literature on successful parenting (on which see now, e.g., Smith and Stern 1997); and Sue Rex and I, in an earlier paper, related the Sinclair findings to the growing research evidence on pro-social modelling (Bottoms and Rex 1998). But thinking again about Sinclair's results in the context of theories of compliance perhaps produces a slightly different insight (though not one that is at all inconsistent with these earlier inter-pretations). Bearing in mind that the hostels studied were typically very small (with only two or three staff, all usually lacking formal training in psychology or social casework), and that the residents were mostly adolescents with disrupted family histories (otherwise a hostel place-ment would not have been deemed necessary), it seems highly probable that *normative attachment* (or lack of it) with the staff could have con-stituted the principal mechanism underpinning the differences in failure rates in the first year of the probation order, when the boys were resident in the hostel. (cf. Sinclair's [1971]) own comment that the findings suggested 'that hostel boys need the knowledge that they are liked, and a clear definition of what they must do to keep this liking': p. 136). However, as the boys' stay in the hostels was (for all residents) limited to twelve months, the opportunity to convert this initial attachment into altered socialisation patterns leading to changed long-term mental dispositions might well have been limited.

Sinclair's study is particularly famous for the fact that, while there were such marked differences in the in-residence failure rates between hostels, these differences almost completely disappeared when post-hostel reconvictions (in the two subsequent years) were considered.[6] But if one interprets the in-residence differences in terms of attachment mechanisms (with limited scope, in the time available, for more deep-rooted socialisation), then of course when those attachments were removed as the boys left the hostels, an obliteration of the initial cross-hostel differences is exactly what one would predict theoretically (notwithstanding that those differences were, in the residential period, so pronounced). As far as I am aware, Sinclair's study has not previously been interpreted in quite this way, and of course given its retrospectivity this interpretation is necessarily tentative and speculative. My aim in developing this example has simply been to try to show how a re-examination of familiar results through the lenses of theories of compliance might have some benefits. Perhaps there is scope for some further re-interpretation of this kind, on a range of other research studies, and then for the testing of some fresh hypotheses arising out of such re-examinations.

For a second application of the conceptual scheme shown in Figure 1, let us consider the present government's policies in the field of community penalties. I think it can reasonably be said that these policies include the following:

(a) A strong emphasis on accredited offender behaviour programmes, mostly with a cognitive-behavioural theoretical basis, aimed particularly at securing longer-term compliance with the criminal law.

(b) For juvenile offenders, a commitment to principles of restorative justice (for a review of this type of response to legal infractions, see Braithwaite 1999), especially in the new 'referral orders' introduced in the Youth Justice and Criminal Evidence Act 1999.[7] Emphasised within this approach are matters such as the offender's acceptance of responsibility for his wrongdoing; encouragement for the offering of apologies by offenders to victims; and the development of informal 'packages' of social control (e.g. involving the offender's family and other supportive networks), all intended to secure longer-term legal compliance.

(c) An attempt to secure higher attendance rates by offenders at community-based programmes, and at appointments with probation officers and others (i.e. enhanced short-term requirement compliance), by making a custodial term the normal outcome when there is a second unjustified breach of requirement of a community order (see Criminal Justice and Court Services Act 2000: section 53).

(d) An attempt to enhance short-term requirement compliance by introducing fresh legal powers whereby compliance with the requirements of community orders can be more extensively checked by means of electronic monitoring (see Criminal Justice and Court Services Act 2000: section 52).

Careful analysis of these various policies shows that they depend upon different anticipated mechanisms of compliance. As previously noted, cognitive-behavioural programmes seek to alter the offender's thinking patterns, or *dispositions,* and thus hopefully to enhance compliance by mechanisms of *habit and routine* (although normative dimensions are also present in many programmes). Restorative justice, it seems clear, relies principally for its intended effects upon mechanisms of *normative compliance*, both through normative challenges to the offender (by, for example, his understanding better the harm he has caused to the victim) and through what it is hoped will be the normative attachments developed in the informal social control packages that are agreed in the restorative justice forum. The readier resort to imprisonment for breaches of community orders is clearly a *deterrent-based strategy*; while the enhanced use of electronic monitoring in support of the requirements of community orders is principally an attempt to enhance short-term compliance through *imposed physical restrictions*, backed up by instrumental-prudential disincentives should the constraint-based requirement be breached.

The government is, then – in different aspects of its policies of community penalties – placing reliance upon *all four* of the principal mechanisms of compliance set out in Figure 1. What is rather less clear, at least to an observer from outside governmental circles, is whether much careful thought has been given *either* to the appropriate weight that should be placed upon one or other of these principal mechanisms within the government's overall strategy, *or* to the possibility of interactive effects as between the different mechanisms (on which see further below). Hopefully, a conceptual analysis of the kind attempted in this chapter might assist in clarifying such issues in future policy discussions.

Compliance: further conceptual exploration

In this section, I aim to take further the preceding analysis of the concept of compliance by focusing on three further issues. The first of these concerns the subjective experience of the potentially compliant person; the second is a fuller exploration of the concept of legitimacy, already briefly alluded to in the previous section; then thirdly I shall turn to the complex topic of interaction effects in the study of compliance.

The individual as subject

Until at least 1970, criminology was dominated by the intellectual approach which can be called, in shorthand, 'scientific positivism'. That approach had and has (for it still flourishes in some circles) many strengths; but it also has some significant weaknesses. (For a brief assessment, within a somewhat different context, see Bottoms 2000). One of positivism's weaknesses has been that it takes very little interest in *subjectivity*: that is, to quote Wollheim (1984: 38) again, in 'how the phenomenon is for the subject … [or] what it is like for the subject to have that particular mental phenomenon'. Because the legacy of criminological positivism has been stronger in treatment evaluation studies than in many other areas of the discipline, there is a particular need to ensure that subjectivity is not ruled out by default in thinking about compliance mechanisms in relation to the treatment of convicted offenders.

Those who seek to induce compliance in others very often think they know what it will be like to be on the receiving end of the measures that they administer. But, as anyone knows who has ever listened to an inappropriate harangue from an authority figure, people in power frequently misjudge their audiences. (Which of us has not been amused and/or angry in such situations, instead of being respectfully contrite, as the speaker wished?) Indeed, whole criminal justice policies have been based on such subjectivity-related mistakes, one of the most famous British examples being the 'short, sharp shock' detention centre experiment of the early 1980s.[8]

Subjectivity is not always immediately relevant in discussions of compliance: most obviously, *compliance based on habit or routine* is unthinking compliance, in which little importance is to be attached to the subject's immediate conscious mental state. But in other kinds of compliance, matters may be very different. In the field of deterrence studies, for example, the importance of the subjective character of deterrence was firmly recognised at least as early as Beyleveld's (1979, 1980) seminal review of the literature, and it was recently expressed by a Cambridge research team in the following manner:

> Criminal deterrence (being concerned with fear of penal consequences) is subjective in two senses. First, it depends not on what the certainty and severity of punishment actually are but on what potential offenders *believe* that they are. To the extent that changes in actual penal policies do not alter potential offenders' beliefs about the likelihood or severity of punishment, they cannot generate any marginal deterrence … Second, criminal deterrence depends not only on what potential offenders believe sanction risks to be, but on how they evaluate those risks in terms of their subjective disutilities. If penalties have increased and potential offenders know this, the change can still have no deterrent effect if those persons do not fear the increased penalties, or fear them but have overriding interests (e.g. financial ones) or inclinations (e.g. a drug addiction) favouring offending. The subjective character of

deterrence is one of its most important characteristics, and one that has not always been fully grasped when introducing policies intended to deter.

(von Hirsch *et al* 1999: 6)

Careful reflection on the subjective character of deterrence leads one to recognise potential uncertainties in the possible effects of the government's new policy of 'imprisonment for a second unjustified breach of requirement' in a community order (see above). One factor suggesting that this policy might well be effective in securing enhanced compliance is that detection rates are likely to be very high, and presumably most offenders will realise this. (Note that this is in marked contrast to, say, the perceived probability of detection when one is considering committing a burglary.) Countervailing factors, potentially weighing against the success of the new policy, might however include the possibilities that: (i) many offenders will not believe that courts will impose a custodial term on them just for failing to visit their probation officer;[9] (ii) even if they do believe that prison terms will be imposed, many offenders might nevertheless adopt a 'don't care' attitude ('let them lock me up if they want to; I'm going to see my girlfriend anyway'). On present research evidence, we simply cannot guess what are the likely overall effects of this new policy – primarily because we lack knowledge of how the relevant factors will be subjectively perceived by the offenders to whom the new policy will apply.[10]

A further example of the importance of subjectivity in legal compliance comes from the field of prison studies, where there are now quite a few indications in the research literature that, as Kevin Wright put it, 'more structured, more authoritarian settings may engender more disruptive behavior' (Wright 1991: 235). The mechanisms involved here appear to be that very physically restrictive control strategies, introduced by prison authorities in order to achieve compliance by imposed physical constraint (see Figure 1, mechanism C(1)(b)), can instead often lead to significant subjective resentment, a consequent loss of legitimacy for the regime of the prison in the eyes of the prisoners, and hence an increase in non-compliant behaviour (see further Bottoms 1999).

This last example, while reinforcing the importance of subjectivity to our developing analysis, reminds us also that a fuller discussion of legitimacy is now required. The example also alerts us to an interesting tension, in the prisons context, between two possible strategies that prison authorities can seek to develop when deciding on the nature of their regimes – namely, physical restrictions and legitimacy. It is time now, therefore, to look more closely both at legitimacy and at possible interaction effects between different mechanisms intended to produce compliance.

Legitimacy

The prestigious Woolf Inquiry into the disturbances at Manchester Prison and elsewhere in 1990 took the view that a widespread sense of *injustice* among prisoners about their general treatment in prison was causally implicated in the scale of the disorders (see Woolf 1991, e.g. at paras. 9.24, 14.437–38).

Woolf did not use the term 'legitimacy', but in the debates following publication of the Woolf Report, colleagues and I took the view that, if indeed 'justice' does help to sustain order in prisons (as Woolf proposed) then it does so because of the contribution that it makes to the legitimation of the prison authorities and the prison regime in the eyes of the prisoners. In our analysis, the acquiescence or otherwise of prisoners to the kinds of authority claimed or exercised over them by officials is a variable matter, centred around a complex matrix of interactions between prisoners' expectations of their captivity, and the experienced reality of that captivity. In particular, the core issue is whether, judged by the reasonable standards of the wider community in which the prison is set, prisoners come to see the behaviour of their custodians as being justifiable, comprehensible, consistent and hence *fair* – or, alternatively, unwarranted, arbitrary, capricious, and overweening (for fuller discussions, see Sparks and Bottoms 1995; Sparks, Bottoms, and Hay 1996).

A main theoretical source drawn on in our analysis was that of the political theorist David Beetham (1991). Beetham argues that virtually all systems of power relations, including ones which are quite autocratic, stand in need of legitimation. Conversely, they encounter particular kinds of problems when power is exercised in non-legitimate ways (see the right-hand column in Figure 2).

As Figure 2 shows, Beetham identifies three separate (but of course interconnected) dimensions of legitimacy, which roughly correspond to the traditional preoccupations of three different academic specialisms that have considered legitimacy as a concept. The three 'dimensions' are thus respectively of special interest to lawyers ('Has power been legally acquired, and is it being exercised within the law?'), to political philosophers ('Are the power relations at issue morally justifiable?'), and finally, to social scientists ('What are the actual beliefs of subjects about issues of legitimacy in that particular society?') (Beetham 1991: 4 ff.).

Figure 2   Beetham's dimensions of legitimacy

Criteria of legitimacy	Coresponding form of non-legitimate power
1 Conformity to rules (legal validity)	Illegitimacy (breach of rules)
2 Justifiability of rules in terms of shared beliefs	Legitimacy deficit (discrepancy between rules and supporting shared beliefs, absence of shared beliefs)
3 Legitimation through expressed consent	Delegitimation (withdrawal of consent)

Source: Beetham (1991): 20.

This scheme usefully reminds us that formal legality is only one aspect of legitimacy, and it is not on its own a sufficient criterion of it. Legitimacy also requires that office holders (such as prison and probation staff) act fairly; and that they can and do justify what they do to those who are affected by their decisions and practices (such as offenders and their families), thus heightening the likelihood that their authority will be assented to.

Empirical support for this last point comes from the work of Tyler (1990). Using data from a panel study of Chicago citizens' encounters with the police and courts, Tyler concluded that people are generally more concerned with issues of *procedural fairness* ('Has their case or situation been treated in a fair way? Are like cases treated similarly?' and so on), and of the *manner* of their treatment (e.g., 'Are they accorded respect by police in on-street encounters?') than they are with the outcome of the case. Tyler's argument is that people view their encounters with authority as 'information about the group that the authority represents and to which the parties to the dispute or allocation belong' (Tyler 1990: 175). Hence, every transaction with an authority figure raises questions that extend 'far beyond those connected with the issue to be decided' (p. 175): to the citizen encountering the police officer (or customs officer, or probation officer, or whoever), that official is not simply dealing with a particular matter in a routine transaction, they are in a real sense *representing*, through their demeanour and behaviour, the whole public service to which they belong. Issues raised in such transactions include 'neutrality, bias, honesty, quality of decision, and consistency' (p. 175) and, more generally, esteem. In short, we can postulate from Tyler's work – when we extrapolate from it into the prisons or community penalties contexts – that *ordinary everyday encounters between staff and offenders can have crucial implications for the nature of the power relations involved, and to the validity of the staff's claims to justified authority* – that is, to legitimacy.

In the prisons context, an analysis of this sort is of most relevance to the day-to-day interactions between prison officers and prisoners. Indeed, empirical analysis in prisons has shown, first, that prisoners' perceptions of staff fairness are the most important component in their overall assessments of the fairness of prison regimes (more important, for instance, than are the actual conditions of imprisonment, or specific regime features such as the arrangements for visits); and secondly, that prisoners' perceptions as to whether the staff are acting fairly are very highly correlated with their assessments as to whether staff–prisoner relationships are good or bad (so much so that, statistically speaking, the two perceptions can be regarded as part of the same construct). (See Ahmad 1996; Bottoms and Rose 1998). It seems very likely that direct analogies that can be drawn, from this body of literature, between the work of prison officers and the approaches adopted by staff involved in the day-to-day enforcement of the more obviously restrictive or demanding aspects of community penalties, notably community service staff and those administering electronic monitoring. An approach by such staff that recognises the human dignity and rights of the offenders being controlled, and affords them procedural fairness (such as the opportunity to state their case in an unhurried way in potentially conflictual situations) would seem likely – on all the evidence – to enhance the perceived legitimacy of the community penalty in question, and consequently to ensure that the offenders will more readily comply with the specific terms of the community penalty (i.e. 'short-term requirement compliance').

But what about longer-term compliance resulting from the legitimate use of authority? Here the empirical evidence is weaker, but there is one study that is especially intriguing. Paternoster *et al* (1997) re-analysed the results of the Milwaukee Domestic Violence Experiment, and found that, among domestic violence suspects who had been arrested in this study, there was statistically significant support for the hypothesis that 'the incidence of repeat spouse assault would be higher for those arrestees who perceived that they had not been treated fairly' by the arresting officers (p. 190). In other words, the fairness or otherwise of the conduct of the arresting officers seems to have had long-term con-sequences for arrestees' subsequent compliance or otherwise with the law prohibiting domestic violence. The authors observe that, from their data, it is not possible to specify the mechanisms that might be underpinning this longer-term compliance, but they point out that the 'most straightforward hypothesis' is a normative one, namely 'that perceptions of unfair procedural due process weaken support for the legal system which, in turn, reduces inhibitions against or proclivities toward future illegal activity' (Paternoster *et al* 1997: 193). This finding clearly requires replication in future research, but its implications are sufficiently interesting to be thought about seriously even prior to such replications.[11]

Interaction effects

The last part of this further exploration of the concept of compliance concerns possible interaction effects. Two separate matters need to be considered in this connection: the first concerns possible interactions between the various mechanisms potentially underpinning compliant behaviour (see Figure 1), while the second concerns possible interactions between compliance mechanisms and different kinds of individuals or social groups.

Perhaps the best-established interaction effect of the first kind might be summarised in the following proposition: *deterrence works best for those persons who have strong ties of attachment to familial or social groups or institutions, in a context where those groups or institutions clearly disapprove normatively of the behaviour at which the deterrent sanction is aimed.* (In terms of Figure 1, notice that this proposition links together, in part, aspects of mechanisms A(b) [disincentives], B(b) [attachment] and B(a) [acceptance of/belief in norm – in this case by the group that is important to the subject]. Those interested in the details of the empirical support for this proposition are directed to the research literature on deterrence (see especially the recent overview by Daniel Nagin 1998); here, I shall simply illustrate the general finding from one important series of research studies, that of Sherman (1992) and his colleagues on domestic violence in the U.S.

Figure 3, taken from Sherman's book, gives the subsequent annual violence rates per 1000 suspects of persons who came to the notice of the police for alleged domestic violence in three US cities (Milwaukee, Colorado Springs, Omaha). The figure distinguishes the subsequent violence rates of those who were arrested for the domestic violence incident, and those who were not, within the context of an experimental research design which ensured that arrests were (with appropriate safeguards for special cases) decided upon on a statistically random

Figure 3 Annual violence rate per thousand domestic violence suspects by arrest and stake in conformity

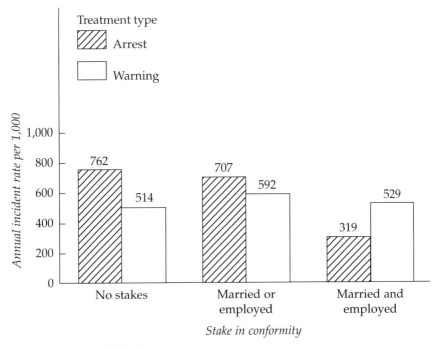

Source: Sherman (1992): 24.

basis. As may be seen, among suspects who were both married and employed, arrest produced lower subsequent violence rates than warnings; while among suspects who were neither married nor employed, the opposite outcome was observed. Sherman (1992: 17) reasonably concludes that this consistent pattern, observed (with minor variations) across several sites, supports the hypothesis that the effects of intendedly deterrent criminal sanctions 'depend upon the suspect's "stakes in conformity", or how much he has to lose from the social consequences of arrest'. Phrasing the results in this way, however, carries the risk of making the compliance sound purely instrumental, whereas in fact it has the mixed normative/instrumental character set out in the italicised phrase in the preceding paragraph. The compliant subject does indeed comply for instrumental reasons, because of what he fears he will lose. But what the subject has to lose, from what Sherman interestingly calls 'the *social* consequences of arrest' (emphasis added), arises from the facts that (i) he regards himself as having a significant attachment to the family/social group/social institution in question (the group is important to him), and (ii) that the members of that family/social group/social institution have certain normative expectations about how people should behave (see von Hirsch *et al* 1999: 40), and may censure the subject if he breaches those expectations. Where such normative factors are not present, instrumental compliance is weaker.

The Sherman example was introduced as an illustration of interaction effects of the first kind (i.e. interactions between the various mechanisms potentially underpinning compliant behaviour, in this case the instrumental and the normative). We may now also note, however, that the research results contain also an example of an interaction effect of the second type (i.e. an interaction effect whereby compliance mechanisms are differentially effective with different kinds of individuals or social groups). In this instance, the interaction effect demonstrated concerns the extent of different individuals' 'stakes in conformity', and how this variable might directly affect the results of an action (arrest) designed to secure enhanced compliance.

Some not dissimilar results were found in the Cambridge Institute of Criminology's evaluation (in five prisons) of the English Prison Service's so-called 'Incentives and Earned Privileges' (IEP) policy (see Liebling *et al* 1997, 1999). This policy was introduced in 1995 'to ensure that prisoners earn privileges by responsible behaviour and participation in constructive activity', to quote the official circular announcing the details of the policy. Hence, the earning of prison privileges was explicitly linked to good prison behaviour; the privileges were seen as an incentive, and a main anticipated outcome of the explicit linking of privileges and behaviour was an aggregate improvement in prisoner behaviour. The research evaluation, however, suggested that, overall, no such improvement in prisoner behaviour could be discerned in the five prisons studied. In seeking to explain this finding, the researchers noted that, in the period from 'before' to 'after' the introduction of the new IEP policy, prisoners' ratings of staff fairness and of regime fairness significantly declined, and it was reasonable to conclude from the data that this decline was causally related to some aspects of the IEP policy then in operation.[12] Possible behavioural improvements from the (instrumental) IEP compliance strategy therefore seemed to have been offset, in practice, by legitimacy deficits, probably leading to reduced normative compliance.[13] Hence as with the Sherman study, the IEP research suggests some quite complex interaction effects between the instrumental and normative mechanisms potentially involved in compliant behaviour (although in this example the instrumental dimension is incentives-based rather than disincentives-based, and the normative dimension is based on legitimacy rather than attachment).

The IEP research additionally contains some evidence of interaction effects of the second type (i.e. differences in responses to the IEP policy from different kinds of offenders): for a summary, see Liebling *et al* 1999: 3).

While both these examples of interaction effects illustrate interactions between the instrumental and normative dimensions in compliance, it is not difficult to imagine interaction effects between some of the other compliance mechanisms listed in Figure 1. An example of a probable interaction effect as between constraint-based compliance and normative compliance has already been noted in the subsection on subjectivity, above (i.e. as regards the legitimacy deficits created by severely restrictive prison regimes); and it is also easy to envisage situations where a new instrumental or constraint-based intervention might break up established routines or habits of thought, thus disturbing traditional patterns of habitual compliance or non-compliance. In short, if we are serious in our quest for an understanding of the mechanisms of compliant behaviour, it is clear that much attention will need to be paid to interaction effects.

'Late modernity' and the enforcement of community penalties

In 1996, Paul Wiles and I published an essay entitled 'Understanding crime prevention in late modern societies' (Bottoms and Wiles 1996), which was subsequently (and generously) described by Ken Pease (1997: 965) as a 'persuasive attempt' to locate recent developments in crime prevention practice within a broader theoretical understanding of societal change. At the beginning of our paper, Wiles and I identified 'four major types of contemporary crime prevention activity' (p.7), giving several examples of each. I shall here provide the barest summary of this categorisation, to give the flavour:

(a) *Defensive strategies*, including neighbourhood watch schemes; the sale of more security protection devices (intruder alarms, rape alarms); and 'target hardening' strategies such as the routine installation of car steering locks.

(b) *Guardianship and monitoring*, including CCTV in public places; the increasing use of private security personnel to guard both private and quasi-public places; and the increasing monitoring of business activity through computerised checking systems.

(c) *The creation of new forms of social order*, including the growth of multi-agency crime prevention partnerships; and the deliberate segregation or exclusion of troublesome groups at specific locations (e.g. schools, shopping malls and football stadia).

(d) *Criminality prevention*, including pre-school education enhancement programmes and youth action programmes.

Taken together, this constitutes an impressive list, which reminds us of the vast changes that have taken place in formal crime prevention activities in the last thirty years or so. For present purposes, the first three categories are of special interest.

Crime prevention strategies are of course an attempt to enhance legal compliance in the community. One might therefore have expected there to have been some considerable cross-fertilisation of ideas between probation managers (and others concerned with effective community penalties) and crime prevention managers about the strategies underpinning some of their respective tasks – especially, in the context of the present discussion, as between the enforcement of community penalties and general crime prevention strategies.

By and large, however, such cross-fertilisation has not been much in evidence. Indeed – and at the risk of being provocative – one might say that at times in the last twenty years leading voices in the field of probation have seemed to wish to preserve as much as possible of the enforcement and compliance ethos of the 1950s and 1960s (see also the related discussion in chapter 2, by Mike Nellis). In an era of CCTV, smart cards and computerised controls, this is an approach that is very difficult to defend.

Some assistance in seeing why this is so might be derived from a consideration of Anthony Giddens's (1990) characterisation of sources of trust in contemporary societies. As may be seen from the column headings in Figure 4, Giddens sees a general move, in contemporary societies, from a context where there is an 'overriding importance of localised trust' to one where, increasingly, trust relations are 'vested in disembedded abstract systems'.

As with all such stark conceptual dichotomies in the social sciences, Giddens's characterisation of sources of trust[14] is best read as a valuable heuristic device, rather than the final word on the subject. With that *caveat* in mind, we can note that, not many decades ago, the context of trust for most people was overwhelmingly *place-based*. Some of its most important manifestations were (as Giddens suggests: see the left-hand column of Figure 4) *kinship relations*, with the extended family being often predominantly clustered in a particular local area, and a real source of trust and support; the *local community*, where many people knew each other within a defined geographical location from which they did not stray very far; *religion* and the local church; and the importance of *tradition* as a guide to action ('we've always done things this way … it's our way'). Accounts of probation officers' practice up to about 1960 make it clear that officers acted as significant figures of authority within this kind of societal framework, seeking to reconnect the offender to the community despite his delinquency.

Increasingly, however, these placed-based contexts of trust have become eroded, though none of them is dead. In the modern world, in order to live our lives sensibly we simply have to trust that various abstract systems, on which we inevitably rely, will function appropriately (note for example the rapidly increasing dependence on computer systems in every walk of life). Additionally (see right-hand

Figure 4 Giddens's characterisation of environments of trust in pre-modern and modern societies

PRE-MODERN	MODERN
General context: overriding importance of localized trust.	*General context:* trust relations vested in disembedded abstract systems.
1 *Kinship relations* as an organizing device for stabilizing social ties across time-space.	1 *Personal relationships* of friendship or sexual intimacy.
2 *The local community* as a *place*, providing a familiar mileu.	2 *Abstract systems* as a means of stabilizing relations across indefinite spans of time-space.
3 *Religious cosmologies* as modes of belief and ritual practice providing a providential interpretation of human life and of nature.	3 *Future-oriented*, counter-factual thought as a mode of connecting past and present.
4 *Tradition* as a means of connecting past and future; past-oriented in reversible time.	

Source: Giddens (1990): 102.

column of Figure 4), instead of doing things 'because we've always done them this way', increasingly people are inclined to ask 'what would happen if we did things in such-and-such a way instead?' – in effect replacing a trust in (past-focused) tradition with an open-ended, future-oriented empirical quest for the 'best' solutions in a given situation. Thus the modern manager relies less on the corporate tradition of their firm or institution, and in a real sense places trust increasingly upon financial and policy projections, and in their ability to manage transitions in a rapidly changing external environment. (This is what Giddens calls 'future-oriented counter-factual thought'.)

Personal relationships of trust also tend to alter in this changed context. People increasingly define themselves *as individuals* rather than in the context of group affiliations (so, membership of a particular family, or living in a particular place, becomes a less important part of most people's self-identity than it used to be). In the field of personal relationships, therefore, trust is increasingly placed, not so much on the extended family or a particular community group, but rather on *personally chosen* ('elective') one-to-one relationships, with a sexual partner or a close friend (of course, such elective relationships have always existed, but they become of enhanced importance to individual identity as place-based group affiliations tend to diminish).

Even a brief acquaintance with any contemporary probation service will quickly throw up many examples of that service operating within the realm of abstract systems (note for example the performance indicators, the risk assessment instruments, the three-year future projections in the service's corporate plan, and so on). But most probation services have found it easier to switch to this mode of thinking at the organisational and managerial level than as regards day-to-day service delivery, notwithstanding that the probation officer him/herself is manifestly no longer the well-known place-based authority figure that he (or occasionally she) was fifty years ago.

If this broad-brush analysis has merit, then its implication must be that, in the contemporary enforcement of community penalties, serious account has to be taken of the societal context of 'late modernity' (Giddens's phrase again) within which we are now all living. The 'late modernity' context is everywhere to be seen in contemporary crime prevention (see categories (a) – (c) in the typology offered earlier in this section, and also chapter 3 by Mark Liddle in this volume). It is of growing importance in the enforcement of community penalties, though still I think too widely resisted (the Probation Service's response to the advent of electronic monitoring, for example, has not been particularly impressive, as is illustrated in chapter 9 by George Mair).

Resisting the arrival of late modernity is as futile as King Canute's legendary battle with the waves. But that does not mean that securing compliance with the aid of abstract systems is now easy, nor that it is easier than it was to secure compliance in the earlier social context of community-based localised trust. It is not easier or harder, it is different. Hence, the contemporary Probation Service needs to think very hard about how, within the context of late modernity (see Figure 4), the various available mechanisms of compliance (see Figure 1) can be best utilised and encouraged to enhance both shorter-term and longer-term compliance. It needs to do this in such a way that counterproductive interaction effects are avoided (see earlier discussion). It is a tough assignment, but – I venture to suggest – one that is both highly relevant and extremely interesting.

Concluding comments

To begin this conclusion, let me recount an incident that occurred during a visit I made to Texas in 1999. With a small group from the University of Texas at Austin, I went to the so-called Estelle Unit at Huntsville, which houses recalcitrant prisoners deemed to require special administrative segregation (or 'Adseg'). 'Adseg' in the Texas prison system comes in three gradings, Adseg 1, 2 and 3, each of enhanced restrictiveness. In Adseg 3, prisoners are completely confined to their cells, except for very short periods of exercise (three half-hour periods per week), such exercise being taken in tiny exercise 'cages', each housing only one prisoner. Food is provided to prisoners by pushing trays through slots in their cell doors. The transition from cell to exercise cage is managed by shackling the prisoner to a guard on each side, with handcuffs and leg-irons. It is the closest thing to attempted total physical constraint-based compliance that I have ever seen (see King 1999 for a much fuller discussion of the growth of such strategies in US prison systems). I asked the warden accompanying our party a question about how Adseg prisoners were prepared for release, assuming that I would receive an answer about gradual reintroduction to more normal prison environ-ments, and so forth. To my astonishment, I was told that there were no strategies of this kind, and that it was not at all uncommon for prisoners to be released direct from Adseg conditions – even Adseg 3 – into the outside community.

Some members of our small party were not criminologists. In the minibus on the way home, they more than anyone were incredulous about these policies. They imagined themselves as having apartments in

Dallas or Houston near to where released Adseg prisoners might settle – and they were appalled at the prospect.

The Texas example provides a stark illustration of the ultimately self-defeating futility of an *exclusive* reliance on constraint-based compliance, at any rate for that vast majority of offenders who will at some stage return to the community. And if exclusively constraint-based compliance is not a sustainable option, then we need to think constructively about integrated penalty 'packages' that will attempt to enhance compliance through a creative mixture of constraint-based, instrumental, normative and habitual mechanisms. In constructing such 'packages', it will be salutary to recall the point made earlier in this chapter that, while community supervision finds it more difficult than does custody to deliver imposed community-based physical restrictions, nevertheless it is actually far *easier* in the community context to think creatively about how the physical restrictions of legal penalties can be linked constructively with other aspects of an offender's life, particularly the *habitual* and the *normative* aspects of his life.

These considerations lead, finally, to the simple recommendation that we should increasingly try to think holistically about compliance in the field of community penalties, based on the framework in Figure 1. I would furthermore wish to contend – for reasons that should by now have become obvious – first, that such holistic thinking is, ultimately, actually required of us if we are to attend with full seriousness to the important question of the effectiveness of community penalties; and secondly, that adequate holistic thinking needs to take full account of the nature and characteristics of the society in which we are attempting to enforce these community penalties.

Notes

1 I am continuing to work on a fuller theoretical account of theories of compliance. A paper on this topic was delivered to the Southern Branch of the British Society of Criminology in January 2001.
2 For a helpful thumbnail comment on the linkages of classical theories of social order to three of the four mechanisms discussed in this section, see the remark by Dennis Wrong (1994: 9): 'Hobbes's solution [to the problem of social order] was coercive, Locke's stressed mutual self-interest, and the Rousseau of *The Social Contract* gave primacy to normative consensus.'
3 Indeed, the law's perceived legitimacy may induce some people to obey even where they regard a particular legal prohibition as being positively morally objectionable. For example, in Britain in the 1980s some of those who disagreed on moral grounds with the so-called Community Charge ('Poll

Tax') nevertheless felt bound to comply because the tax was a validly-enacted measure, piloted through Parliament by a democratically elected government.

4 Part of the purpose of Foucault's *Discipline and Punish* (Foucault 1977) is to emphasise the power-infused processes that produce discipline, and thus habitual obedience, in (for example) the family, the school and the factory as well as the prison. Note also, however, David Garland's (1986: 878) shrewd comment that Foucault's 'sweeping cultural critique' of the oppressive character of such processes is only rhetorically possible because it is focused on obedience. Garland continues: 'Had it focused on some of the other norms which social … agencies try to inculcate – such as literacy, cleanliness, health, responsibility, independence, stability, etc. – its critique would not have been so easily made.'

5 Two technical terms are used in this sentence. 'Failure rate' is the percentage of all residents in a given hostel regime who *either* left the hostel as a result of a further offence *or* left after absconding. 'Hostel regime' is the term used by Sinclair to denote the tenure of one hostel warden: hence one hostel might over time have had more than one 'hostel regime'. Sinclair (1971: 73) shows that the 'failure rate' was closely correlated with the reconviction rate during the first (hostel residence) year of the probation order.

6 Sinclair's reconviction data are limited to a dichotomy of 'reconvicted' or 'not reconvicted'. Given this, the best way of looking at post-hostel criminality was to consider the reconviction rates, in the two years after leaving the hostel, *of those who had not been reconvicted during the hostel year*. Using this measure, no significant differences between hostel regimes were found (p. 74), except in the case of one such regime (p. 99).

7 'Referral orders' are available for persons with no previous convictions, appearing at the Youth Court and pleading guilty, and on whom the Youth Court is not proposing to impose either a custodial sentence or an absolute discharge. Referral orders involve referral to a 'Youth Offender Panel', a version of a restorative justice 'conference' of the sort now familiar in juvenile jurisdictions in Australia and New Zealand (on which see Braithwaite 1999). The relevant statutory provisions now appear, in England, in the 2000 consolidation statute (Powers of Criminal Courts (Sentencing) Act 2000, Part III).

8 The 'short, sharp shock' detention centres placed a special emphasis on activities such as drill and extra physical education, in the expectation that these would be disliked. ('These will be no holiday camps', as the then Home Secretary put it). The subjective reaction of the prisoners was, however, quite different. For example, in one of the experimental centres it was reported by researchers that 'the "new" activities (drill, extra physical education, etc) reduced the amount of time spent on work. Work tended to be less popular than these new activities, hence the change [of regime] *involved the displacement of a relatively unpopular activity by a relatively popular one'* (Thornton *et al* 1984: 203, emphasis added).

9 Offenders might have some justification for such a belief. For example, the development of mandatory minimum sentencing laws in various US jurisdictions has led to widespread circumvention through practices such as plea bargaining (see von Hirsch *et al* 1999, Appendix); and the new English statutory provision allows a convicting court to avoid imprisonment for a second unjustified breach of requirement if it is of the opinion *either* that 'the offender is likely to comply with the requirements' for the remaining duration of the order *or* if there are 'exceptional circumstances' that justify not passing a sentence of imprisonment (Criminal Justice and Court Services Act 2000, s. 53).

10 This emphasises that while the Government's policy in the field of community penalties is in some respects strongly evidence-led (notably in the field of offending behaviour programmes), that is not the case for all aspects of the policy.

11 A possible limitation of the research, that would require attention in any replication study, is that there is no systematic analysis of the characteristics of the cases in which the arresting officers were perceived to act fairly or not fairly. It is theoretically possible that certain case characteristics *both* predict later offending *and* are more likely to elicit practices by arresting officers that are perceived as unfair.

12 Though this could not be definitively established, because the Home Secretary insisted on introducing the IEP policy simultaneously in all Prison Service establishments; hence, no control group was available in the research.

13 It was also the case that the instrumental dimension of the IEP policy was imperfect in the five prisons studied, because inconsistencies in practice meant that prisoners were sometimes unsure what exactly they had to do to be promoted to a higher privilege grade. However, it seemed probable from the research data that the losses in fairness, as well as the imperfections in the incentives structures, were related to the absence of the anticipated improvements in prisoners' behaviour.

14 It is important to emphasise that Giddens is not claiming any overall change in the amount of trust, nor that 'traditional settings were comforting and psychologically snug, while modern ones are not' (Giddens 1990: 105). The claim is rather that the *sources* of trust have changed, with important social consequences.

References

Ahmad, S. (1996) Fairness in Prison. Unpublished Ph.D. thesis, University of Cambridge.

Beetham, D. (1991) *The Legitimation of Power.* London: Macmillan.

Beyleveld, D. (1979) 'Identifying, Explaining and Predicting Deterrence', *British Journal of Criminology*, 19, 205–224.

Beyleveld, D. (1980) *A Bibliography on General Deterrence Research*. Farnborough: Saxon House.

Bottoms, A.E. (1999) 'Interpersonal Violence and Social Order in Prisons', *Crime and Justice: A Review of Research*, 26, 205–281.

Bottoms, A.E. (2000) 'The Relationship between Theory and Research in Criminology', in R.D. King and E. Wincup (eds) *Doing Research in Crime and Justice*. Oxford: Oxford University Press.

Bottoms, A.E. and Rex, S. (1998) 'Pro-Social Modelling and Legitimacy: Their Potential Contribution to Effective Probation Practice', in S. Rex and A. Matravers (eds) *Pro-Social Modelling and Legitimacy: The Clarke Hall Day Conference*. Cambridge: University of Cambridge, Institute of Criminology.

Bottoms, A.E. and Rose, G. (1998) 'The Importance of Staff–Prisoner Relationships: Results from a Study in Three Male Prisons', Appendix A in D. Price and A. Liebling, *Staff–Prisoner Relationships: A Review of the Literature*. Research Report to the Home Office by the University of Cambridge, Institute of Criminology.

Bottoms, A.E. and Wiles, P. (1996) 'Understanding Crime Prevention in Late Modern Societies', in T. Bennett (ed.) *Preventing Crime and Disorder*. Cambridge: University of Cambridge, Institute of Criminology.

Braithwaite, J. (1999) 'Restorative Justice: Assessing Optimistic and Pessimistic Accounts', *Crime and Justice, A Review of Research*, 25, 1–126. Chicago: The University of Chicago Press.

Clarke, R.V.G. (1995) 'Situational Crime Prevention', *Crime and Justice: A Review of Research*, 19, 91–150.

Cohen, P.S. (1968) *Modern Social Theory*. London: Heinemann.

Foucault, M. (1977) *Discipline and Punish: The Birth of the Prison*. London: Allen Lane.

Garland, D. (1986) 'Foucault's *Discipline and Punish*: An Exposition and Critique', *American Bar Foundation Research Journal*, 847–880.

Giddens, A. (1990) *The Consequences of Modernity*. Cambridge: Polity Press.

Harrell, A. (1999) *Understanding the Impact of Drug Courts*. Washington, D.C.: The Urban Institute.

Hirschi, T. (1969) *Causes of Delinquency*. Berkeley and Los Angeles: University of California Press.

King, R.D. (1999) 'The Rise and Rise of Supermax: An American Solution in Search of a Problem?' *Punishment and Society*, 1, 163–186.

Liebling, A., Muir, G., Rose, G. and Bottoms, A.E. (1997) *An Evaluation of Incentives and Earned Privileges*. Research Report to the Home Office by the University of Cambridge, Institute of Criminology.

Liebling, A., Muir, G., Rose, G. and Bottoms, A.E. (1999) 'Incentives and Earned Privileges for Prisoners: An Evaluation', *Research Findings No. 87*. London: Home Office.

Nagin, D. (1998) 'Criminal Deterrence Research at the Outset of the Twenty-First Century', *Crime and Justice: A Review of Research*, 23, 51–91.

Nelson, K. (2000) Drug Courts and their Implications for Criminal Justice

Policy, unpublished M. Phil. thesis, University of Cambridge (available in the Radzinowicz Library of Criminology, University of Cambridge, Institute of Criminology).

Paternoster, R., Brame, R., Bachman, R. and Sherman, L.W. (1997) 'Do Fair Procedures Matter? The Effect of Procedural Justice on Spouse Assault', *Law and Society Review*, 31, 163–204.

Pease, K. (1997) 'Crime Prevention', in M. Maguire, R. Morgan and R. Reiner (eds) *The Oxford Handbook of Criminology* (second edition). Oxford: Clarendon Press.

Sampson, R.J. and Laub, J.H. (1993) *Crime in the Making: Pathways and Turning Points Through Life*. Cambridge, Mass.: Harvard University Press.

Sherman, L.W. (1992) *Policing Domestic Violence*. New York: Free Press.

Sinclair, I. (1971) *Hostels for Probationers*, Home Office Research Study No. 6. London: HMSO.

Smith, C.A. and Stern, S.B. (1997) 'Delinquency and Family Behavior: A Review of Family Processes and Intervention Research', *Social Service Review*, 71, 382–420.

Sparks, R. and Bottoms, A.E. (1995) 'Legitimacy and Order in Prisons', *British Journal of Sociology*, 46, 45–62.

Sparks, R., Bottoms, A.E. and Hay, W. (1996) *Prisons and the Problem of Order*. Oxford: Clarendon Press.

Thornton, D., Curran, L. Grayson, D. and Holloway, V. (1984) *Tougher Regimes in Detention Centres*. London: HMSO.

Tyler,T. R. (1990) *Why People Obey the Law*. New Haven: Yale University Press.

von Hirsch, A., Bottoms, A.E., Burney, E. and Wikström, P-O.H. (1999) *Criminal Deterrence and Sentence Severity*. Oxford: Hart Publishing.

West, D.J. (1963) *The Habitual Prisoner*. London: Macmillan.

Wollheim, R. (1984) *The Thread of Life*. Cambridge: Cambridge University Press [Republished 1999, New Haven: Yale University Press].

Woolf, Lord (1991) *Prison Disturbances, April 1990*, Cm.1456. London: HMSO.

Wright, K.N. (1991) 'A Study of Individual, Environmental and Interactive Effects in Explaining Adjustment to Prison', *Justice Quarterly*, 8, 217–242.

Wrong, D. (1994) *The Problem of Order: What Unites and Divides Society*. Cambridge, Mass.: Harvard University Press.

Chapter 6

Making 'What Works' work: challenges in the delivery of community penalties

Andrew Underdown

Context is often crucial. As the Probation Service moves to apply 'What Works' in offender rehabilitation, what is crucial about the context? The 'community' setting of 'community' penalties presents both special challenges and rich opportunities. In some of these Cropwood papers there are important insights, which could help the Probation Service to overcome the challenges and exploit the potential of its community setting.[1]

The launch of a major policy initiative is arguably the moment for the greatest attention to the challenges and risks presented. The 1990s saw a string of criminal justice policy initiatives, which were promoted with commitment and much resource, but perhaps little attention to their areas of potential weakness. The Criminal Justice Act 1991 provided striking examples of this shortfall; reforms creating unit fines and circumscribing custodial sentencing proved not to be durable (Crow *et al* 1996). The 'What Works' initiatives for probation services, launched by ministerial commitment in the summer of 1998 and massively resourced within the outcome of the Comprehensive Spending Review 2000, are a major policy initiative of comparable significance. The broad shape of these initiatives has been well grounded in research evidence. The initiatives form part of the government's Crime Reduction Programme, a programme shaped by seeking to draw on the best of international research relevant to crime reduction (Nuttall 1998; Sherman *et al* 1997).

If probation's 'What Works' strategy is evidence-based, what risks or areas of weakness could it nevertheless face? Certainly, there are a host of management and implementation challenges. The strategy requires local probation areas to introduce new methods of work with offenders, recruit and train appropriate staff, adopt new processes, collect new information and refocus and restructure their organisations, all at a pace and a scale that is truly challenging. Crucially, a new accreditation system for treatment programmes is scrutinising proposed programmes against available research evidence, and is providing detailed guidance on practice, frameworks for staffing and staff development, monitoring and evaluation (Home Office 2000a).

Implementation on this scale cannot run altogether smoothly, but there is room for optimism that there will be a good proportion of high quality practice from the start. Some staff will be able to refine and reuse expertise developed within the previous range of probation pro-grammes.[2] A massive programme of staff training in new working methods is under way. A comprehensive audit system will clarify where practice is falling short and should clearly point up the improvements required. There is also increasing understanding of the organisational development within probation services that is needed to support staff delivery on effective practice.

A central challenge to the probation 'What Works' initiatives lies, I believe, not so much in the service's ability to use these evidenced methods with skill and commitment, but rather in an issue central to rehabilitative work in a community setting, the issue of compliance and engagement. For a moment, let us explore the challenges faced.

One approach is to look at the issue through the simple (perhaps simplistic) perspective of 'mental maths'. Suppose 100 offenders begin a community-based rehabilitation programme, all with the same statistical chance of re-offending (as measured by a group prediction instrument, or 'risk assessment score' [RAS]). Seventy of them complete the programme, and their re-offending rate is ten percentage points less than that predicted by the RAS. Thirty fail to complete the programme, and their re-offending rate is 20 percentage points worse than predicted. What is the overall impact of the programme? The answer is that it would reduce re-offending by one percentage point, just one tenth of what would have been achieved if all the offenders had completed the programme. The real world is, of course, much more complex than this. Nevertheless, the crude calculation gives food for thought, against the context of declared targets for successful completion of probation programmes of 70 per cent rising to 80 per cent. At these real-life levels, there is every chance that the positive impact on programme completers will be substantially reduced by the poor outcomes associated with failure to complete.[3] Improving completion rates through higher offender compliance will be crucial to outcomes in a community context.

The need for urgent attention to the issue of completion is also driven by the interplay between tighter enforcement policies for community sentences and demanding attendance requirements required by 'What Works' programmes. A typical offending behaviour programme operating within a probation order will require an offender to comply with instructions to attend and participate on between 30 and 50 occasions within the first year of supervision. Under National Standards revised in 2000 (Home Office 2000b), the challenge is to achieve attendance with no more than one unauthorised absence, since a second will involve breach proceedings with a serious consideration of custodial sentencing. This requires that offenders achieve an attendance rate of 96–98 per cent. Within this total attendance commitment, the offender's participation in accredited programmes is governed by rules designed to safeguard programme and treatment integrity. These would typically require offender attendance at about 25 sessions with a maximum of two sessions missed for any reason (again an attendance target of over 90 per cent, but applied to sessions operating on a fixed schedule, and including, for example, sickness as well as unauthorised absences). These are most demanding levels; it is worth comparing their assumptions of absence with the following:

		%
(a)	Sickness levels in manual employment[4]	5.6
(b)	Authorised/unauthorised absence from secondary education[5]	9.0
(c)	Unacceptable absence for probation appointments	8.7
(d)	Total absence for probation appointments[6]	22.6

Achievement of high attendance and completion rates requires a major improvement on past service performance, and will be critical to achieving adequate reductions in offending from these programmes. In this context, Anthony Bottoms's discussion of compliance points up the need to make use of a 'creative mixture of instrumental, normative and habitual mechanisms', taking into account 'the nature and characteristics of the society in which we are attempting to enforce these penalties' (see p. 112 above).

Some key elements of a convincing compliance strategy are already present, others need to be urgently developed.

The most evident strand of existing policy is the emphasis on timely breach action – reflected in the revised National Standards (Home Office 2000b) and the Home Secretary's reasonable determination that these standards are rigorously adhered to. Monitoring and audit results indicate that attendance rates have been raised by this instrumental compliance approach. Referral for breach proceedings before a court represents a significant disincentive; this will be increased by the provisions regarding imprisonment for breach of community orders contained in Criminal Justice and Court Services Act 2000.

However, the later stages of enforcement proceedings remain less certain and predictable. The vagaries of warrant enforcement must be evident to at least a proportion of offenders.[7] So there remain opportunities to improve the predictability of there being a timely sanction in response to breach. As Hedderman and Hearnden (2000) have argued, there is also a risk, in tighter enforcement standards and severe sentencing, of losing any graduation in the response. Our understanding of criminal behaviour includes a recognition that substantial numbers of offenders commence a period of supervision with poor reasoning skills or drug or alcohol dependency. For offenders who could demonstrate progress within a rehabilitative programme, a graduated response would provide gradually escalating sanctions which might also encourage more completions.

The heavy emphasis on disincentives needs also to be enriched by some balancing incentives – often remarkable by their absence from the community penalties system. Some probation services have shown initiative in marking and celebrating programme completion – awards ceremonies and Teesside's 'Big Breakfast' (providing breakfast for offenders attending their last session of the 'Think First' programme) are examples. Stronger incentives would preferably be consistent and predictable, and established within a legislative framework. They could reward compliance and purposeful engagement with rehabilitative programmes, perhaps by reducing the restrictions or lessening the demands that the overall community penalty imposes. The experience of operating the Drug Treatment and Testing Order may trigger further developments of the courts' role in overseeing those orders, and provide a model for court roles in oversight or review of other community penalties (cf. the strong role of incentives in the American drug court experiments: see Harrell 1999). The government's current Sentencing Review presents wider opportunities still. However, no effective strategy for compliance can rest on an instrumental approach alone.

Within probation's rehabilitative programmes, there are important opportunities to improve normative compliance, as well as the cognitive skills that are likely to make instrumental compliance more effective. Several 'What Works' approaches have potential in this way. Cognitive training programmes aim to improve cause–effect thinking and understanding of social obligations through values enhancement.[8] Motivational interviewing approaches seek to explore dissonance within expressed attitudes and behaviour, and use this to promote a more pro-social approach (HM Inspectorate of Probation 1998). A pro-social modelling approach would include probation staff encouraging and recognising punctual attendance and positive engagement; this could reward through the incentive of recognition and might achieve desired behaviour through a measure of attachment, where offenders value and even enjoy the time spent with supervising staff.[9] As Sue Rex discusses in chapter 4, there is significant evidence that such approaches improve attendance and completion rates. Wider organisational initiatives, including those that address race and gender equality, will help to promote 'legitimacy' in how probation authority is exercised. All of this is productive, and worthwhile, and, by its nature, slow to develop. Pursued with energy, it can provide a plausible mechanism for sustaining compliance, once an offender is engaged with and learning from a rehabilitative programme. However, such approaches will be too slow to have impact on compliance in the early weeks of supervision.

What, then, from Anthony Bottoms' framework, could probation managers use to drive up compliance rates in those crucial early weeks of an order? Internal monitoring reports show that 20 per cent of community supervision cases can have breach initiated within the first three months due to non-compliance. Little attention has been given to the mundane, situational and routine factors that determine punctual attendance. Success with a community penalty could depend on how compliant behaviour fits into lifestyles, daily routine and the ordinary exchanges of social relationships. Thoughtful probation staff have long attempted to make some use of such factors – for example by enlisting a parent to remind their son or daughter of their appointment, or in linking appointment times to an offender's daily or weekly routines, where they exist. Such approaches, though, have had little organisational attention. Any such approach needs to be empirically tested and cost effective. Fairly straightforward examples would include using telephone calls to wake up or remind offenders of their attendance obligations, or contacts with mentors or volunteers, timed to trigger compliance with a statutory appointment. More speculatively, how could electronic monitoring conditions establish a daily routine that makes attendance more likely? Could that technology be used to confirm departure from home to meet a morning attendance requirement? Would other private sector organisations be willing to sponsor initiatives which improve compliance, punctuality and employability? Such initiatives could include sponsoring practical arrangements to encourage punctuality – from providing alarm clocks to exploiting new communications technology.

If community-based programmes are delivered with integrity and high engagement and completion rates, then significant reductions in re-offending should be achievable.

Several meta-analytic studies have found a positive association between delivering in a community setting, compared with an institutional setting.[10] The potential advantages of a community context for rehabilitative programmes have been widely discussed; these include greater opportunities to generalise what has been learnt and to apply and rehearse new behaviours (Losel 1995). Against this encouraging background, the Probation Service has formulated a broad-based 'What Works' strategy (Home Office 2000d). The strategy is consistent with the messages from research about a broad-based approach, highlighted in chapter 4. As well as large-scale deployment of cognitive-behavioural programmes, there is a major emphasis on the supporting conditions for those programmes, on initiatives that tackle social circumstances linked to offending and on the potential of community service. The strategy embraces the implementation of research-based programmes, and the encouragement of further research to widen the evidence base.

If the strategy is broad-based and impressive, where might the risks lie? The writer would single out two inter-related issues – time scales and integration. Whilst the strategy is broad-based, the early emphasis is on cognitive behavioural programmes. Early results from the large-scale implementation of those programmes will be subject to public and political scrutiny, long before later elements of the strategy, such as accredited community service, come into play. So the challenge lies in achieving integration at each step of the way and at each level of the organisation. The Service's first national director has entitled her first strategic plans as an 'integrated strategy for the National Probation Service'. Probation officers need to achieve close integration between the new cognitive-behavioural programmes which offenders will be attending and the other elements of supervision, which will be less closely shaped by these national initiatives in these early years. The emphasis should be on the individual application and reinforcement of changed behaviour patterns and attention to crucial social issues, especially employment and unstable accommodation,[11] in the supervision of offenders during and after programme attendance.

To conclude, these first years of the twenty-first century are a period of special opportunity for community penalties. Strategies for offender compliance will be crucial to achieving rehabilitative impact. At each stage of the emerging 'What Works' strategy, the different elements of community supervision will need to be linked and integrated in order to make the most of that community context. If we meet these challenges, then this could indeed prove to be the time 'when "What Works" will work'.

Notes

1 This chapter is a developed and reworked version of comments originally made at the Cropwood Conference, where the author was the discussant in the session considering the papers by Sue Rex and Anthony Bottoms (see chapters 4 and 5, above).

2 HM Inspectorate's Thematic Inspection on Probation Orders with additional requirements found 'impressive work with difficult and disparate groups of offenders' (HM Inspectorate of Probation 1996). Similar results were found in the fieldwork of the HMIP What Works Project (Underdown 1998). Indeed it is common for reviewers or inspectors of probation practice to find impressive examples of skilled practice by probation staff working directly with offenders. But, as in the 1996 and 1998 studies, such practice has also often been judged to be 'inconsistent'.

3 For example, in the Mid-Glamorgan STOP evaluation, those who completed the programme showed, after twelve months, and after adjusting for 'pseudo-reconvictions', reconviction rates seven percentage points lower than predicted. However, this positive effect was offset in full by higher than predicted offending by those who did not start or did not complete the programme, so that the overall reconviction rate after twelve months for the whole STOP group was exactly as predicted (Raynor and Vanstone 1997, Table 4: 36). In other studies, non-completers typically perform poorly, although the significance for overall outcomes varies greatly.

4 Local Government Sickness Absence levels 1999/2000 for manual staff; Employers' Organisation.

5 DfEE *Statistical Bulletin*, December 1998.

6 Greater Manchester Probation Service Enforcement Audit, January 2001 (internal report).

7 A survey about the execution of warrants for breach of community orders (Home Office 2000c) showed that, where a warrant was issued to institute breach proceedings, 92 days was the average time for warrant execution. The Access to Justice Act 1999 changes the arrangements for warrant execution; its impact is yet to be seen.

8 James McGuire's 'Think First' programme contains sessions on moral reasoning; Robert Ross' 'Reasoning and Rehabilitation' programme includes 'Values Enhancement'.

9 Perhaps in a way not dissimilar to Sinclair's hostel wardens of the 1960s (Sinclair 1971).

10 For example, Andrews *et al* (1990) found an effect size for appropriate correctional service of 0.35 in a community setting compared with 0.20 in a residential/institutional setting.

11 Research into McGuire's 'Think First' programme in Devon, Greater Manchester and Teesside found higher than expected drop-out rates for offenders without suitable or stable accommodation (Home Office 2000e).

References

Andrews, D.A., Singer, I., Hoge, R.D., Bonta, J., Gendreau, P. and Cullen, F.T. (1990) 'Does Correctional Treatment Work? A Clinically Relevant and Psychologically Informed Meta-Analysis', *Criminology*, 28 (3), 369–404.

Crow, I., Cavadino, M., Dignan, J., Johnston, V. and Walker, M. (1996) *Changing Criminal Justice.* Sheffield: Centre for Criminological and Legal Research, University of Sheffield.

Department for Education and Employment (1998) *Statistical Bulletin.* London: HMSO.

Greater Manchester Probation Service (2001) Enforcement Audit (internal report, January).

Harrell, A. (1999) *Understanding the Impact of Drug Courts.* Washington, D.C.: The Urban Institute.

Hedderman, C. and Hearnden, I. (2000) 'The Missing Link: Effective Enforcement and Effective Supervision'; *Probation Journal*, 47 (2), 126–128.

HM Inspectorate of Probation (1996) *Probation Orders with Additional Requirements: Report of a Thematic Inspection 1995.* London: Home Office.

HM Inspectorate of Probation (1998). *Evidence-based Practice: a Guide to Effective Practice.* London: Home Office.

Home Office (2000a) *First Annual Report of Joint Prison/Probation Accreditation Panel.* London: Home Office.

Home Office (2000b) *National Standards for the Supervision of Offenders in the Community.* London: Home Office.

Home Office (2000c) *Survey of Time Taken by Courts to Complete Action on Community Penalties.* London: Home Office.

Home Office (2000d) *What Works Strategy for the Probation Service.* London: Home Office.

Home Office (2000e) Research briefing: A Retrospective Study of the McGuire Programme by the Probation Studies Unit, University of Oxford. Paper presented to What Works Conference, Manchester. September 2000.

Losel, F. (1995) 'The Efficacy of Correctional Treatment: A Review and Synthesis of Meta-Evaluations', in J. McGuire (ed.) *What Works: Reducing Re-offending.* Chichester: John Wiley.

Nuttall, C.P. (ed.) (1998) *Reducing Offending: An Assessment of Research Evidence on Ways of Dealing with Offending Behaviour.* Home Office Research Study No. 187. London: Home Office.

Raynor, P. and Vanstone, M. (1997) *Straight Thinking on Probation (STOP): the Mid-Glamorgan Experiment*. Oxford: University of Oxford, Centre for Criminological Research, Probation Studies Unit No. 4.

Sherman, L.W., Gottfredson, D., Mackenzie, D., Eck, J., Reuter, P. and Bushway, S. (1998) *Preventing Crime: What Works, What Doesn't, What's Promising*. Washington DC: US Department of Justice, Office of Justice Programs.

Sinclair, I. (1971) *Hostels for Probationers*. Home Office Research Study No. 6. London: HMSO.

Underdown, A.W. (1998) *Strategies for Effective Offender Supervision: Report of the HMIP What Works Project*. London: Home Office.

Chapter 7

Accountability in the delivery of community penalties: to whom, for what, and why?

Judith Rumgay

Introduction

An increasing number of agencies and individuals perceive a legitimate claim on their local probation service for accountable management of the community penalties. For example: the delivery of supervision programmes is becoming a complex multi-agency exercise as the Service develops its range of financial partnerships with non-statutory organisations, its participation in youth justice teams and its role in implementing new forms of coerced intervention in offenders' lives; its presence in Drug Action Teams and crime prevention and community safety groups raises questions about the nature of the contribution which its development of the community penalties is supposed to make to the achievement of these bodies' goals; requirements that the Service represent the interests of real and potential victims in its advice to sentencers constrains the legitimacy of proposals for community penalties in pre-sentence reports. The way in which the Probation Service defines its obligations towards these diverse parties must, therefore, impact on the style and content of the community penalties meted out to offenders.

Yet such relationships to parties with a stake in community penalties are not only increasing in number and variety, but their very nature is vulnerable to shifts in policy perspectives and emphases. For example, the Home Office's 'partnership' initiative for the Probation Service, announced in 1992, conveyed a specific, and much more limited meaning than did its broader use of the term in crime prevention policy (Crawford 1999). As far as the Probation Service was concerned, it appeared that its partners were henceforth to be identified by their engagement in a financial relationship for delivery of discrete parts of supervision programmes (Home Office 1992). Although the reality of partnership development was considerably more complex, the Service tussled with the implications of this new role as a purchaser of services and its impact on relationships with non-statutory agencies which traditionally had been based on goodwill (Rumgay 2000a). Yet, while the Service and its new partners struggled to come to terms with this imposed redefinition of inter-agency relations, the policy environment was already changing. In 1998, the government's consultation document, which considered the Probation Service's future, referred to its partners almost exclusively as the statutory agencies of police, Crown Prosecution Service, prisons and local authorities, with barely a nod in the direction of 'those other local bodies which help to deliver public protection services' (Home Office 1998a: 11–12). Even were we to overlook this extraordinary vision of the role of voluntary sector organisations within their communities, the question remains: what is the Service and its variously defined partners supposed to make of this shift, which carries clear implications for the relative priorities now to be attached to statutory and enforcement-oriented relationships and voluntaristic, rehabilitative associations with the non-statutory sector?

Similarly, the Probation Service was closely connected to the emergence of the 'forgotten' victim in criminal justice debate and the development of victim support services (Rock 1990). This provided the Service with an opportunity to extend its concern for, and skills in the relief of human distress, beyond the population of offenders, on the splendidly straightforward premise that the pain caused by crime should be assuaged, wherever it is felt. Yet recent requirements that the Service represent the concerns of victims in its pre-sentence advice to sentencers (Home Office 1995), with the implication that those concerns should bear directly on the treatment of the offender, shatters the common identity of victims and offenders as individuals whose lives are touched by crime, creating them instead as rivals for the Service's compassion.

Forced into choices between enforcement and voluntarism, victims and offenders, statutory and non-statutory allegiances, the Probation Service finds itself struggling with multiple, fragmented account-abilities. As the pivotal agency in the delivery of the community penalties, their fate and that of the Probation Service itself are inseparably bound together. Fragmentation of the Service's account-abilities leads to a loss of coherence for the community penalties. For example, in the Drug Treatment and Testing Order, and the planned

Abstinence Order, the technology and skills of drug treatment have become conflated with those of law enforcement, leading to ambiguity of purpose (Rumgay 2000a), with potentially damaging impact on inter-agency collaboration (Barton 1999).

Confusion as to the meaning of the community penalties strikes to the heart of the Probation Service's sense of mission. It is the contention of this chapter that questions of accountability – to whom, for what and why – cannot be answered in piecemeal fashion as the Service and its associated partners react to what has become a tidal wave of penal innovations. They can only be resolved within a clear sense of mission from which principles for practice may be coherently derived. Lacking that, the consequent fragmentation of purpose and priorities promotes a view of different parties as competitors for recognition and accountable service, who can be satisfied only at the expense of other claimants. Moreover, constant pre-occupation with the Probation Service's obligations towards this population of multiple claimants fosters the illusion that accountability is a uni-directional responsibility. Few have dwelt for long on the question of what might be the reciprocal obligations of any of these claimants towards the Probation Service. This chapter explores the potential of one possible vision of the Probation Service's mission for clarifying the nature of its accountable relationships and the implications of that clarification for delivery of the community penalties.

Harm minimisation: an acceptable mission?

When Ken Pease, at the first Bill McWilliams Memorial Lecture, proposed 'transforming the Probation Service into a generic helping service for all those whose experience of criminal justice impoverishes them, materially, emotionally or spiritually' (1999: 14), he allied a vision of the Probation Service's mission to a broader conceptualisation which resonates strongly with a theme in contemporary public policy debate. Recognition of the 'harm' inflicted on communities by a variety of social problems has encouraged considerable interest in the application of this concept to policy formation and implementation.

The field of drug misuse was an early leader in embracing harm as an energising concept in pragmatic policy development, fuelled by the discovery of the HIV virus among intravenous injectors in 1985. The stimulation of voluntary sector initiatives in drug-related harm reduction (Dorn 1990) testified to the need for an expanded multi-agency enterprise, with a strong non-statutory component, in reaching those groups whose activities placed them most at risk and, by extension, threatened the health of local communities in which drug abuse thrived. Subsequently, several publications by the Advisory Council on the Misuse of Drugs (1991, 1994, 1996) challenged the primary agencies of the criminal justice system to develop strategies for integrating harm minimisation into their daily practice.

The success of the field of illicit drug addiction in deriving practice principles from the goal of harm minimisation encouraged transference of that objective to prevention and treatment of alcohol problems. The 'practical desire simply to reduce the level of tragedy, harm, pain and misery' (Plant, Single and Stockwell 1997: 4) associated with 'the most widely used recreational psychoactive drug in most countries of the world' (Plant, Single and Stockwell 1997: 3) has proved to have implications for a wide range of organisations, embracing activities, for example, in health promotion, taxation, licensing and management of public drinking environments, urban design and policing of public order.

In criminal justice debate, attempts to develop policy initiatives around the concept of harm are perhaps most well established in discussions of restorative, and relational justice. To perceive crime in terms of its 'harm to people and relationships' (Zehr 1990) has clear implications for reinstating the victim as central to criminal justice concerns. A narrow focus on victimisation in policy and practice development, however, constrains our imaginations, since victims are created in the public consciousness almost entirely by violent crime (Rubin 1999). Yet by considering the 'relational damage' (Schluter 1994) of even allegedly 'victimless' crimes such as illicit drug use, we begin to appreciate the damage inflicted on the partners, children, employers and neighbours of the user.

We are further required through this inventory of the multi-faceted harms of crime, to recognise the damage which it inflicts even upon its perpetrators. The probability of becoming an offender is increased by early exposure to crime as victim or onlooker in families and neighbourhoods (Widom 1994). Adolescent involvement in illicit drug use has been found to impair social functioning (Baumrind and Moselle 1985; Newcomb and Bentler 1988) and to predict criminal activity (Stacy and Newcomb 1995) in adulthood. However, although alcohol and drug misuse are commonly thought to cause crime, criminal involvement and lifestyles often appear to precede and to fuel substance abuse (Collins 1982; Elliott, Huizinga and Menard 1989; Kandel, Simcha-Fagan and Davies 1986; Kerner et al 1997; McCord 1995; Parker, Bakx and Newcombe 1988). Moreover, criminal lifestyles are embued with the risk of victimisation and its consequences, including premature death (Baskin and Sommers 1998; Cohen *et al* 1998; Goldstein *et al* 1997; Kennedy and Braga 1998). Finally, perhaps the most terrible in this inventory of harms suffered by offenders, the perpetrators of domestic homicides are faced with the appalling reality of having bereaved themselves and their families by their own hand (e.g. Alder and Baker 1997; Ahluwalia and Gupta 1997; Mishcon *et al* 1996).

A full-blooded analysis of the harm of crime would, therefore, extend to *all* those whose lives are spoiled by it, including offenders and communities (Zehr 1990) – a point which is recognised by proponents of restorative approaches, but rather rarely pursued in policy rhetoric which draws upon them. This line of argument brings criminal justice debate into touch with wider social policy issues. It is well recognised that the harms of crime are disproportionately concentrated in areas afflicted with multiple disadvantages of poverty, poor housing and poor opportunities in education, employment and health care (Social Exclusion Unit 1998). In an examination of the field of social housing, Burney (1999) exposes the self-defeating enterprise of excluding individuals and families on grounds of nuisance and criminality, when these same parties are particularly likely to meet criteria for housing priority on the basis of need. Indeed, amongst the homeless, involvement in the penal system is only one aspect of lives marked by unemployment, substance dependence, illness and disability (Kemp 1997). The harms of crime, then, are tangled with multiple social and personal harms which impact upon poor communities and excluded individuals. In this context, the identities of the harmers and the harmed become inextricably confused.

Alternative discussions in criminal justice have applied different perspectives to the concept of harm. Clear, for example, asserts the essential harmfulness of the penal system itself, complaining that 'when other writers have used value-positive terms such as *punishment* or *sanctions* to investigate this topic, it enables them to sidestep the harming intent and harmful content of the actions they seek to justify' (1994: 3). A particularly vivid account of some of the 'penal harms' to which Clear refers is offered in a recent study which exposes the role of imprisonment in producing mental health and substance misuse problems (Singleton *et al* 1998). Even were we to accept the extraordinary premise that mental illness and addiction were reasonable consequences of deserved punishment, we still must consider the economic and social costs of deliberately exposing offenders to iatrogenic experiences. Thus, in an increasingly vengeful policy climate, Clear exposes the confidence trick which is visited on the public generally, and the victims of crime in particular, by portraying the resolution of criminal harm narrowly in terms of reciprocal harms delivered to offenders (see also Elias 1993).

In his critique of the futility of policy which views the wisdoms of a rational, scientific criminology and the imperatives of public concern, however ill-founded, as irreconcileable, Rubin (1999) offers harm mini-misation as a pragmatic compromise for constructive policy development. In this context, the community penalties, when well targeted and managed, offer a cost-effective approach to reducing the harm of unnecessary incarceration, which is felt by families and communities attempting to absorb prisoners discharged into their midst, bringing with them the expensive consequences of their confinement in terms of poverty, joblessness and homelessness. By illuminating the true social harms of excessive imprisonment, 'we might be able to agree upon reasonable intermediate sanctions for nonviolent offenders, not out of misguided sympathy for criminals but rather for the sake of citizens who deserve protection from violent criminals and more effective, less-bankrupting penalties for the rest' (Petersilia 1999: 147).

This brief exploration of harm as a central concept underpinning policy development, and its minimisation as a goal of such policy, is not intended to be exhaustive. It attempts to draw attention to the potential utility of placing harm minimisation at the centre of the Probation Service's modern mission. The literature which has been mentioned also illuminates certain core benefits of such an approach:

1 It links the Probation Service's activity to a broader range of endeavour, in which harm minimisation has illuminated and invigorated approaches to a variety of social problems, thus neutralising the recurrent political criticism that its mission is idiosyncratic, poorly understood and, consequently, of limited utility (Patten 1988; Straw 1997; Home Office 1998a).

2 It establishes common cause between the Probation Service and the variety of statutory and non-statutory agencies which it may view as partners. This is not to suggest that such diverse agencies as, for example, the police, youth clubs and alcohol counselling services would always embrace the minimisation of harm caused by crime as their over-arching objective, but neither would any be likely to reject it as an element in their enterprise.

3 It resolves the Service's conflict of choice between victim and offender priorities for style and content of service, by confirming their common identity as individuals whose lives are damaged by crime, and

perceiving the alleviation of that damage to be in the interests of both parties.

4 None of the perspectives considered above condones the activities of those individuals whose behaviour brings about the infliction of harm. To describe drug misuse, alcoholism and crime as social problems is not to deny that those problems are manifested in the choices and actions of individuals. If anything, a harm minimisation perspective assumes that such individuals are likely to possess sufficient self-interest to be motivated to avail themselves of opportunities to reduce the harms to which they expose themselves. It further exploits the possibility that they may be swayed by recognition of the suffering of meaningful others. Thus, the approach pursues the reduction of levels of harm experienced in the community through influencing the harm-inducing choices and activities of individuals. Harm minimisation, then, pursues accountability in individual conduct for alleviating the impact of damaging behaviours.

5 Equally, harm minimisation is characterised in all the approaches noted here as an essentially *pragmatic* approach to policy development. Harm minimisation, as a policy strategy, acknowledges the intractability of certain social problems, including crime, without conceding defeat. The analysis of harm, and pursuit of its alleviation, offers a principle for coherent practice development in an increasingly complex social world and amid the destabilising fluctuations of penal policy and legislation.

An accountable mission?

Harm minimisation, then, has certain identifiable advantages as a central objective for the Probation Service, in re-unifying what is fast becoming an impossibly fragmented battery of claims on its allegiance and offering a principle for coherent practice development. Yet, in conferring these benefits, what implications does the pursuit of harm minimisation carry for accountability in the development and delivery of the community penalties? The ways in which a harm minimisation approach and its specific benefits may clarify issues in accountability remain to be explored.

The broad community enterprise

The creation of an explicit link between the Probation Service's mission and that of other agencies concerned with the minimisation of harm caused by particular social problems, illuminates the relationship between community-based provision for offenders and for the general public. Communities suffer the harms of problems such as alcohol and drug misuse whether or not the individuals who engage in those behaviours enter the penal system. Communities also suffer the harms of crime whether or not there are personal victims and, moreover, whether or not the offenders are identified. This enables us to understand why harm reducing services must firstly be openly accessible to *all* members of communities and only secondarily, and by virtue of their membership of that wider group, to those members of communities who are identifiable by their connection to the criminal justice system. Provision for offenders, therefore, must be embedded within the framework of those services which support local communities.

This perspective calls for active embracement of a role for the Probation Service in strengthening the broader mission of its partner agencies in local communities to provide for non-offenders, rooting services for offenders *within* that provision rather than placing them in competition. Programmes for offenders make no coherent sense unless they are embedded within locally defined responses to need (Petersilia 1990; Rumgay 2000a).

The distortion of this relationship between offender-focused and community-wide provision appears in a contemporary trend towards the criminalisation of social policy and social problems (Crawford 1999). This trend has enabled policy makers to indulge in the co-option of the Probation Service's non-statutory partners as agencies of public protection, noted above. It is a trend which must be resisted, and can only be resisted, by allegiance to a broader community enterprise.

The harm which is perpetrated on individuals, families and communities by identifying criminality, or the risk of criminality, as the primary route to services for treatment and support is already documented in the fields of child protection and mental health. The preoccupation with identifying abuse within families seeking help for problems in child rearing has created alienation and hostility among parents who find themselves under investigation as potential abusers while their struggles attract little assistance (Department of Health 1995; Munro 1999). Ironically, the huge investment in screening for abuse has impoverished the support services available even to the identified abusers (Farmer and Owen 1995). Similarly, the 'risk technology' industry which has burgeoned in the wake of inquiries after homicides by mentally disordered people overlooks the collective message from these reports that the public would be better protected from such tragedies by general improvements in the quality of care for psychiatric patients and their families (Munro and Rumgay 2000).

The progressive incursion of penal priorities into the field of drug misuse seems likely to follow a similar path of dislocating communities from the services which they need for their disadvantaged and vulnerable members. Yet, as the studies mentioned above suggest, and Zimring and Hawkins (1999), examining the expansion of the American penal system, confirm, huge investment of resources into the management of crime predicated on anxiety about the prevalence of serious personal violence, has the paradoxical effect of reducing the proportion of those increased resources which is in reality dedicated to protecting the public from those most serious offences. This, they observe, is true even for the United States, where the prevalence of personal violence is indeed a very serious crime problem in comparison with England.

Co-option of community support services as penal services is thus neither equitable nor cost-effective, but creates harm. A harm minimisation perspective, therefore, demands that provision for offenders *reflects*, rather than drives, responses to social problems, and commits the Probation Service to active participation in the development of community-based provision which is primarily accessible to all on the basis of need.

The common cause

It has been argued that harm minimisation offers a common cause for the Probation Service and its partners, since all might accept that as a goal of their activities, at least partially. But this is not to assert a common *role* for the Service and either its statutory or its voluntary sector partners. To require the Service to work 'in partnership' is to ask it to work co-operatively with those agencies with which it shares common cause. It is not to demand that it performs the same tasks.

Thus, probation officers should neither voluntarily assume the role of, nor be required by other agencies to become catchers, prosecutors or incapacitators of criminals. The tendency of some agencies to confuse the priorities and tasks of the Probation Service with their own is observed by Crawford (1999), who notes the police view of inter-agency collaboration as a source of information on offenders. A harm minimisation perspective by no means requires the Probation Service to withhold all information on offenders under its supervision from police, but rather demands that it accepts responsibility for sharing that information which serves the goal of reducing harm. For example, to offer the information that an offender with a history of violence has issued threats against a specific individual, is not to participate in general intelligence gathering, which is properly a policing function.

Similarly, although it has been argued here that the Probation Service should participate in the development of community support services, it is not required in so doing to abandon its special focus on offenders. While the Service should draw on general provision, it also has a responsibility to assist services to respond to offenders. Successful partnerships with voluntary sector agencies have utilised the framework of support which is in place imaginatively to enhance provision for offenders, in ways which partners similarly perceive as extending their self-defined role in the community (Rumgay 2000a).

Thus, the Service may derive its accountabilities to its partners through a clear delineation of its specific harm-reducing role in developing community-based supervision opportunities for offenders. Confusion of that role with those of other agencies cannot promote greater inter-agency harmony, since it will inevitably force the Service into choices of allegiance to selected partners at the expense of co-operative relationships with others.

Common identities

The recent unedifying spectacle of the hounding of paedophiles, with the consequence of forcing government *both* to provide special accommodation and protection *and* to impose their presence on communities which had been encouraged to believe that exclusion was an option, exposes the futility of attempts to deny offenders any identity as members of communities. Banishment does *not* appear to be an option in modern British society. Equally, to deny offenders any identity as victims has led to the kinds of injustices meted out to women whose involvement in crime may be traced to victimisation experiences (Ahluwalia and Gupta 1997; Hamberger and Potente 1994; Rumgay 2000b).

It is a matter of everyday observation for probation officers that the lives of victims and offenders are deeply entwined. To acquiesce in the fragmentation of identities which is encouraged by pitting real and potential victims and offenders, and offenders and communities, against each other is to prevent the Probation Service from engaging properly in the very tasks with which it is currently charged: protecting the public and challenging offending behaviour (Home Office 1998a). A few examples help to illustrate this point. Offending lifestyles and victimisation experiences are closely connected (Baron 1997; Baskin and Somers 1998; Jacobs, Topalli and Wright 2000): one cannot realistically challenge the former without confronting the latter. Offenders commonly live in communities in which the boundaries between moral and immoral choices, and between morality and strict legality are routinely blurred in everyday experience (Foster 1990; Parker, Bakx and Newcombe 1988): one cannot challenge offending choices in isolation from the social worlds in which they arise. Mentally ill people who become violent predominantly attack those with whom they are in close connection (Estroff and Zimmer 1994), who are often attempting to provide care in the absence of effective professional support (see, for example, Harbour *et al* 1996; Keating, Collins and Walmsley 1997; Mishcon *et al* 1996): one cannot protect the most common victims of fatal assault by the mentally disordered by predicating risk management on an assumption of random stranger victimisation.

These realities, however, do not imply that the victims of crime must merge their interests with those of offenders, yielding up any entitlement to anger and a desire for justice. Nor do they mean that such entitlements may accrue only to those individuals who fit the required portrait of the totally innocent victim (Shapland, Willmore and Duff 1985). Crime victims are not assisted by our apparent need, as onlookers to their plight, to differentiate between the deserving and the undeserving among them (Lerner 1980). Rather, agencies involved in the support of victims need to be willing to recognise the psychological complexity of the victim experience. For example, this commonly involves self-blame (Janoff-Bulman and Frieze 1983; Miller and Porter 1983) and denial of the severity of one's victimisation, even in the face of the objective evidence (Taylor, Wood and Lichtman 1983). These psychological reactions are not evidence of a victim's complicity, nor are they maladaptive, but appear to be part of the process of reasserting a healthy identity. Anger, then is only one element in the process of recovery from victimisation (Wortman 1983), nor is revenge a universal feature of victims' responses (Dicks 1991; Elias 1993; Henderson 1992). Strong criticism has been levelled against criminal justice processes which seek only to appease victims' anger, neglecting the complexity of their experience, and counterproductively intensifying their rage rather than assisting its healthy resolution (see Wiebe 1996). Pillsbury (1998) observes that this distortion of anger is facilitated in the forced separation of victim and offender in the criminal justice process: in everyday life, anger at the wrongs we suffer more commonly arises in the context of caring relationships between family, friends and colleagues, which naturally limit our 'tendency to exaggerate evil' (p. 69).

Fragmentation is thus not only predicated on a series of false dichotomies, but is also harmful. A perspective which acknowledges the need for an integrated approach to victimisation and offending alleviates the pressure to make false choices of allegiance. For example, it is very clear that restorative justice, if reduced to victim–offender mediation programmes, cannot address the multi-faceted needs and identities of victims. Services for the victims of crime must include provision for victims in their own right rather than solely in their relation to offenders. So, for example, trauma recovery counselling should be available as an open access service within communities, irrespective of a victim's identification through the criminal justice system. Agencies should extend the offer of such help to those insatiably angry victims whose rage has become a barrier to recovery, rather than holding out the false promise of appeasement through punishment. Moreover, such provision should be extended to offenders whose criminal involvement is linked to victimisation. Until the Probation Service, with its partners, can testify to such holistic provision, initiatives such as victim-offender mediation and victim impact statements will continue to risk co-option of victims' interests in the narrow sighted delivery of penal sanctions to offenders (Clear 1994).

Accountable offenders

To assume the accountability of offenders for limiting or assuaging the harm which they inflict on others is not a mandate to engage in indiscriminate coercion. A harm minimisation perspective may begin to open up real choices between enforcement and voluntarism of treatment opportunities. It has already been argued that provision for offenders should be based in community-wide services. It follows, therefore, that the Probation Service should assist treatment agencies to avoid becoming extensions of the penal system, by encouraging voluntarism where possible. Indeed, as Clear remarks: 'Offenders who volunteer for risk reduction programmes are more likely to succeed in them ... . To deny an offender who wants one a risk-related treatment is worse than short-sighted: it is self-defeating.' (1994: 185).

Moreover, engagement of offenders in rehabilitative treatment is rarely, if ever, achieved by force alone. Enabling offenders to honour their accountability for modifying their damaging behaviours requires professional skills in stimulating and sustaining their motivation (see, for example, Prochaska and Diclemente 1986; Miller and Rollnick 1991). Winick (1991) and Wexler (1996) both explore frameworks which acknowledge that coercion is neither the only, nor the most successful tool available in the legal process for securing co-operation in treatment.

This is not to deny that coercion has any role in the delivery of treatment opportunities. Well targeted and well managed coerced supervision programmes may play an important part in engaging high risk offenders in treatment (Rumgay 2000a). However, at a time when the anxieties of the 1980s of net-widening and entrapment of offenders in the criminal justice system (Cohen 1985), which stimulated activity in the areas of targeting and gatekeeping (Bottoms and Stelman 1988), are at last becoming reality (Home Office 1998b), the Probation Service is curiously reticent on the visitation of its coerced community penalties on a caseload of decreasing seriousness. Yet it is not part of the mission of non-statutory agencies to extend the net of coerced intrusion into individuals' lives. This perspective exposes the Service's obligations to those partners to assist them to avoid co-option in such an enterprise. The reciprocal, and complementary, obligation of partners should be to assist the Probation Service to resist narrow, harm-inducing definitions of its task in terms of enforcement.

Pragmatism and the community penalties

What we do to offenders by way of delivering the community penalties cannot provide a total answer to the claims of victims and communities on the resources of the criminal justice system and allied services. Indeed, these claims are clearly too complex to be answered satisfactorily by anything that the penal system might do to offenders. They reflect social and personal needs which are distributed within communities, and which should be addressed in their own right. The community penalties, then, are necessarily pragmatic, partial and limited approaches to the harms of crime. And while the community penalties should be embedded within the broader range of provision, rather than diluting and distorting its availability, then, in so far as that provision is weak, so too must be the community penalties.

While this is an argument for realistic expectations of the community penalties, it is *not* an argument for passive resignation to excessive use of imprisonment. The harms which are inflicted on offenders' families through disruption and stigmatisation, on victims whose complex needs are overlooked, on communities required to rectify the damage of confinement and on broader social provision through massive investment in incarceration with its diminishing returns, compel the Probation Service to compete energetically at the margins of the custody threshold for those offenders who are needlessly prison bound.

Amidst this tension between the constraints on community-based provision and the imperatives of developing supervision opportunities, the Probation Service with its partners may adopt an approach which pools complementary skills and resources to address locally defined problems. Such creative adaptations to local opportunities and constraints have led to imaginative and successful partnership programmes which not only increase offenders' engagement in harm-reducing opportunities, but also contribute to the health of communities (Chapman 1995; Gadd 1996; Petersilia 1990; Rumgay 2000a, 2000b).

It is precisely through such local co-operative enterprise that the harm minimisation approach to the community penalties can gain acceptance, through bringing recognisable benefits to those individuals and agencies who hold a stake in them. For example, sentencers seek ways to avoid exacting harsh penalties which appear to offend against true justice (Gould 1996): well managed community-based programmes offer one such avenue. Even in a generally punitive policy climate, it is possible at local level to work with courts and other interested parties to secure agreement on realistic, acceptable aims for the community penalties (Schall and Neises 1999). At this level also it becomes possible to introduce changes incrementally, rather than pursuing all-or-nothing global strategies: 'Management of the political environment is not simply advertising or sales, but a *problem-solving tool* that facilitates development of intermediate sanctions that fit their local contexts and assists the public in tackling tough problems' (Schall and Neises 1999: 73, emphasis added). Paradoxically, such pro-active local negotiation and investment in harm minimisation approaches brings its clearest reward in *reducing* the troublesome, anxiety-provoking public visibility of street lifestyles through offering offenders the means to moderate their damaging behaviours (Cohen 1997).

Conclusion

In 1998, the government declared a bold enterprise for a modern Probation Service: 'the protection of the public from predictably dangerous offenders under supervision in the community and from those who pose a more general risk of re-offending' (Home Office 1998a: 7). Two years later, a curiously royally phrased announcement by the Minister for Prisons and Probation fronted the revised National Standards for offender supervision: 'We are a law enforcement agency. It's what we are. It's what we do' (Paul Boateng, in Home Office 2000). These activities are not the same. For the Probation Service, law enforcement largely boils down to ensuring the delivery of more and harsher punishments to offenders who transgress the terms of increasingly stringent supervision requirements. The American experimentation with intensive coerced supervision has well established this result (Clear and Hardyman 1990; Petersilia and Turner 1990), demonstrating the capability of penal sanctions to deliver expensive harms to offenders which are not effectively counterbalanced by reciprocal benefits to the communities in which they live, *unless* backed by access to high quality rehabilitation opportunities (Petersilia 1999).

Penal rhetoric is incapable, contemporarily at least, of spelling out a stable, coherent message for the Probation Service's policy and practice. To acquiesce in destabilisation and confusion, given the tenor of current penal initiatives, will transform the Service into an agency for the enforcement of social exclusion: its task, to implement the denial of citizenship to those whose entrapment in broader social disadvantage has helped to bring them to the attention of the criminal justice system. This penal drift, with its false guarantee of public safety, leads to an approach to offender management characterised by 'searchlight supervision', in which increasingly powerful coerced intrusion is directed into the lives of individuals identified as 'risky', who must continue to suffer the harms of community-wide disadvantage *along with* their real and potential victims. This trend conveys the policy message that the social problems of local communities are to be endured, while provision is directed at control, punishment and treatment of those who have attracted attention through crime. Concurrently, the Probation Service's relationships with its partners will be impoverished, as it withdraws its contribution to the overall health of local communities in order to focus its attentions on the narrow enforcement of penal sanctions.

Alternatively, as this chapter has tried to show, an explicit common interest in avoiding this future may promote healthy, accountable partnerships between the Probation Service and allied agencies, which embrace an integrated perspective on the relationships between offenders, victims and their communities. Only such an integrated approach can fully illuminate the accountability of *all* parties to crime and its resolution, not only the statutory and voluntary agencies, but also offenders and victims. High quality, fully accountable supervision programmes are not produced through participating in false dichotomies which force choices between rival claimants for priority, but by basing such opportunities for offenders within the range of activities which reduce the harms inflicted on communities by crime and its penal consequences.

References

Advisory Council on the Misuse of Drugs (1991) *Drug Misusers and the Criminal Justice System. Part I: Community Resources and the Probation Service*. London: HMSO.

Advisory Council on the Misuse of Drugs (1994) *Drug Misusers and the Criminal Justice System. Part II: Police, Drug Misusers and the Community*. London: HMSO.

Advisory Council on the Misuse of Drugs (1996) *Drug Misusers and the Criminal Justice System. Part III: Drug Misusers and the Prison System: An Integrated Approach*. London: HMSO.

Ahluwalia, K. and Gupta, R. (1997) *Circle of Light: The Autobiography of Kiranjit Ahluwalia*. London: HarperCollins.

Alder, C.M. and Baker, J. (1997) 'Maternal Filicide: More than One Story to be Told', *Women and Criminal Justice*, 9 (2), 15–39.

Baron, S.W. (1997) 'Risky Lifestyles and the Link Between Offending and Victimisation', *Studies on Crime and Crime Prevention*, 6 (1), 53–71.

Barton, A. (1999) 'Breaking the Crime/Drugs Cycle: The Birth of a New Approach?', *The Howard Journal*, 38 (2), 144–157.

Baskin, D.R. and Sommers, I.B. (1998) *Casualties of Community Disorder: Women's Careers in Violent Crime*. Boulder, CO: Westview Press.

Baumrind, D. and Moselle, K.A. (1985) 'A Developmental Perspective on Adolescent Drug Use', *Advances in Alcohol and Substance Use*, 5, 41–67.

Bottoms, A.E. and Stelman, A. (1988) *Social Inquiry Reports: A Framework for Practice Development*. Aldershot: Wildwood House.

Burney, E. (1999) *Crime and Banishment: Nuisance and Exclusion in Social Housing*. Winchester: Waterside Press.

Chapman, T. (1995) 'Creating a Culture of Change: A Case Study of a Car Crime Project in Belfast', in J. McGuire (ed.) *What Works: Reducing Offending. Guidelines from Research and Practice*. Chichester: John Wiley and Sons, pp. 127–138.

Clear, T. (1994) *Harm in American Penology: Offenders, Victims and Their Communities*. Albany, NY: State University of New York Press.

Clear, T.R. and Hardyman, P.L. (1990) 'The New Intensive Supervision Movement', *Crime and Deliquency*, 36 (1), 42–60.

Cohen, J., Cork, D., Engberg, J. and Tita, G. (1998) 'The Role of Drug Markets and Gangs in Local Homicide Rates', *Homicide Studies*, 2 (3), 241–62.

Cohen, P. (1997) 'Crack in the Netherlands: Effective Social Policy is Effective Drugs Policy', in C. Reinarman and H.G. Levine (eds) *Crack in America: Demon Drugs and Social Justice*. Berkeley, CA: University of California Press, pp. 214–224.

Cohen, S. (1985) *Visions of Social Control: Crime, Punishment and Classification*. Cambridge: Polity Press.

Collins, J.J. (1982) 'Alcohol Careers and Criminal Careers', in J.J. Collins (ed.) *Drinking and Crime: Perspectives on the Relationships Between Alcohol*

Consumption and Criminal Behaviour. London: Tavistock, pp. 152–206.

Crawford, A. (1999) *The Local Governance of Crime: Appeals to Community and Partnerships.* Oxford: Oxford University Press.

Department of Health (1995) *Child Protection: Messages from Research.* London: HMSO.

Dicks, S. (1991) *Victims of Crime and Punishment: Interviews with Victims, Convicts, Their Families and Support Groups.* Jefferson, North Carolina: McFarland and Company.

Dorn, N. (1990) 'Substance Abuse and Prevention Strategies', in H. Ghodse and D. Maxwell (eds) *Substance Abuse and Dependence: An Introduction for the Caring Professions.* Basingstoke: Macmillan, pp. 232–43.

Elias, R. (1993) *Victims Still: The Political Manipulation of Crime Victims.* Newbury Park, CA: Sage.

Elliot, D.S., Huizinga, D. and Menard, S. (1989) *Multiple Problem Youth: Deliquency, Substance Use and Mental Health Problems.* New York: Springer-Verlag.

Estroff, S.E. and Zimmer, C. (1994) 'Social Networks, Social Support, and Violence Among Persons with Severe, Persistent Mental Illness', in J. Monahan and H. Steadman (eds) *Violence and Mental Disorder: Developments in Risk Assessment.* Chicago: University of Chicago Press.

Farmer, E. and Owen, M. (1995) *Child Protection Practice: Private Risks and Public Remedies.* London: HMSO.

Foster, J. (1990) *Villains: Crime and Community in the Inner City.* London: Routledge.

Gadd, B. (1996) 'Probation in Northern Ireland', in G. McIvor (ed.) *Working with Offenders.* London: Jessica Kingsley, pp. 53–68.

Goldstein, P.J., Brownstein, H.H., Ryan, P.J. and Bellucci, P.A. (1997) 'Crack and Homicide in New York City: A Case Study in the Epidemiology of Violence', in C. Reinarman and H.G. Levine (eds) *Crack in America: Demon Drugs and Social Justice.* Berkeley, CA: University of California Press, pp. 113–130.

Gould, K.A. (1996) 'Turning Rat and Doing Time for Uncharged, Dismissed, or Acquitted Crimes: Do the Federal Sentencing Guidelines Promote Respect for the Law?', in D.B. Wexler and B.J. Winick (eds) *Law in a Therapeutic Key: Developments in Therapeutic Jurisprudence.* Durham, North Carolina: Carolina Academic Press, pp. 171–201.

Hamberger, L.K. and Potente, T. (1994) 'Counseling Heterosexual Women Arrested for Domestic Violence: Implications for Theory and Practice', *Violence and Victims*, 9 (2), 125–137.

Harbour, A., Brunning, J., Bolter, L. and Hally, H. (1996) *The Viner Report: The Report of the Independent Inquiry into the Circumstances Surrounding the Deaths of Robert and Muriel Viner.* Ferndown: Dorset Health Commission.

Henderson, L.N. (1992) 'The Wrongs of Victims' Rights', in E.A. Fattah (ed.) *Towards a Critical Victimology*, New York: St Martin's Press, pp. 100–192

Home Office (1992) *Partnership in Dealing with Offenders in the Community: A Decision Document.* London: Home Office.

Home Office (1995) *National Standards for the Supervision of Offenders in the Community*. London: Home Office.

Home Office (1998a) *Joining Forces to Protect the Public: Prisons–Probation. A Consultation Document*. London: Home Office.

Home Office (1998b) *Probation Statistics England and Wales 1997*. London: Government Statistical Service.

Home Office (2000) *National Standards for the Supervision of Offenders in the Community*. London: Home Office.

Jacobs, B.A., Topalli, V. and Wright, R. (2000) 'Managing Retaliation: Drug Robbery and Informal Sanction Threats', *Criminology*, 38 (1), 171–197.

Janoff-Bulman, R. and Frieze, I.H. (1983) 'A Theoretical Perspective for Understanding Reactions to Victimisation', *Journal of Social Issues*, 39 (2), 1–17.

Kandel, D.B., Simcha-Fagan, R. and Davies, M. (1986) 'Risk Factors of Delinquency and Illicit Drug Use from Adolescence to Young Childhood', *Journal of Drug Issues*, 16, 67–90.

Keating, D., Collins, P. and Walmsley, S. (1997) *Report of the Independent Inquiry into the Treatment and Care of Norman Dunn*. Newcastle upon Tyne: Newcastle and North Tyneside Health Authority.

Kemp, P.A. (1997) 'The Characteristics of Single Homeless People in England', in R. Burrows, N. Pleace and D. Quilgars (eds) *Homelessness and Social Policy*. London: Routledge, pp. 69–87.

Kennedy, D.M. and Braga, A.A. (1998) 'Homicide in Minneapolis: Research for Problem Solving', *Homicide Studies*, 2 (3), 263–290.

Kerner, H., Weitekamp, E.G.M., Stelly, W. and Thomas, J. (1997) 'Patterns of Criminality and Alcohol Abuse: Results of the Tuebingen Criminal Behaviour Development Study', *Criminal Behaviour and Mental Health*, 7, 401–420.

Lerner, M.J. (1980) *The Belief in a Just World: A Fundamental Delusion*. New York: Plenum Press.

McCord, J. (1995) 'Relationship Between Alcoholism and Crime Over the Life Course', in H.B. Kaplan (ed.) *Drugs, Crime, and Other Deviant Adaptations: Longitudinal Studies*. New York: Plenum Press, pp. 129–141.

Miller, D.T. and Porter, C.A. (1983) 'Self-blame in Victims of Violence', *Journal of Social Issues*, 39 (2), 139–152.

Miller, W.R. and Rollnick, S. (1991) *Motivational Interviewing: Preparing People to Change Addictive Behavior*. New York: Guilford Press.

Mishcon, J., Dick, D., Milne, I., Beard, P. and Mackay, J. (1996) *The Hampshire Report: Report of the Independent Inquiry into the Care and Treatment of Francis Hampshire*. Ilford: Redbridge and Waltham Forest Health Authority.

Munro, E.M. (1999) 'Protecting Children in an Anxious Society', *Health, Risk and Society*, 1 (1), 117–127.

Munro, E. and Rumgay, J. (2000) 'Role of Risk Assessment in Reducing Homicides by People with Mental Illness', *British Journal of Psychiatry*, 176, 116–120.

Newcomb, M.D. and Bentler, P.M. (1988) *Consequences of Adolescent Drug Use:*

Impact on the Lives of Young Adults. Beverley Hills, CA: Sage.

Parker, H., Bakx, K. and Newcombe, R. (1988) *Living with Heroin: The Impact of a Drugs 'Epidemic' on an English Community.* Milton Keynes: Open University Press.

Patten, J. (1988) *Punishment, the Probation Service and the Community.* London: Home Office.

Pease, K. (1999) 'The Probation Career of Al Truism', *The Howard Journal,* 38 (1), 2–16.

Petersilia, J. (1990) 'Conditions that Permit Intensive Supervision Programs to Survive', *Crime and Delinquency,* 36 (1), 126–145.

Petersilia, J. (1999) 'Alternative Sanctions: Diverting Nonviolent Prisoners to Intermediate Sanctions: The Impact on Prison Admissions and Corrections Costs', in E.L. Rubin (ed.) *Minimizing Harm: A New Crime Policy for Modern America.* Boulder, CO: Westview Press, pp. 115–49.

Petersilia, J. and Turner, S. (1990) 'Comparing Intensive and Regular Supervision for High-risk Probationers: Early Results from an Experiment in California', *Crime and Deliquency,* 36 (1), 87–111.

Pillsbury, S.H. (1998) *Judging Evil: Rethinking the Law of Murder and Manslaughter.* New York: New York University Press.

Plant, M., Single, E. and Stockwell, T. (1997) 'Introduction: Harm Minimisation and Alcohol', in M. Plant, E. Single and T. Stockwell (eds) *Alcohol: Minimising the Harm. What Works?* London: Free Association Books, pp. 3–9.

Prochaska, J. and Diclemente, C. (1986) 'Toward a Comprehensive Model of Change', in W.R. Miller and N. Heather (eds) *Treating Addictive Behaviors: Processes of Change.* New York: Plenum Press, pp. 3–27.

Rock, P. (1990) *Helping Victims of Crime: The Home Office and the Rise of Victim Support in England and Wales.* Oxford: Clarendon Press.

Rubin, E.L. (1999) 'Introduction: Minimizing Harm as a Solution to the Crime Policy Conundrum', in E.L. Rubin (ed.) *Minimizing Harm: A New Crime Policy for Modern America.* Boulder, CO: Westview Press, pp. 1–34.

Rumgay, J. (2000a) *The Addicted Offender: Developments in British Policy and Practice.* Basingstoke: Palgrave.

Rumgay, J. (2000b) 'Policies of Neglect: Female Offenders and the Probation Service', in H. Kemshall and R. Littlechild (eds) *User Involvement and Participation in Social Care: Research Informing Practice.* London: Jessica Kingsley, pp. 193–213.

Schall, E. and Neises, E. (1999) 'Managing the Risk of Innovation: Strategies for Leadership', in P.M. Harris (ed.) *Research to Results: Effective Community Corrections.* Lanham, MD: American Correctional Association, pp. 57–74.

Schluter, M. (1994) 'What is Relational Justice?', in J. Burnside and N. Baker (eds) *Relational Justice: Repairing the Breach.* Winchester: Waterside Press, pp. 17–27.

Shapland, J., Willmore, J. and Duff, P. (1985) *Victims in the Criminal Justice System.* Aldershot: Gower.

Singleton, N., Meltzer, H., Gatward, R., Coid, J. and Deasy, D. (1998) *Psychiatric Morbidity Among Prisoners in England and Wales.* London: HMSO.

Social Exclusion Unit (1998) *Bringing Britain Together: A National Strategy for Neighbourhood Renewal*, Cmnd 4045. London: HMSO.

Stacy, A.W. and Newcomb, M.D. (1995) 'Long-term Social-psychological Influences on Deviant Attitudes and Criminal Behavior', in H.B. Kaplan (ed.) *Drugs, Crime, and Other Deviant Adaptations: Longitudinal Studies*. New York: Plenum Press, pp. 99–127.

Straw, J. (1997) Speech to the National Probation Convention. London, November.

Taylor, S.E., Wood, J.V. and Lichtman, R.R. (1983) 'It Could be Worse: Selective Evaluation as a Response to Victimisation', *Journal of Social Issues*, 39 (2), 19–40.

Wexler, D.B. (1996) 'Therapeutic Jurisprudence and the Criminal Courts', in D.B. Wexler and B.J. Winick (eds) *Law in a Therapeutic Key: Developments in Therapeutic Jurisprudence*. Durham, North Carolina: Carolina Academic Press, pp. 157–169.

Widom, C. (1994) 'Childhood Victimization and Risk for Adolescent Problem Behaviors', in M.E. Lamb and R. Ketterlinus (eds) *Adolescent Problem Behaviors*. New York: Erlbaum, pp. 127–164.

Wiebe, R. (1996) 'The Mental Health Implications of Crime Victims' Rights', in D.B. Wexler and B.J. Winick (eds) *Law in a Therapeutic Key: Developments in Therapeutic Jurisprudence*. Durham, North Carolina: Carolina Academic Press, pp. 213–141.

Winick, B.J. (1991) 'Harnessing the Power of the Bet: Wagering with the Government as a Mechanism for Social and Individual Change', in D.B. Wexler and B.J. Winick *Essays in Therapeutic Jurisprudence*. Durham, North Carolina: Carolina Academic Press, pp. 219–290.

Wortman, C.B. (1983) 'Coping with Victimisation: Conclusions and Implications for Future Research', *Journal of Social Issues*, 39 (2), 195–221.

Zehr, H. (1990) *Changing Lenses: A New Focus for Crime and Justice*. Scottdale, PA: Herald Press.

Zimring, F.E. and Hawkins, G. (1999) 'Public Attitudes Toward Crime: Is American Violence a Crime Problem?', in E.L. Rubin (ed.) *Minimizing Harm: A New Crime Policy for Modern America*. Boulder, CO: Westview Press, pp. 35–57.

Chapter 8

Accountability: difference and diversity in the delivery of community penalties

Loraine Gelsthorpe

Introduction

The aim this chapter is to reflect on certain dimensions of the notion of accountability which affect the offender. Much of the general criminal justice discourse of accountability revolves around managerial and cost issues (good stewardship of tax-payers' money) and around obligations towards 'the community' (Clarke and Newman 1997; Rutherford 1993). Equally, debates about accountability often include an important focus on responsibilities towards victims (Zedner 1997; Crawford and Goodey 2000; Sanders 1999), the development of multiple forms of crime control in the community, the reciprocal obligations of those agencies involved in the delivery of community penalties, and, in particular, on the utility of the principle of harm reduction for coherent and accountable practice developments (see chapter 7 in this book). Thus in one way, a focus on the offender completes the picture and at the same time can help to avoid the false dichotomy which is sometimes drawn between offenders and victims. Indeed, it can be plausibly argued that attention to the 'personhood' or experiences of the offender can ultimately benefit victims (especially bearing in mind that offenders and victims are often drawn from one and the same social group).

To focus on the offender is of course a high risk strategy, for there are those who would argue that an offender deserves no consideration and should be denied 'citizen's rights' (insofar as these can be defined, see the Human Rights Act 1998; see also Nash 1997 regarding the rights of probation service clients for instance). At the same time, it is arguable that by its very intervention into offenders' lives the criminal justice system is seeking to inculcate values which we would associate with 'good citizenship'. To focus on possible duties towards the offender which go beyond the rights and responsibilities expressed in Probation Service National Standards – and similar principles which govern other penalties in the community – is therefore arguably but a small piece of 'pro-social modelling' and a small step towards social inclusion. One particularly important issue in this regard is that of respect for offenders' individuality and cultural diversity, while in no way condoning their offending behaviour. A strong argument can be mounted to the effect that respect for individuality and social diversity is a key corollary both of an adequate concept of citizenship, and of the principle of social inclusion. The main focus of this chapter then concerns the need to accommodate social differences in order to facilitate 'good citizenship'.

Accountability towards the offender

One route into such issues concerns the human rights route. In October 2000 the Human Rights Act 1998 came into full effect. From that point onwards, all UK laws are required to be framed and interpreted in a way that is compatible with the European Convention of Human Rights. The Convention, of course, inspired by the horrors of the second world war, derives from the Declaration of Human Rights which was adopted by the General Assembly of the United Nations in 1948. Once a state joined the Council of Europe and submitted to the jurisdiction of its courts in Strasbourg, its citizens could apply to that court if all other avenues in their home state had been exhausted. Failure to comply with the Convention can result in the offending state being required to pay compensation to the citizen whose rights have been violated or, in extreme cases, expulsion from the Council of Europe. Put simply, the Convention establishes basic civil and political rights to all within the jurisdiction of a member state of the Council of Europe. As Cheney *et al* (1999) describe, the rights and freedoms the states undertake to secure include the right, without discrimination, to life, liberty and security of the person; the right not to be subjected to torture, or to inhuman or degrading treatment or punishment; the right to a fair trial and the presumption of innocence; the rights to respect for private life, home and correspondence; the right to freedom of expression; the right to freedom of thought, conscience and religion; the rights to freedom of assembly and association, and the right to the peaceful enjoyment of a person's possessions. Needless to say, there are some small print clauses that allow interference in some of these rights in certain circumstances (Brooke 1999).

Article 3 of the European Convention, which guarantees protection against inhuman or degrading treatment, is potentially particularly relevant to community penalties. For example, one can imagine that, if those who are subject to a community service order were treated in a certain way (such as being required to carry out their community service while wearing leg-irons and humiliating clothing) then this would be in breach of Article 3. One mechanism for enforcement of community penalties that might require scrutiny in his regard is electronic tagging, which has been growing in popularity (despite initial research findings which encouraged caution; see Mair and Mortimer 1996) and is again promoted in the Criminal Justice and Court Services Act 2000. It has yet to be tested in Strasbourg, but it is possible that an objection could be mounted under Article 3 against the imposition of such a monitoring device, at least in some circumstances. A Prison Reform Trust report on the monitoring trials noted that:

> ... some offenders have objected to the use of the tag. One woman who refused to be tagged felt it was potentially stigmatising in her work as a publican. Another offender cut off his tag and threw it in a pond because he claimed that it made him feel like a dog. In December 1995, a 22-year-old tagged man was assaulted by youths who believed he was a convicted sex offender.
>
> (Prison Reform Trust 1997: para. 44)

The Report went on to argue that tagging places particular pressure on the tagged offender's family. Indeed, the confinement of offenders at home can not only lead to aggression and frustration which may be directed at those close at hand, but may also result in confusion as to who is responsible for the offender's care (Prison Reform Trust 1997: para 55). It is possible then that the imposition of such a device could also result in a breach of Article 8 which guarantees respect for private and family life. If a person's life is disrupted to a sufficient degree and the family breaks down as a result, it is possible to suggest that such an application could be made. But matters are complicated, not least by the fact that 'tagging' can actually be popular with offenders where it leads to the early release of prisoners for example; and although early research reports referred to family difficulties as a result of 'tagging', later research reports indicated that these were perhaps less signficant than first thought (Mortimer and May 1997). In other words, it is at present far from clear how the Human Rights legislation will be interpreted in the sphere of community penalties. Nevertheless, as the Human Rights Act 1998 becomes embedded within the criminal justice system, accountability towards the offender (including children) in these respects and the implications for conceptions of citizenship are set to become increasingly important. There is much to be discussed and much to be decided at this stage, but some of the issues here open up more general considerations of accountability towards the offender in the community.

In terms of the application of the Human Rights legislation itself, it may well be that cases involving offenders who are in custody will always be seen as a priority over offenders on non-custodial penalties, their claims of mistreatment or neglect being seen as more legitimate since the hardships are perceived to be greater in the first place. But these complex debates about sentencing provisions for offenders in the community and human rights prompt broader consideration of accountability towards the offender, and issues about social differences and accountability, to which I now turn.

Social differences and accountability towards the offender

Few would dispute the fact that many criminal justice practices are imbued with particular sets of social and cultural values which seemingly do not tolerate social differences. And yet it is arguable that social differences are an intrinsic part of human rights. Whether or not the system should always accommodate such differences, of course, is another question, and such matters have been resolved differently. In its aspirations, the legal and criminal justice system appears not to tolerate the abduction of young women in order to facilitate arranged marriages, or tolerate spousal abuse even where this is a family or cultural tradition, but does allow difference on religious grounds when it comes to the wearing of crash-helmets on motorbikes (Road Traffic Act 1988 s16.[2]). Leaving these longstanding legal battles aside, I describe below three situations where one can argue that recognition of social and cultural differences may be important: pro-social modelling, probation programmes based on cognitive behavioural approaches, and parenting orders, as one of the new generation of community penalties.

First, some preliminary comments concerning race and gender issues, given that this is the unifying theme underlying these three examples. The components of white (male) culture have been usefully described as: rugged individualism (the individual is the primary unit), competition (there is a win/lose dichotomy), time (time is viewed as a commodity), family structure (the nuclear family is the ideal social unit), and status and power (measured by economic power and material possessions) and so on (Anthias and Yuval-Davis 1992; Modood 1992). It is easy to discern such values in the legal and criminal justice system – with the emphasis on individual responsibility, legal contests, the measurement of punishment in terms of time, the recognition of the nuclear family, and of employment (and thus material means) as an important social control. Critics have long since argued that both criminological knowledge and criminal justice practices are imbued with white, western concepts (see, for example, Rice 1990; Cook and Hudson 1993; Chigwada-Bailey 1997). In relation to community penalties, we might remind ourselves that social inquiry reports and pre-sentence reports as their successors, have come under critical scrutiny with regard to the dominance of particular race and gender issues (see Waters 1983; Whitehouse 1983; Horsley 1984; Eaton 1986; Gelsthorpe 1992).

To pursue this further, there are numerous claims about a masculinist dominance of both criminological theory and practice which have at times penetrated the core of debates about 'criminal justice' (see, for example, Leonard 1982; Morris 1987; Gelsthorpe and Morris 1990; Daly 1994b; Naffine 1997). Further, Carol Gilligan's (1982) 'different voice' spoke of caring rather than of justice, of moral decisions based on an empathic and concrete sense of actual human relationships rather than on abstract and universal principles of justice as fairness. This counter-poising of caring and justice has been taken up by various criminologists as well as philosophers and psychologists. Frances Heidensohn (1997) for example, has described the implications of Gilligan's work for criminal justice practices – suggesting that there are two models at play – the 'Portia' model of justice (abstract, rational, rights-based, masculine) and the 'Persephone' model (concrete, relational, expressive, feminine). The idea that interventions are most effective in reducing reconviction risks when in a more relational and individualised form certainly finds support in Gill McIvor's (1992) work on Community Service Orders in Scotland. It is also fair to say that there is currently renewed faith in relational justice practices more generally (*viz* the emphasis on restorative justice in the Crime and Disorder Act (Dignan 1999; c.f. Morris and Gelsthorpe 2000) with great hopes for effectiveness.

What is of chief relevance here are the two simple points that: (a) it is important to recognise and respect individuality (with due respect for social differences whether these be age, gender, race, ethnicity, culture or whatever) in criminal justice practices since this is arguably an important dimension of citizenship and therefore accountability, and (b) it is important to recognise that identities are produced, consumed and regulated within culture – therefore one has to critically examine and reflect on knowledges and practices within the sphere of criminal justice, which in turn reflect cultural perspectives. The three examples which follow then are all areas where I think that there is scope for greater recognition of social differences.

Pro-social modelling

Christopher Trotter has described pro-social modelling in the following way:

> Pro-social modelling or anti-criminal modelling and reinforcement involves the practice of offering praise and rewards for clients' pro-social expressions or actions. The probation officer becomes a positive role model acting to reinforce pro-social or non-criminal behaviour.
>
> (Trotter 1993: 4)

In its broadest sense it means:

> ... anti-criminal modelling and reinforcement, problem-solving and the quality of inter-personal relationships [are] important characteristics of effective correctional practice.
>
> (Trotter 1993: 5)

In sum,

> pro-social expressions or activities which are seen as appropriate to reinforce include: keeping appointments, being punctual, under-taking community work or other special conditions such as maintaining contact with drug treatment agencies, attempting to solve problems, discussing issues in an open manner, recognising the harm that criminal behaviour can cause, accepting responsi-bility for your own actions or behaviour, understanding other people's point of view, being considerate of other people's feelings, placing importance on personal and family relationships, seeking work, visiting the employment service, controlling your anger, controlling drinking, etc.
>
> (Trotter 1993: 22)

A number of questions emerge from these characterisations of pro-social modelling. For example:

(i) What sorts of cultural values are being expressed in the 'positive role modelling'? (and whose cultural values are they?) How can pro-social and in contrast anti-social behaviour be characterised and in what ways, if any, do these characterisations reflect social, cultural or gender differences?

(ii) What sorts of 'social differences' are relevant to the discussion? (age, sex/gender, class, ethnic/cultural, sexual orientation, religious, occupation, education, disabled/non-disabled and so on?) What differences are there between younger or older notions or experiences of authority for instance, and what relevance might these have for notions of pro-social modelling? What differences, if any, are there between male and female notions and experiences of authority? What relevance might these have for pro-social modelling?

(iii) How might we best characterise these differences without being essentialist in the process? That is, without assuming that certain beliefs about different groups of people are fundamental differences.

(iv) Are any of the 'social differences' identified in tension with the core elements of pro-social modelling? Are there any particular issues for the probation officer or community service organiser? Are there issues for the offender? What language is used to convey the principles of pro-social modelling and legitimacy? Are there any reasons why male or female probation officers or offenders would find pro-social modelling easier or more difficult than those of the opposite sex?

(v) How can social differences be accommodated within 'pro-social modelling'? And to what extent should they be? How can officers minimise threats to 'personal identity' in the process of modelling pro-social behaviour? How can practitioners ensure that they are able to 'hear across social cleavages'?

These questions are not easily answerable, but they perhaps help present a case for what might be termed as *reflexive probation practice*, by which I mean a practice which reflects consciousness of what the practitioner (probation officer, or community service officer, for instance) is bringing to the relationship in which pro-social modelling is practised, and perhaps anticipation of how the offender might read, hear or otherwise receive messages from the practitioner. A reflexive probation practice also means respecting the offender as an individual and avoids homo-genising processes, whereby from a heterogeneity of types of wrong-doing and types of wrongdoer, the people trapped in the penalising circuit are treated more and more alike. A reflexive probation practice might further involve cultural awareness whereby practitioners are comfortable with differences that exist between themselves and offenders in terms of race, ethnicity, culture and beliefs and so on. Of course, some kinds of attempts to accommodate broad social differences would be constrained by the law, and nothing that is said here should be read as challenging those constraints. Within that, however, it can be argued that attempts to accommodate individual social differences are intrinsic to the very meaning and spirit of pro-social modelling.

The key point in relation to accountability is that a reflexive probation practice which is aware of social and cultural differences, and of the need to avoid discriminatory practice, may help move us some way towards transparency and thus accountability towards the offender. Indeed, such a move may be considered essential to integrative practice (Smith and Stewart 1998). Moreover, fulfilment of an obligation to respect cultural differences amongst offenders may ultimately enhance offenders' beliefs regarding the legitimacy of the criminal justice system.

Cognitive skills programmes

There has recently been a revival of interest in rehabilitation and particularly claims that the use of cognitive skills in probation pro-grammes and other community interventions can be effective in reducing reoffending (McGuire 1995). Inspired by North American research (for example, Gendreau and Ross 1979, 1987; Ross, Fabiano and Ewels 1988; Lipton 1998), these programmes are generally grounded in cognitive psychology and notions that short-term work in controlled group settings can facilitate a change in thinking patterns and thus behaviour – particularly behaviour which is associated with re-offending. Indeed, we can discern a clear push to promote such programmes within the English criminal justice system, not least by policy-makers charged with the task of making probation practice more effective; the very introduction of probation 'Pathfinder Programmes' reflects the theoretical precepts of cognitive skills training, and the accreditation criteria (Home Office 1999) indicate full support for these.

The evidence suggests that the cognitive deficits most obviously identified with offending behaviour appear to be: impulsivity associated with poor verbal self-regulation, impairment in means–end reasoning, a concrete thinking style that impinges on the ability to appreciate the thoughts and feelings of others, conceptual rigidity that inclines people to a repetitive pattern of self-defeating behaviour, poor inter-personal problem-solving skills, egocentricity, poor critical reasoning, and a selfish perspective that tends to make people focus only on how their actions affect themselves instead of considering the effects of their actions on others (Ross, Fabian and Ewels 1988).

The key principles for intervention derived from meta-analyses have been well-rehearsed and need no repetition here (see, for example, McGuire 1995; Underdown 1998; Gaes *et al* 1999). These principles, taken together, are seen to form the basis of a psychological model of behavioural change. The model is not without criticism, however, partly because of the failure to fully address the interconnections between different factors and different levels of analyses, as Gaes *et al* (1999) reflect:

> While other social sciences predict behavioural change on the basis of structural, cultural, or economic principles, those ideas are not easy to translate into individual-based intervention strategies … One limitation of the psychological perspective is that there may be many contexts in which behavioral changes, despite the best treatments, are limited by structural and cultural obstacles beyond the control of the treatment provider.
>
> (1999: 366)

Additionally, notions of success may have been exaggerated due to methodological problems and biases in measurements of success (Mair 1997; Gaes *et al* 1999). Leaving such criticisms aside, the evidence from outcome studies suggests that treatment intervention programmes based on cognitive thinking skills (CTSP) provide some modest evidence of the effectiveness of the approach for reducing reconviction for adult offenders. Most of the successes are in probation settings. However, the evidence for effectiveness appears to derive largely from meta-analyses which are based on evaluation of treatment interventions *with white males* . This leads to the questions: what is the relevance of such programmes for women?; and, although I am unable to deal with the issue in any depth in this chapter for reasons of space, what is the relevance of such programmes for ethnic minority offenders?

We must bear in mind that it has been argued that our knowledge of female offenders is beset with myths, muddles and misconceptions because of ideological reasoning (Smart 1976; Leonard 1982; Morris 1987; Heidensohn 1997; Naffine 1997). It is also relevant to add that there is a problem in deriving our knowledge of female offending from convicted offenders because sentencing is complicated by the fact that it often reflects magistrates' (and judges') perceptions of women's needs and circumstances as well as offence-based factors (Hedderman and Gelsthorpe 1997).

Nevertheless, whether looking at prison- or community-based samples (for it is argued that there is little to choose between them, Mair and May 1997) much of the literature on the needs and experiences of women offenders and on their pathways into crime indicates that there are differences between men and women. Women's health needs, substance abuse, poor educational and job levels, and experiences of sexual and physical abuse are all different from those of men (Walmsley *et al* 1992; Morris *et al* 1995; HM Inspectorate of Prisons for England and Wales 1997). A 1997 Home Office research study involving a sample of 1,986 offenders on probation in 1994 (Mair and May 1997) similarly confirms the picture of female offenders as having distinctive needs which relate to their general poverty and deprivation.

The recent review of women prisoners' needs by Howden-Windell and Clark (1999) suggests a similar range of needs: it includes reference to high levels of victimisation (sexual/physical violence) during childhood, adolescence and adulthood for instance. Further evidence from studies of convicted women also points to adverse effects from family pressures to conform to gender roles and expectations (Chesney-Lind 1997); child-care responsibilities (Bonta *et al* 1995); difficulty in achieving healthy intimate relationships (Pollock 1998), and low self-esteem (Morris *et al* 1995; Rumgay 1996). Factors which are noted to be more prevalent among imprisoned women than men include personality disorders, history of self-injury, and psychiatric orders (Bolger 1994; Bonta *et al* 1995; Maden 1996; Hannah-Moffat 1999). Blanchette and Motiuk (1997) found the following factors more prevalent among women than men in Canadian federal prisons: previous suicide attempts, marital/family relationship problems, communication problems in relationships, problems with family relationships in childhood, high levels of victimisation in social relationships, assertiveness problems, financial and accommodation problems (with high dependency on social assistance), and mental health problems (see also, Steffensmeier and Allan 1998; Bloom and Covington 1998; Kendall 1998; Hannah-Moffat and Shaw 2000a and b).

In sum, there are numerous studies which confirm differences between the social circumstances, needs, and possible motivations of male and female offenders whether considering typical low-risk women offenders (who have committed property-related crimes, for instance) or exceptional female offenders (the violent, persistent, or serious offender) (Chesney-Lind and Laidler 1997; Daly 1992; 1994b). A key question, of course, is the extent to which these broad social characteristics can be said to be offending-related. The specific contributory factors in women's offending have received comparatively little research attention in Britain, as elsewhere, beyond what might be termed as the 'broad pathways into crime' described above. Lack of money, or a lack of opportunity to gain sufficient income through legitimate means, is cited by many women as a major explanation for their offending (Carlen *et al* 1985; Carlen and Cook 1989; Cook 1997), but these studies are small-scale or otherwise inadequate as a basis for generalisation. Essentially, there is an urgent need for research in the area of motivation and the onset of offending. The general indications drawn from Prison Service work in this area (Howden-Windell and Clarke 1999) and the literature more generally (such as it is) are that dynamic risk factors include: involvement in relationships supportive of anti-social behaviour, cognitive deficits, drug misuse, and financial difficulties, but these are tentative findings; for the most part there is a lack of conclusive evidence regarding 'criminogenic' factors. At best, I would suggest that all we can say is that there is little evidence about whether women share some or all of men's dynamic risk factors or whether they have similar pathways into and out of offending.

The lack of conclusive evidence with regard to women, however, seems to have encouraged a focus on similarities between men and women in terms of what might be appropriate interventions. The case for similarity in the thinking skills (cognitive deficits) of males and females is by no means clear for instance, and yet similarities are often assumed in intervention programme design. It *is* the case that com-prehensive literature reviews on moral development have concluded that most studies do not show a significant sex difference in levels of moral judgement (Friedman, Robinson and Friedman 1987; Walker 1984; Palmer and Hollin 1998). But lack of difference in moral judgement is not the same thing as lack of difference in thinking skills, and all the early work from which English models of intervention with offenders have evolved was based on samples of men, tools designed for men and so on. Even Dowden and Andrews' (1999) meta-analysis of programmes (whereby they argue that the principles of risk, need and responsivity can be addressed through social learning and cognitive-behavioural approaches) includes acknowledgement that much more research is needed before interventions of this kind can be adopted with con-fidence. This is, of course, to leave aside the argument that in the case of women (and arguably in the case of men too) there are indications that broad *sources* of crime may need to be tackled as well as any immediate psychological motivation. Indeed, as intimated earlier, it may be argued that the need to address underlying issues is fundamental to attempts to reduce crime; that is, the broad social factors as well as immediate dynamic risk factors. As Rumgay (1996) has argued, the backgrounds and circumstances of women's lives may be inseparable from their involvement in crime. Far from being irrelevant to an understanding of women's offending, personal difficulties and welfare problems are inextricable from it.

There are two simple points to make. First, the development of some of the national community-based programmes for male and female offenders which focus on effective thinking skills are based on limited evidence of similarities in the psychological functioning of males and females; and they have been developed negatively. That is, they have been developed on the basis that there is little evidence to suggest the dynamic risk factors are different for women and men, and therefore that the two genders require a different approach. In other words, to put it bluntly, nationally recommended programmes are largely based on an act of faith that programmes for men will work for women. Secondly, notwithstanding the urgent need for further detailed research in this area, there is at least a possibility that it may be important to address broad social factors as indicative of pathways into crime. Generally then, social (gender) differences have been somewhat neglected in the design and delivery of community-based programmes (as those commenting on the development of programmes in Canada have shown; for example, McMahon 1998; Zaplin 1998; Kendall 1998; Shaw and Hannah-Moffat 2000).

We can add to this neglect of women a point about ethnicity, although there is no space to pursue the issue here. Given that most of the evaluative research which provided the basis for English developments in effective practice was based on intervention programmes with *white* males, there are also a number of problems with the assumption that such programmes are appropriate for ethnic minority offenders (Dominelli *et al* 1995; Bhui 1999; Campbell and Johnson 2000).

A key issue is whether the promotion of 'generic' programmes is proper in terms of fairness and equality of access to treatment programmes which have the same likelihood of effectiveness – given that the evidence regarding effectiveness is largely based on white males. In other words, is there procedural and substantive justice in access to, and the delivery of such programmes? And, what are the implications of not being accountable to offenders in this way? There is a strong case to suggest that the promotion of effectiveness requires recognition of possible social and cultural differences between men and women, and thus far, there has been too little attention given to this issue.

Parenting Orders

Section 2.25 Section 8 of the 1998 Crime and Disorder Act provides that the court may make a Parenting Order where (i) a Child Safety Order is made, (ii) an Anti-social Behaviour Order or a Sex Offender Order is made in respect of a child or a young person, (iii) a child or young person is convicted of an offence, or (iv) a person is convicted of offences under ss.443 or ss.444 of the Education Act 1996. In essence, the parenting order requires a parent to attend counselling or guidance sessions no more than once a week for a maximum of twelve weeks (but this can, on a discretionary basis, be waived where the parent has previously been through a parenting course); the parenting order may also include additional requirements (e.g. ensure that the child regularly attends school; ensure that the child is home by a certain time each night) for a period up to twelve months. Parents may be fined for failing to comply with any requirements in a parenting order. Where a person under sixteen is convicted of an offence, the court *shall* make a parenting order (if the desirability condition is fulfilled), or, if no order is made, court shall state in open court why an order is not being made.

The government's proposal for this method of increasing parental responsibility by no means found widespread support as it was debated in Parliament (see the description of the passing of the Bill by Gelsthorpe 1999). But criticisms were pushed aside. Put simply, the order embodied in the Crime and Disorder Act 1998 flies in the face of expert views. In response to Home Secretary Jack Straw's announcement of plans for a National Family and Planning Institute to oversee parent classes and helplines, *Guardian* feature writer Heather Welford, drawing heavily on the Save the Children (Scotland) report on Positive Parenting (1998), questioned the government's strategy on parenting (*Guardian*, 9 September 1998). She pointed out some of the dangers of dictating to people how they must raise their children, arguing that informal support groups and networks are more likely to have impact with parents than didactic approaches. As the Save the Children (Scotland) indicates, 'some parents have been deterred from attending because they associate *parenting courses* with *bad parenting* and feel that attendance would be stigmatising' (1998:39). The parents did not want a pre-set curriculum, or the feeling of obligation to attend. But they did want access to expertise and the chance to set their own priorities.

Leaving aside the question what is meant by 'a parent' in a practical sense (as opposed to a legal sense) and leaving aside the relative merits or otherwise of this measure as a supportive mechanism, the core question here is once again, what social and cultural precepts underpin the order? How are social and cultural differences with regard to parenting to be accommodated with the programmes for 'delinquent parents'. Whatever the legal difficulties, we know that the parents of young people in trouble are disproportionately drawn from homes where all responsibilities have been devolved to one remaining adult (see, for example, Rutherford 1986; Hagell and Newburn 1994). As women so overwhelmingly occupy this position, where parents are punished for failing, these punishments inevitably fall upon them in similarly unequal proportions (Mann and Roseneil 1994). Interestingly, the whole issue of parenting orders coincides with a broad social policy thrust regarding not only general support for parents (for example, better financial support), but support for marriage (Ministerial Group on the Family 1998; Utting 1995). One can discern a distinct image of what a 'proper family' and 'proper parents' do in preparatory debates. As Jack Straw, then Shadow Home Secretary, and Janet Anderson, then Shadow Minister for Women, describe in their consultation paper on parenting:

> In the 1990s we expect modern parents to engage with their children on at least the following: Respect for others; Lying; Stealing; Family and personal relationships; Personal care and hygiene, Diet and exercise; Sex education; Drinking; Smoking; Drugs; Education – school and homework; TV, video and cinema violence; Bullying; Truancy; Vandalism; Household participation; Work and career motivation.
>
> (Straw and Anderson 1996)

Thus Lord Thomas of Gresford seemed to put his finger on the issue in relation to 'parenting orders' in a very perceptive way:

> The orders seem to be wonderfully idealistic. We have before us the template of the new Labour family where no doubt the mother smilingly greets her children as they come from school with her arms covered in flour from baking scones for their tea, and the father is ready to help with the homework, and so on – and if they are not, we shall jolly well make them so because we shall train them in the proper duties of how to be a mother and father. People are not like that. The puritanical, almost Cromwellian, zeal with which the order is introduced is typical of other measures which may be found within the Bill.
>
> (HL Official Report, 10 February 1998, Col. 1068–70)

The reality of parenthood in many cases where young people are in trouble, undoubtedly involves vulnerability and poverty (Drakeford 1996), with many parents (especially mothers) living on state benefits and experiencing housing problems, though we should acknowledge that the statistically significant predictors of delinquency (*inter alia* social status, family size, suffering a broken home before the age of five, low family income, a parent with a criminal record, poor parenting skills, birth order) rarely approach the realms of certainty (Utting *et al* 1993). There *are* clear signs that what seems to happen is that adverse social and environmental factors, combined with family management practices, educational under-achievement, conflict in the home, delinquent peers and so on, add stresses that *may well* result in delinquency (Sampson and Laub 1993), but any intervention strategies that set about stigmatising individual children or their parents known to be statistically 'at risk' would arguably have as many dangers as benefits, especially if such interventions promote white, middle-class notions of parenthood without recognition that this may not, perhaps even cannot, be the norm.

There is obvious need for support and encouragement for the parents of young offenders. It is arguable that a chief problem with the Parenting Order revolves around the context in which such 'support' is to be delivered, that is, a punitive, court room context (Gelsthorpe 1999). But just as important perhaps is the point that measures will only carry legitimacy if they are respectful of social differences in both the notion and practice of parenting. Here too there is need for accountability towards the offender.

Conclusion

This chapter has set out the case for more attention to be given to social and cultural differences in the conception and delivery of community penalties. Importantly, I have argued that, at the very least, there needs to be further research on the nature of social and cultural differences with regard to pathways into, and out of, crime before 'generic programmes' become established as the norm. Without such research there is the danger of missing the point, thus limiting the potential for effective intervention.

Accountability towards the offender can perhaps be conceptualised in three different ways:

(i) *legally*, in terms of human rights;

(ii) *socially and culturally*, in terms of recognising social differences in the conception and delivery of community penalties in order to maximise the potential for effectiveness, and

(iii) *inclusively*, in terms of recognising social and cultural differences amongst offenders so as to avoid alienating them, and more particularly, to promote respect for the law.

Whilst a human rights perspective sets out important matters of principle, this is perhaps a fairly limited approach; not only are attempts to limit harm at some distance from the promotion of 'good' (effective) practice, but the complexities of the issues suggest that there is to be no quick or simple recourse to the law. I would place rather more importance on the need to recognise social and cultural differences because attention here may increase the possibility of effectiveness, and crucially, because it holds out the prospect of enhancing normative compliance. As Tyler (1990) has suggested, normative compliance may arise from an individual's general moral sense, or from a changed perspective on the world due to some life event (like marriage). It may also come from a morally-based perception that the demand for compliance derives from a law, or from legal authorities, that are *legitimate*. In this regard, there is already clear evidence that a perception that legal authorities are acting fairly (procedural justice) has a significant impact on notions of legitimacy (Tyler 1990; Paternoster *et al* 1997). Paternoster *et al* helpfully spell out the essential ingredients of procedural justice which appear to facilitate legitimacy: representation, consistency, impartiality, accuracy, correctability and *ethicality*. It is this last point that is of most interest in this context, for if legitimacy demands that legal authorities treat offenders with respect and dignity, we might argue that recognition of social and cultural differences in the delivery of community penalties is an essential part of the required respect for offenders in order to facilitate active citizenship on their part.

Citizenship education in England has received considerable attention since 1997, resulting in the introduction of programmes of study for citizenship in secondary schools from the year 2002 (McLaughlin 2000). Whilst there is an apparent ongoing lively debate about the purposes of citizenship education, the essence of citizenship appears to go well beyond knowledge of political institutions. Indeed, 'good neighbourliness', 'social and moral responsibility', 'political literacy' and 'community involvement' are all mentioned as key ingredients (Qualifications and Curriculum Authority 1998); abstinence from crime is taken for granted. In a sense, the term 'citizenship' signifies what may be described as a 'politics of attachment' (Kraemer and Roberts 1996). In other words, the 'social bonds' (Sampson and Laub 1993). Whilst much has been written about social bonding and delinquency or crime prevention (Utting 1996; Roshier 1989; Graham and Bowling 1996) particularly through the quality of parenting through successive stages of children's development, much less attention has been given to notions of attachment or social bonding through community and relationships, which arguably have a symbolic as well as a grounded existence (Rustin 1996).

'Attachment' beyond childhood, of course, is undoubtedly complex. Individuals will be tied to different representations, memories, principles and ideals and not only to what they, as individuals, have experienced. But it is here, in this interconnection of social bonding or attachment and citizenship, that I would posit the need to take cognisance of cultural and social differences and diversity in professional criminal justice system practice. Or at least, posit the need to explore the relevance of these connections in securing perceptions of the criminal justice authorities as legitimate. To be treated not as a composite offender with a risk/need score, but as a fully human, socially and culturally differentiated offender, is perhaps to engender reciprocal 'respect'.

This is but a sketch of ideas, but a lack of responsiveness to social and cultural differences between offenders (relevant to their pathways into and out of crime) may limit effectiveness by diminishing the legitimacy of the criminal justice authorities in offenders' eyes and therefore cut across the promotion of good citizenship. A community penalties agenda for the future should perhaps demonstrate accountability towards the offender, in transparent fashion, by recognising these differences. The promotion of 'good citizenship' arguably depends on treating offenders *as* citizens who are differentiated socially and culturally.

prison takes away identity
you become a "prisoner" adopting another
identity.

References

Allen, R. (2000) 'Putting the community back into community sentences', *Criminal Justice Matters*, 39, Spring, 4.

Anthias, F. and Yuval-Davis, N. (1992) *Racialised Boundaries: Race, Nation, Gender, Colour and Class and the Anti-Racist Struggle.* London: Routledge.

Bhui, H. (1999) 'Race, racism and risk assessment: linking theory to practice with Black mentally disordered offenders', *Probation Journal*, 46 (3), 171–181.

Blanchette, K. and Motiuk, L. (1997) Maximum-security female and male federal offenders: a comparison. Report. Research Branch: Correctional Service Canada.

Bloom, B. and Covington, S. (1998) 'Gender-specific programming for female offenders: what is it and why is it important?' Paper presented to American Society of Criminology, Washington DC, November 1998.

Bolger, L. (1994) The prevalence of personality disorder in a women's prison. Unpublished MSc. dissertation cited in J. Howden-Windell and D. Clarke (1999) 'The Criminogenic Needs of Women. A Literature Review'. Unpublished Paper. London: HM Prison Service.

Bonta, J., Pang, B. and Wallace-Capretta, S. (1995) 'Predictors of recidivism among incarcerated female offenders', *The Prison Journal*, 75, 277–294.

Bottoms, A.E. (1997) 'The philosophy and politics of punishment and sentencing' in C. Clarkson and R. Morgan (eds) *The Politics of Sentencing Reform*. Oxford: Clarendon Press.

Brooke, H. (1999) 'The Human Rights Act 1998', *Criminal Justice Matters*, 38, Winter, 29.

Campbell, D. and Johnson, G. (2000) 'Anansi and the offending behaviour programme', *Criminal Justice Matters*, 39, Spring, 17–18.

Carlen, P., Hicks, J., O'Dwyer, J. Christina, D. and Tchaikovsky, C. (1985) *Criminal Women: Autobiographical Accounts.* Oxford: Basil Blackwell.

Carlen, P. and Cook, D. (1989) *Paying for Crime.* Milton Keynes: Open University Press.

Cheney, D., Dickson, L., Fitzpatrick, J. and Uglow, S. (1999) *Criminal Justice and the Human Rights Act 1998.* Bristol: Jordans.

Chesney-Lind, M. (ed.) (1997) *The Female Offender. Girls, Women and Crime.* Thousand Oaks, CA: Sage.

Chesney-Lind, M. and Laidler, K. (1997) 'Drugs, Violence, and Women's Crime' in M. Chesney-Lind (ed.) (1997) *The Female Offender. Girls, Women and Crime.* Thousand Oaks, CA: Sage.

Chigwada-Bailey, R. (1997) *Black Women's Experiences of Criminal Justice.* Winchester: Waterside Press.

Clarke, J. and Newman, J. (1997) *The Managerial State.* London: Sage.

Cook, D. (1997) *Poverty, Crime and Punishment.* London: Child Poverty Action Group.

Cook, D. and Hudson, B. (eds) (1993) *Racism and Criminology.* London: Sage.

Crawford, A. and Goodey, J. (eds) (2000) *Integrating a Victim Perspective within Criminal Justice.* Aldershot: Ashgate.

Daly, K. (1992) 'Women's Pathways to Felony Court: Feminist Theories of Lawbreaking and Problems of Representation', *Review of Law and Women's Studies*, 2, 11–52.

Daly, K. (1994a) 'Criminal Law and Justice Practices as Racist, White and Racialised', *Washington and Lee Law Review*, 15 (2), 431–464.

Daly, K. (1994b) *Gender, Crime and Punishment.* New Haven: Yale University Press.

Dignan, J. (1999) 'The Crime and Disorder Act and the prospects for restorative justice', *Criminal Law Review* (January), 48–60.

Dominelli, L., Jeffers, L., Jones, G., Sibanda, S. and Williams, B. (1995) *Anti-Racist Probation Practice*. Aldershot: Arena.

Dowden, C. and Andrews, D. (1999) 'What works for Female Offenders: A Meta-Analytic Review', *Crime and Delinquency*, 45 (4), 438–452.

Drakeford, M (1996) 'Parents of young people in trouble', *The Howard Journal of Criminal Justice*, 35, 242–255.

Eaton, M. (1986) *Justice for Women?* Milton Keynes: Open University Press.

Eaton, M. (1993) *Women After Prison*. Buckingham: Open University Press.

Friedman, W., Robinson, A. and Friedman, B. (1987) 'Sex differences in moral judgement? A test of Gilligan's theory', *Psychology of Women Quarterly*, 11, 37–46.

Gaes, G., Flanagan, T., Motiuk, L. and Stewart, L. (1999) 'Adult Correctional Treatment', in M. Tonry and J. Petersilia (eds) *Prisons*. Chicago: University of Chicago Press.

Gelsthorpe, L. (1992) 'Social Inquiry Reports: race and gender considerations', *Home Office Research and Statistics Department Research Bulletin*, 32.

Gelsthorpe, L. (1999) 'Youth Crime and Parental Responsibility' in A. Bainham, S. Day-Sclater and M. Richards (eds) *What is a Parent?* Oxford: Hart Publishing.

Gelsthorpe, L. and Morris, A. (eds) (1990) *Feminist Perspectives in Criminology*. Buckingham: Open University Press.

Gendreau, P. and Ross, R. (1979) 'Effectiveness of Correctional Treatment: Bibliotherapy for Cynics', *Crime and Delinquency*, 25, 463–489.

Gendreau, P. and Ross, R. (1987) ' Revification of Rehabilitation: Evidence from the 1980s', *Justice Quarterly*, 4, 349–407.

Gilligan, C. (1982) *In A Different Voice. Psychological Theory and Women's Development*. Cambridge, MA: Harvard University Press.

Gilroy, P. (1997) 'Diaspora and the Detours of Identity', in K. Woodward (ed.) *Identity and Difference*. London: Sage.

Graham, J. and Bowling, B. (1995) *Young People and Crime*. Home Office Research Study 145. London: Home Office.

Hagell, A. and Newburn, T. (1994) *Persistent Young Offenders*. London: Policy Studies Institute.

Hannah-Moffat, K. (1999) 'Moral Agent or Actuarial Subject: Risk and Canadian Women's Imprisonment', *Theoretical Criminology*, 3 (1), 71–94.

Hannah-Moffat, K. and Shaw, M. (2000a) 'Thinking about Cognitive Skills? Think again!', *Criminal Justice Matters*, 39, Spring, 8–9.

Hannah-Moffat, K. and Shaw, M. (2000b) 'Gender, Diversity, Risk and Need Classifying and Assessing Federally Sentenced Women', Final Report. Ottawa: Status of Women Canada.

Hedderman, C. and Gelsthorpe, L. (eds) (1997) *Understanding the Sentencing of Women*. Home Office Research Study 170, London: Home Office.

Heidensohn, F. (1997) 'Gender and Crime', in M. Maguire, R. Morgan and R.

Reiner (eds) *The Oxford Handbook of Criminology.* Oxford: Oxford University Press.

HM Inspectorate of Prisons for England and Wales (1997) *Women in Prison. A Thematic Review by HM Chief Inspector of Prisons.* London: HMSO.

Home Office (1999) *What Works. Reducing Re-offending: Evidence-Based Practice.* London: Home Office Communications Directorate.

Horsley, G. (1984) *The Language of Social Enquiry Reports.* Social Work Monograph 27. Norwich: University of East Anglia

Howden-Windell, J. and Clarke, D. (1999) 'The Criminogenic Needs of Women. A Literature Review.' Unpublished Paper. London: HM Prison Service.

Kendall, K. (1998) 'Evaluations of Programs for Female Offenders', in R. Zaplin (ed.) *Female Offenders: Critical Perspectives and Effective Interventions.* Baltimore, Maryland: Aspen Publishers.

Kraemer, S. and Roberts, J. (eds) (1996) *The Politics of Attachment. Towards a Secure Society.* London: Free Association Books.

Leonard, E. (1982) *Women, Crime and Society: a Critique of Theoretical Criminology.* New York: Longman.

Lipton, D. (1998) How Do Cognitive Skills Training Programs for Offenders Compare with Other Modalities? A Meta-analytic Perspective', Paper presented at the Stop and Think Conference, York, England.

McGuire, J. (1995) *What Works: Reducing Re-offending.* Chichester: John Wiley.

McLaughlin, T. (2000) 'Citizenship Education in England: The Crick Report and Beyond', *Journal of Philosophy of Education,* 34 (4), 541–570.

McIvor, G. (1992) *Sentenced to Serve: The Operation and Impact of Community Service Orders by Offenders.* Aldershot: Avebury.

McMahon, M. (1998) 'Assisting Female Offenders: Art or Science?' Paper (Chairperson's commentary), Annual Conference of the International Community Corrections Association, Arlington, Virginia (September 27–30).

McWilliams, W. (1993) 'The Mission to the English Police Courts' 1976–1936', *The Howard Journal of Criminal Justice,* 22, 129–147.

Maden, T. (1996) *Women, Prisons and Psychiatry.* Oxford: Butterworth-Heinemann.

Mair, G. (1997) 'Community Penalties and the Probation Service' in M. Maguire, R. Morgan and R. Reiner (eds). *The Oxford Handbook of Criminology.* Oxford: Clarendon Press.

Mair, G. and May, C. (1997) *Offenders on Probation.* Home Office Research Study 167. London: Home Office.

Mair, G. and Mortimer, E. (1996) *Curfew Orders with Electronic Monitoring.* Home Office Research Study 163. London: Home Office.

Mann, K. and Roseneil, S. (1994) 'Some Mothers do 'ave 'em: Backlash and the Gender Politics of the Underclass Debate', *Journal of Gender Studies,* 3 (3), 317–331.

Ministerial Group on the Family (1998) *Supporting Families.* A Consultation Document. London: Home Office.

Modood, T. (1992) *Not Easy Being British: Colour, Culture and Citizenship.* London: Runnymede Trust and Trentham Books.

Morris, A. (1987) *Women, Crime and Criminal Justice.* Oxford: Blackwell.

Morris, A., Wilkinson, C., Tisi, A., Woodrow, J. and Rockley, A. (1995) *Managing the Needs of Female Prisoners.* London: Home Office.

Morris, A. and Gelsthorpe, L. (2000) 'Something Old, Something Borrowed, Something Blue, but Something New? A comment on the prospects for restorative justice under the Crime and Disorder Act 1998', *Criminal Law Review,* January, 18–30.

Mortimer, E. and May, C. (1997) *Electronic Monitoring in Practice: the Second Year of the Trials of Curfew Orders.* Home Office Research Study 177, London: Home Office.

Naffine, N. (1997) *Feminism and Criminology.* Cambridge: Polity Press.

Nash, M. (1997) 'Consumers Without Teeth: Can Probation Service "Clients" have a Say in the Service They Receive?', *International Journal of Public Sector Management,* 4 (9), 12–19.

Palmer, E. and Hollin, C. (1998) 'A Comparison of Patterns of Moral Development in Young Offenders and Non-offenders', *Legal and Criminological Psychology,* 3, 225–235.

Paternoster, R., Bachman, R., Brame, R. and Sherman, L. (1997) 'Do Fair Procedures Matter? The Effect of Procedural Justice on Spouse Assault', *Law and Society Review,* 31, 163–204.

Pollock, J. (1998) *Counselling Women in Prison. Women's Mental Health and Development,* 3. Thousand Oaks, CA: Sage.

Qualifications and Curriculum Authority (1998) *Education for Citizenship and the Teaching of Democracy in Schools: Final Report of the Advisory Group on Citizenship.* London: Qualifications and Curriculum Authority (Advisory Group Chaired by B. Crick).

Prison Reform Trust (1997) *Electronic Tagging: Viable Option or Expensive Diversion?* London: Prison Reform Trust.

Rice, M. (1990) 'Challenging Orthodoxies in Feminist Theory: a Black Feminist Critique', in L. Gelsthorpe and A. Morris (eds) (1990) *Feminist Perspectives in Criminology.* Buckingham: Open University Press.

Roshier, B. (1989) *Controlling Crime.* Milton Keynes: Open University Press.

Ross, R., Fabiano, E. and Ewels, D. (1988) 'Reasoning and Rehabilitation', *International Journal of Offender Therapy and Comparative Criminology,* 32, 29–35.

Rumgay, J. (1996) 'Women Offenders: Towards Needs-based Policy', *Vista,* September, 104–115.

Rustin, M. (1996) 'Attachment in Context' in S. Kraemer and J. Roberts (eds) *The Politics of Attachment. Towards a Secure Society.* London: Free Association Books.

Rutherford, A. (1986) *Growing Out of Crime: Society and Young People in Trouble.* Harmondsworth: Penguin.

Rutherford, A. (1993) *Criminal Justice and the Pursuit of Decency.* Oxford: Oxford University Press.

Sampson, R. and Laub, J. (1993) *Crime in the Making: Pathways and Turning Points Through Life*. Cambridge, Mass.: Harvard University Press.

Sanders, A. (1999) *Taking Account of Victims in the Criminal Justice System: A Review of the Literature*. Social Work Research Findings, 32. Edinburgh: HMSO.

Save the Children, Scotland (1998) *Supporting Parents, Supporting Parenting. Positive Parenting*, First Year Report. London: Save the Children.

Shaw, M. and Hannah-Moffat, K. (2000) 'Women and Risk: A Genealogy of Classification', in M. Shaw (ed.) *Conflicting Agendas: Evaluating Feminist Programmes for Offending Women*. New York: SUNY Press.

Smart, C. (1976) *Women, Crime and Criminology*. London: RKP.

Smith, D. and Stewart, J. (1998) 'Probation and Social Exclusion', in C. Jones Finer and M. Nellis (eds) *Crime and Social Exclusion*. Oxford: Blackwell Publishers.

Steffensmeier, D. and Allan, E. (1998) 'The Nature of Female Offending: Patterns and Explanations' in R. Zaplin (ed.) *Female Offenders: Critical Perspectives and Effective Interventions*. Baltimore, Maryland: Aspen Publishers.

Straw, J. and Anderson, J. (1996) *Parenting. A Discussion Paper*. London: The Labour Party.

Trotter, C. (1993) *The Supervision of Offenders – What Works?* A Report to the Australian Criminology Research Council.

Tyler, T. (1990) *Why People Obey the Law*. New Haven: Yale University Press.

Underdown, A. (1998) *Strategies for Effective Offender Supervision*. Report of the HMIP What Works Project. London: Home Office.

Utting, D. (1995) *Family and Parenthood*. York: Joseph Rowntree Foundation.

Utting, D. (1996) 'Tough on the Causes of Crime? Social Bonding and Delinquency Prevention', in S. Kraemer and J. Roberts (eds) *The Politics of Attachment. Towards a Secure Society*. London: Free Association Books.

Utting, D., Bright, J. and Henricson, C. (1993) *Crime and the Family. Improving child-rearing and preventing delinquency*. London: Family Policy Studies Centre, NACRO and Crime Concern.

Walker, L. (1984) 'Sex Differences in the Development of Moral Reasoning', *Child Development*, 55, 677–691.

Walmsley, R., Howard, L., and White, S. (1992) *The National Prison Survey 1990*. Home Office Research Study 128. London: HMSO.

Waters, R. (1983) *Ethnic Minorities and the Criminal Justice System*. Aldershot: Avebury.

Whitehouse, P. (1983) 'Race, Bias and Social Inquiry Reports', *Probation Journal*, 30 (2), 43–49.

Woodward, K. (ed.) (1997) *Identity and Difference*. London: Sage.

Young, J. (1992) 'Ten Points of Realism' in J. Young and R. Matthews (eds) *Rethinking Criminology*. London: Sage.

Zaplin, R. (ed.) (1998) *Female Offenders: Critical Perspectives and Effective Interventions*. Baltimore, Maryland: Aspen Publishers.

Zedner, L. (1997) 'Victims', in M. Maguire, R. Morgan and R. Reiner (eds) *The Oxford Handbook of Criminology*. Oxford: Clarendon Press.

Chapter 9

Technology and the future of community penalties

George Mair

We need a service better able to take forward new national strategic developments. New technologies offer opportunities for service to be delivered in new ways and more cost-effectively. For example, electronic monitoring can provide a cheap and effective means of imposing tighter supervision on offenders; of imposing discipline on chaotic lives; of reintegrating offenders more effectively into society; and an inescapable means of detecting breaches of court orders. A new service needs to embrace such technologies and to incorporate the opportunities they offer into their strategies for confronting and impacting on offending behaviour, thus making better and more focused use of probation core competences and skills.

(Home Office 1998: 8)

Introduction

Traditionally, the Probation Service has been seen as (and happy to acknowledge itself as being) the caring end of the criminal justice process. For most of its existence this has not been a problem, but since the project of probation restructuring and reorganisation began in 1984 with the Statement of National Objectives and Priorities (SNOP) (Home Office 1984), this compassionate image has become increasingly problematic and indeed has been used as a stick with which to beat probation officers. Advise, assist and befriend as the objectives of the service with their soft, understanding and rather passive connotations have been replaced by confront, challenge and change – suggesting a much more active, aggressive and hard-nosed stance.

Despite all of the developments that have affected the Probation Service in the past twenty years (and a selection of these developments might include the introduction of new community penalties, more work with prisoners, changes to pre-sentence reports, the introduction of national standards and performance indicators, increased use of group-work with offenders, the introduction of cash limits, the requirement to enter into partnership agreements with other organisations, working with the victims of crime), I would argue that fundamentally probation officers still work in the same ways with offenders. The reality of probation practice has probably changed little in the past twenty years; it is not difficult to see how advise, assist and befriend and confront, challenge and change might be reconciled in everyday work with offenders.

Two developments, however, have – in symbolic terms alone – much more profound potential implications for community penalties and the work of probation officers: the electronic monitoring of offenders (cur-few orders) and computerisation. I have previously described the former as having 'the potential to become a major player in the community penalty arena' (Mair 2000: 260) and the latter as 'a development which is often forgotten, but which is likely to have both profound and long-term consequences for probation work' (Mair 1996: 30–31). Both develop-ments, of course, are based upon new technology and while we often hear about the application of the latest technological developments to police work (the use of computers to manage large amounts of data; the introduction of DNA data-bases) and to prisons (central locking of cells; the use of Barringer machines to test visitors for contact with drugs), the probation service and new technology are rarely seen as compatible.

In this chapter, I propose to take a fairly wide-ranging look at tech-nology in the context of community penalties. I will first discuss two recent experiences of what might be termed the collision of new technology and community penalties and then go on to speculate on what the future might hold for this somewhat unlikely partnership.

When worlds collide

The two early experiences of new technology coming into contact with the Probation Service that I wish to discuss are the introduction of the electronic monitoring (EM) of offenders, first via a condition of bail and subsequently as part of a sentence of the court (the curfew order), and the use of computers to calculate risk assessment using OGRS (the Offender Group Reconviction Scale). Neither case makes one feel comfortable about the ability or willingness of the Probation Service to take on board with confidence initiatives based on new technology. There is certainly a place for a degree of scepticism and caution about new schemes that are introduced quickly and without adequate consultation. But this is not to say that such schemes should be obstructed and their success jeopardised by a refusal to give them a fair chance. John Donne in his poem 'Satyre III' states that we should 'Doubt wisely' – a piece of advice that probation officers (as well as researchers) would do well to heed. A knee-jerk response to new technology as alien to the traditions of the Probation Service and unhelpful to community penalties would not be a wise position to take – especially in the light of the quotation at the head of this paper and the Foresight Consultation Paper on crime prevention and the new technology (Department of Trade and Industry 2000).

Electronic monitoring

The first use in England and Wales of electronic monitoring as a tool in the criminal justice process took place during 1989–90 in the course of a six-month trial of electronic monitoring as a condition of bail (for a full report on the trial see Mair and Nee 1990). In the course of discussing how the trial might be organised, Home Office officials held meetings with representatives of the Probation Service to elicit their views about electronic monitoring. It is no exaggeration to state that these views were negative; the National Association of Probation Officers (NAPO) and the Association of Chief Officers of Probation (ACOP) were in agreement on this (see Nellis 1991). Electronic monitoring was seen as controlling, oppressive, an infringement of civil rights and not something that the Probation Service should be involved with.

Now the particular context in which electronic monitoring was being introduced played a part in this reaction. The Green Paper, *Punishment, Custody and the Community* (Home Office 1988), had recently been published and was received by probation officers as posing not only a serious threat to the traditional caring, welfare-oriented role of the service but also a threat to the very existence of the service itself (it is fair to say that the Green Paper opened serious hostilities on the Probation Service by the Conservative government; since the publication of SNOP four years earlier there had been a 'phoney war'). But there is little doubt that – given their background and training – probation officers were deeply unsympathetic in any event to the very idea of using technology to keep tabs on the whereabouts of offenders. From this perspective, probation work dealt in human beings; electronic monitoring meant treating humans as objects.

As a result of this stance on the part of the Probation Service towards electronic monitoring, the Home Office used the private sector not only to provide the equipment but also staff to organise and operate the scheme. The Probation Service role was limited; members of the local services were invited to sit on the project liaison groups but their involvement was minimal (indeed in one trial site the probation representative failed to attend any of the meetings of the liaison group). The results of the trial were somewhat ambivalent and given the considerable time that elapsed between the end of the trial (1990) and the re-introduction of electronic monitoring as part of a curfew order (1995), the Probation Service may have felt that their stance towards this new technology had succeeded in halting its further development. In truth, incompetent drafting of legislation was responsible for the delay (Mair 1998) which may even have been an additional factor in the success of the new trials (Mair and Mortimer 1996; Mortimer and May 1997).

Because of the attitude of probation service organisations towards electronic monitoring in 1989–90, probation officers were not seriously considered for the role of responsible officer for those who would be subject to curfew orders in the new trial. Again, this went to the staff of the private companies who supplied the equipment. The probation response to the first twelve months of the 1995 trial was 'at best equivocal and at worst obstructive' (Mair and Mortimer 1996: 29). The power of probation officers not to consider a curfew order or to dismiss it as an option in pre-sentence reports was certainly a contributory factor in the low number of curfew orders made in the early stages of the trial.

Despite the unofficial low-level campaign against the electronic monitoring of offenders carried on by the Probation Service, it now looks fairly certain that EM is here to stay: the curfew order is now available nationally, electronic monitoring is used as part of the Home Detention Curfew for prisoners on early release, trials are underway for the use of EM in relation to persistent petty offenders, fine defaulters, and offenders aged 10–15. The probation *volte-face* has been quite remarkable. Even by the end of the first year of the 1995 trial there were signs that probation officers were having to come to terms with electronic monitoring; this may not have been so much a genuine change of heart as a matter of political expediency as it became clear that EM was not going away. Indeed, there is some evidence that probation officers now favour the use of a curfew order made jointly with a community penalty

(Mortimer, Pereira and Walter 1999). And in 1997 a Chief Probation Office published a book which – while not positively advocating the use of EM – certainly took a much more balanced position than would have been possible a few years earlier: 'It seems to me that tagging is neither more nor less liable to oppressive use than any other sanction' (Whitfield 1997: 121).

No matter how profound this change of heart really is, the fact remains that because of its initial suspicion of the technology, the Probation Service has lost out on being responsible for operating this new tool which may become an increasingly significant part of dealing with offenders. The potential repercussions of this for the Service may be serious.

Actuarial risk assessment

Probation officers have always had to assess risk in relation to the offenders they dealt with. At least implicitly in social inquiry reports (the predecessor to pre-sentence reports) and in the work carried on with offenders under a probation order, risk was a key factor to be considered.

Whether adequate risk assessment always took place, however, or took place consistently and always took account of the same factors is another matter given the relatively unfettered discretion probation officers had in the past. The problems associated with such faulty risk assessment were increased risk to the public and inequity in dealing with offenders. While the history of actuarial risk assessment in the Probation Service in this country has yet to be written, it developed seriously in the second half of the 1980s and by the mid-90s we had OGRS – a risk of reconviction scale that had been devised by a leading statistician and was simple to use.

Once again the context in which OGRS was introduced was critical. By the mid-90s the Probation Service was feeling embattled as the Conservative government warned of privatisation, demanded the recruitment of ex-service personnel, and cut probation budgets; ACOP were no longer welcomed to cosy meetings at the Home Office to discuss proposed new developments. The way was not prepared well for OGRS, despite warnings from the Home Office Research and Planning Unit that considerable care would be necessary in introducing any risk prediction technique (Mair 1989), but the press reaction came as a surprise. Even before OGRS was made available to the Probation Service, encouraged by NAPO, the *Independent* newspaper sneered at OGRS as 'a magic equation that is supposed to sort out the incorrigible from the redeemable', 'a fiendishly complicated sum' and as being 'about as discriminating as a policeman's truncheon at a football riot' (24 July 1995). Three years later when OGRS had been released for use, the *Sunday Mirror* headline (29 November 1998) with considerable mis-representation read:

$$X = (31-a) - (b+c) + (\sqrt{d \div (e+5)} \times 75) \pm f$$

It's the magic formula to get out of jail free.

In fact, this so-called 'fiendishly complicated sum' only took a few minutes at most to calculate (and I write as one who might be described as quantitatively challenged), and a computer software package was designed to make it even easier and faster to calculate the score. Using a computer was, however, seen as distancing the probation officer even further from the offender who was being assessed. Probation officers' understandable apprehensions about this new, scientific, technical approach which would aid in assessing offenders were exacerbated by the Home Office decision to make OGRS available for national use without a concerted effort to explain the background to the scale, how it was developed, and how it should be used. Nor was there any research effort put into finding how the scale was used in practice, despite research demonstrating that the introduction of such novel techniques could lead to all sorts of problems (Cochran, Corbett and Byrne 1986; Aubrey and Hough 1997). OGRS is now history and a new assessment system – OASys – has been developed and is about to be released to the Probation Service. It will be interesting to follow its implementation although one might be forgiven a feeling of history repeating itself when reading a *Guardian* editorial (21 August, 2000) that began:

> **Postcode sentencing – computers cannot deliver justice**
> It sounds like a George Orwell story: Britain is to use
> computers to help fix the sentences of criminals
> and their release dates

The future

It would be no exaggeration then to claim that the track record of the Probation Service with regard to new technology is not good. Indeed, it could be argued that the Service has often – at least initially – been deeply resistant to change of any kind (e.g. neither community service nor day centres were welcomed with enthusiasm), although it has proved ineffectual in halting such changes. But that was in the past, and the speed of change – and the need to keep up with it – has continued to make demands on all criminal justice agencies. The Probation Service cannot afford to be left behind. In this section I wish to discuss a series of issues around the relationship between the Probation Service and new technology. My speculations will not be focused on how new technology can be built into existing community penalties – on its own this would be a somewhat bloodless exercise – but will also be concerned with how probation staff might deal with this new world. For as long as we have probation officers – and electronic monitoring staff – the key issue is surely not how sophisticated the technology can be and what it is capable of doing, but how humans respond to that technology, how they come to terms with it, how they interact with it, how they use it, how they misuse it, how they might subvert it, how they incorporate it to their own needs.

The Probation Service of the near-future is likely to be similar to what we currently have, at least in terms of the sentences it operates (it is, of course, possible that the Sentencing Review might lead to changes, perhaps in the direction of one generic community order but this would certainly include the options of probation supervision and community service). The most relevant piece of technology to the operation and organisation of community penalties is the use of CCTV and video. It has recently been claimed that someone moving around a UK city will, on average, be caught on CCTV camera 300 times in a day – which raises some important issues about the depth and intensity of surveillance that is going on almost unnoticed. Forms of intensive probation involve probation staff seeing offenders several times a day at different pre-arranged locations and the potential of CCTV here may be considerable. Instead of having a probation worker travel to a location and talk to the offender there, the offender could be seen on camera and his or her movements monitored. Offenders might have to report to a specific point where they can be viewed on camera (a form of these – 'Help Points' – are already in place in some European cities and are beginning to appear in this country); or a smart card with voice identification might be used. Interestingly, some years ago the probation service in New York was in the process of planning to introduce special booths where offenders could check in electronically with their probation officers. This measure was one response to a serious budget problem and was aimed at low-risk offenders; nevertheless it was mocked by those British academics and probation staff who were aware of it. Coincidentally, as the paper on which this chapter is based was being written, the Home

Secretary announced a new package of measures designed to curb persistent young offenders:

> The whereabouts of each young offender will be checked at least twice daily with 24 hours a day, seven days a week surveillance where this is necessary. Surveillance techniques, including in the late evenings and the weekends, may include electronic monitoring, voice verification, tracking by probation and social work staff and policing.
>
> (*Guardian*, 25 September 2000)

Some banks are currently handing out mobile phones to their customers to encourage internet banking, and offenders could be issued with these so that they might be contacted by their probation officer at any time. Such phones would have to be personalised but that should not be an insurmountable problem. In any event, videophone technology will soon be widely available which will overcome the identification issue and might mean that offenders do not need to turn up to the probation office to see their probation officer – supervision sessions could be carried out over the phone. CCTV might be especially effective in monitoring community service group work placements as these tend to be situated in one geographical location.

For the most part, these uses of cameras and mobile phones are not really aids to the supervision process as such; although if one-to-one work can be carried out via a videophone this will change dramatically the nature of the contact between probation officer and offender. They are, however, aids to monitoring compliance and thereby making enforcement more rigorous. A perennial complaint of sentencers is that the enforcement of community penalties is not strict enough, that this in turn makes sentencers lose confidence in such penalties and thus not use them as often as they might. The introduction of national standards and increasingly strict rules about breach are evidence of how seriously enforcement is perceived by the Home Office. By using cameras and mobile phones, compliance with the rules of a community penalty could be enforced even more strictly.

A rigid approach to enforcement relying on new technology has its drawbacks (apart from the obvious problem of breakdown of the equipment). In the first place, more offenders may fail on these measures and be breached. This could lead to more custodial sentences and a resultant loss of confidence in the efficacy of community penalties by sentencers. It might also engender a purely mechanical approach to checking in with one's probation officer, which would not be in keeping with the spirit of probation supervision. And it would also erode further the discretion of probation officers to discuss failures to appear with offenders, to negotiate over matters of compliance. It would be possible to construct a powerful account of the Probation Service over the past twenty years which focused on the erosion of discretion, and the application of technology would appear to offer an end to discretion over enforcement. CCTV offers an illusion of certainty that an offender was not present at a location when they state the opposite. A mobile phone makes it very difficult for an offender to claim they forgot about the appointment with the probation officer. In the same way, the technology for on-the-spot drug testing offers the perception of accuracy about whether or not an offender has been using drugs recently. The probation officer can no longer collude with the offender (for whatever reasons – because the supervision is going well, because the period of the order is almost complete, because state benefits might be lost with serious consequences for the offender's family) to ensure that they do not transgress the trip-wire of breach.

This (seemingly) clear line, however, is rather fuzzy in practice. With regard to drugs testing, for example, initially hard-line proponents argued that a positive test meant failure and that meant custody (if the offender was serving a community sentence). Over time, this stance softened as interpreted literally it meant increasing numbers going into prison thereby contributing to overcrowding, and also that no help was available to the offender who would almost inevitably be thrown off any programme they were on to tackle drug use (relapse was not recognised as part of the process). So discretion re-entered. For many drug-testing schemes now, offenders can have more than one positive test and these are seen as posing problems that need resolution and issues to be discussed rather than as outright failure that requires sanctioning via increased punishment. It is difficult for an offender to deny the evidence of a positive drug test when the result is in front of them, and the situation can be exploited by the probation officer to confront and challenge (and this is to ignore the possibility of false positive or false negative tests as a result of equipment failure, and the scope for cheating). A similar situation can be envisaged with regard to the use of CCTV/video/mobile phone.

But it is not only probation officers who might have to confront such technologies in their work. Sentencers might well decide that as it is such a simple matter to monitor offenders they can add various exclusionary requirements to probation or combination orders so that an offender is faced with a number of places or times that are restricted. Richard Jones has recently noted the 'withdrawal of system access authorisation' as a sanction:

Electronic monitoring of curfew compliance can be understood as an attempt to withdraw the societal 'privilege' of doing certain activities, through restrictions in time and/or space, such as spending the evening drinking in a pub or bar. Indeed, the sanction of an electronically monitored curfew is itself often presented by the criminal justice system as a 'privilege' to offenders, in the sense that such offenders might instead have faced a custodial sentence, and that failure to comply could lead them to prison.

(Jones 2000: 18)

Probation officers have always worried about 'setting offenders up to fail' and if sentencers load requirements on to offenders simply because they are easy to monitor as a result of technological advances, this may have unintended consequences. However, the attitudes of sentencers towards the use of new technology in community penalties will be crucial. In the electronic monitoring trials sentencers were by no means enthusiastic about the introduction of 'tagging'. A few were very keen, some were completely opposed to the idea, while probably the majority were sceptical and adopted a 'wait-and-see' attitude which meant that they were cautious about using EM as a condition of bail (in the first trial) or as a sentence (in the second trial). Interestingly, sentencers were not generally happy about the Home Office marketing of the technology. They will have to be convinced of the benefits of applying new technology to exisiting community penalties, otherwise they may refuse to use them.

Some of the developments currently being urged on the Probation Service would seem to have an affinity with new technology which might prove to be fertile ground for its further penetration of probation work. First, there is the policy that cognitive behaviouralism should be the preferred approach to working with offenders. It may be an over-simplification, but the delivery of cognitive behavioural programmes is very much an educational approach, and there is little choice for the deliverer of the programme to deviate from the programme manual. Thus, is there any reason why one or two members of staff have to be in a room with a group of offenders to deliver the programme? Surely it would be possible to use videos to deliver the material effectively to a group of offenders. Or the programme could be used in this way with individual offenders – the Open University has followed such an approach for decades, and distance-learning courses are now an option at many universities and colleges. Many such probation programmes are already monitored by video in an effort to keep a firm grip on programme integrity. Using videos to deliver the programme would solve at a stroke the question of programme integrity as consistent delivery would be guaranteed every time. The efforts being put into Pathfinder programmes and the work of the Joint Prison Probation Accreditation Panel would not be inimical to such an approach to programme delivery. Indeed, this kind of approach seems to be currently envisaged in a Pathfinder Programme for one-to-one work; the Priestley 1:1 programme is noted to have the 'potential for a cost-effective multi-media version which could be self-administered' (Home Office 1999).

Second, accountability has become a pressing concern in the Probation Service for various reasons to do with efficiency, effectiveness and value-for-money. The need to account for how one spends one's work time becomes ever important, and while the question of the effectiveness of individual probation officers has never been openly posed it is surely only a matter of time before this particular nettle is grasped. It is quite possible that the work of probation staff could be subject to regular monitoring in order to assess effectiveness; it is already recorded on video in order to check on the delivery of cognitive behavioural programmes. Such a record would not only have implications for management, but could change the work of the Probation Inspectorate who would no longer have to visit probation areas and sit in on sessions with offenders. Indeed, if all files and documents were to be kept electronically rather than on paper (and it is surely only a matter of time before this happens), the nature of inspections would change completely.

Third, probation officers are moving slowly but inexorably towards becoming case managers and technology will contribute towards this by making it easier to keep tabs on offenders as they participate in various specialised activities and programmes. While data exchange protocols can mean lengthy discussion with other agencies (criminal justice as well as non-criminal justice), technically it has become a simple matter to pass on information quickly. This could speed up risk assessment and the preparation of pre-sentence reports.

A final key issue for new technologies and the future of community penalties is training. What do the new training courses for potential probation officers (and we should not ignore the training needs of probation service officers who are taking on increasing responsibilities for offenders) offer in the way of education in the possibilities of new technology? Is this material adequate? If probation staff (and sentencers) are not trained to understand the potential of new technologies and how these might be utilised to make community penalties more effective without any negative effects (e.g. one might achieve low reconviction rates at a high financial cost and an unacceptable level of surveillance and intrusion), then the full benefits of technological developments will not be realised. This might have implications for offenders, but will also have implications for the Probation Service itself and community penalties. There has always been something old-fashioned about the probation order and the idea of supervision, although this has been breaking down recently. If probation staff are unable or unwilling to confront the opportunities offered by new technologies they will almost certainly be condemning themselves to a backwater. And there will be no shortage of other organisations or agencies offering themselves to develop and operate community penalties as the example of electronic monitoring shows.

Conclusions

The challenge of new technology to community penalties and the Probation Service is considerable. The spirit and traditions of probation work would seem to be at odds with the kind of vision associated with new technology – mechanical, inhuman, uncaring. But there is no reason why the Service should remain trapped by outmoded traditions; that such technology is already being used in association with probation work is only too evident with the Curfew Order and Home Detention Curfews. This could quite easily spread to becoming an integral part of the Probation Order, Community Service and the Combination Order. New community penalties might be developed based purely on surveillance – the Curfew Order is only a small step in this direction – and this may happen sooner rather than later if the ambitious 'What Works' initiative is found to have failed in a few years time. Some of the issues that would require consideration have been discussed above, but in this concluding section I wish to note briefly several other matters relating to the use of new technology and community penalties.

Richard Jones has already pointed to the potential for exclusion to be used as punishment (Jones 2000) by the use of CCTV, smart cards and electronic monitoring. Offenders are already excluded in many ways – they tend to be poor, unemployed, have low educational attainments, are badly housed or even homeless – and to further exclude them as a form of punishment would go against the grain of government thinking. It would also go against the deepest principles of probation work, which has always struggled to reintegrate offenders into their 'communities'. And it would be profoundly ironic if new technology were to be used to further exclude a group of people who are already excluded from the possible benefits of such technology.

While we currently see widespread development of CCTV systems across the country as a whole, their impact upon crime and community safety remains unclear. Indeed, the possible cultural impact of living in a society where we are constantly 'on camera' has not been seriously debated. The potential for dehumanisation, objectification, distancing and categorisation in new technology is considerable and we should not simply see it as a positive advance. The final scene of Francis Ford Coppola's 'The Conversation', where Gene Hackman as Harry Caul ('Harry's the best bugger in the business') literally tears his apartment apart in a desperate and unsuccessful effort to find an electronic bug may be prescient. In this kind of scenario *Quis custodiet custodies* becomes a critical question.

It is also worth remembering that technology does not come to us without a context. For the Probation Service, technology will arrive in a political context and an economic context; it may be further wrapped in moral and personal contexts. Thus the technology itself is mediated by other factors and these are likely to be at least as important as the technology in determining how the package is received. Much more careful work will be required of the Home Office in 'selling' new technology to the Probation Service.

Finally, the role of the new National Probation Service will be crucial. This development will undoubtedly lead to greater consistency and systematisation in community penalties; this has been an ongoing theme of policy for some years, but it will be accelerated by the existence of a national service. Probation work will become more visible and it would be wise to be more proactive about new technology. One of the first tasks of the Director of the Service should be to convene a working group to consider new technology and its applications to community penalties. Such a group could consider the potential uses of pieces of new technology as well as the overall impact of this on community penalties. Certain limited uses of CCTV or video is unlikely to change the fundamental nature of probation work but there will come a point when an increased level of technology will change the nature of such work, and this would have serious implications for offenders, probation staff and sentencers.

At the present time, the future of community penalties does not depend on new technology but this is becoming an increasingly significant factor and developments will need constant monitoring by those responsible for running such penalties. Community penalties are a key part of the sentencing framework of the courts and while ten years ago in this country new technology may not have been seen as having much of a contribution to make in this field, it is now clear that this is not the case. Community penalties and new technology cannot be left to make fragmented and partial accommodations to each other; if this happens both are likely to suffer and it will be offenders who lose out.

References

Aubrey, R. and Hough, M. (1997) *Assessing Offenders' Needs: Assessment Scales for the Probation Service*. Home Office Research Study No.166. London: Home Office.

Cochran, D., Corbett, R.P. and Byrne, J.M. (1986) 'Intensive Probation Supervision in Massachusetts: a Case Study in Change', *Federal Probation*, 50 (2), 32–41.

Department of Trade and Industry (2000) *Foresight Crime Prevention Panel: Just Around the Corner – a Consultation Document*. London: Department of Trade and Industry.

Guardian, 21 August 2000 'Postcode Sentencing'.

Guardian, 25 September 2000 'Surveillance Curbs on Young Offenders'.

Home Office (1984) *Probation Service in England and Wales: Statement of National Objectives and Priorities*. London: Home Office.

Home Office (1988) *Punishment, Custody and the Community*. London: Home Office.

Home Office (1998) *Joining Forces to Protect the Public – Prisons-Probation: A Consultation Document*. London: Home Office.

Home Office (1999) *Probation Circular 35/1999: Crime Reduction Programme – Pathfinder Selection*. London: Home Office.

Independent, 24 July 1995 'Prison is not a Numbers Game'.

Jones, R. (2000) 'Digital Rule: Punishment, Control and Technology', *Punishment and Society*, 2 (1), 5–22.

Mair, G. (1989) 'Some Implications of the Use of Predictive Scales by the Probation Service', in G. Mair (ed.) *Risk Prediction and Probation: Papers from a Research and Planning Unit Workshop*. Research and Planning Unit Paper 56. London: Home Office.

Mair, G. (1996) 'Developments in Probation in England and Wales 1984–1993', in G. McIvor (ed.) *Working with Offenders*. London: Jessica Kingsley.

Mair, G. (1998) 'The Electronic Monitoring of Offenders in England and Wales, 1988–1998', *Journal of Offender Monitoring*, 11 (3), 21–23.

Mair, G. (2000) 'Research on Community Penalties', in R. King and E. Wincup (eds) *Doing Research on Crime and Justice*. Oxford: Oxford University Press.

Mair, G. and Mortimer, E. (1996) *Curfew Orders with Electronic Monitoring*. Home Office Research Study No.163. London: Home Office.

Mair, G. and Nee, C. (1990) *Electronic Monitoring: The Trials and their Results*. Home Office Research Study No.120. London: HMSO.

Mortimer, E. and May, C. (1997) *Electronic Monitoring in Practice: the Second Year of the Trials of Curfew Orders*. Home Office Research Study No.177. London: Home Office.

Mortimer, E., Pereira, E. and Walter, I. (1999) *Making the Tag Fit: Further Analysis from the First Two Years of the Trials of Curfew Orders*. Home Office Research Finding No.105. London: Home Office.

Nellis, M. (1991) 'The Electronic Monitoring of Offenders in England and Wales: recent developments and future prospects', *British Journal of Criminology*, 31 (2), 165–185.

Sunday Mirror, 29 November 1998, 'X=(31–a) – (b+c) + ($\sqrt{d \div (e + 5)}$ × 75) ± f. It's the Magic Formula to Get Out of Jail Free.'

Whitfield, D. (1997) *Tackling the Tag: The Electronic Monitoring of Offenders*. Winchester: Waterside Press.

Chapter 10

Community penalties and social integration: 'community' as solution and as problem

Peter Raynor

When I was invited to contribute this chapter to an examination of the relationship between 'community safety' and 'community justice', my first reaction was that both terms seem to have the kind of inexact and disputed meaning that characteristically accompanies the word 'community'. We all like to use the word, generally in a positive way, and there is a constant risk that we will imagine we mean the same thing when in reality we could be unwittingly following completely different paths in a network of concepts which may be only loosely related. Taking just a few examples from the field of social policy, we might mean 'not in institutions' (as in 'care in the community' or 'community nurse'), or 'in small institutions rather than large ones' ('care in the community' again), or 'provided largely by non-professionals organised on a neigh-bourhood basis' (as in 'community social work'). In our own field we have 'community sentences' (meaning outside prison), 'community policing' (meaning more communication between the police and the public) and many others. The very popularity of the word stands as a warning that it is expected to carry the weight of many different and perhaps conflicting expectations. As Robert Pinker put it in a discussion of 'community social work':

> It is one of the most stubbornly persistent illusions in social policy studies that eventually the concept of community – as a basis of shared values – will resolve all our policy dilemmas. The very fact that this notion is cherished from left to right across the political spectrum makes it highly suspect.
>
> (Barclay 1992: 241)

(It is of course unusual these days to refer to social work when discussing probation in England and Wales, but it would be less unusual in most of the rest of Europe, or indeed the rest of the British Isles. It is far from clear who represents the mainstream on this issue.)

Other usages of 'community' seem to refer more to an ideal of community to which we aspire, and which we hope to achieve as a result of various kinds of social or political change effort (as in 'community development', or communitarianism). This usage is often enriched with a heavy dose of nostalgia for real or imagined communities of the past. The essential distinction we often fail to make is between the descriptive use of 'community' to refer simply to existing living arrangements outside institutions, and its normative use to advocate a greater degree of cooperation, social bonding and mutual help. The rhetorical force of appeals to 'community' sometimes depends on confusing these two, and we need to bear this distinction in mind throughout this discussion. 'Community' has even been described as an aerosol word, which we spray over social problems in the hope that it will make them disappear. Policies based on an appeal to idealised 'community' may fail in the real community because the necessary social resources and relationships are not available; conversely, policies may gain support and popularity by exploiting the rhetoric of 'community' to appeal to diverse audiences with different preoccupations and interests. A clear example of this is the broad appeal of the Community Service Order, to which I will return later. Both our themes in this session, 'community safety' and 'community justice', lend themselves to discussion based on various mixtures of actual, potential and ideal 'community'. In an attempt to limit the risks presented by venturing into this minefield, I am focusing my contribution on three questions which I think are particularly relevant to the development of 'community' penalties and probation in Britain:

1 How far do current initiatives based on effective supervision practice, risk assessment and 'What Works' threaten the principles of proportionality and desert which were fundamental to the vision of 'justice' embodied in the 1991 Criminal Justice Act?

2 How far do 'community justice' concepts such as restorative approaches or social integration offer a practical alternative?

3 Are there ways of understanding and presenting rehabilitative community penalties within the restorative 'community justice' paradigm which might confer greater perceived legitimacy and support?

'What Works' and just deserts

To begin to address the first question, it is now clear that Home Office policy for the new National Probation Service will give high priority to the development of new evidence-based forms of supervision which will be effective in reducing offending (Chapman and Hough 1998). Indeed this policy extends across the whole correctional field, embracing programmes offered to prisoners, and supported by an accreditation process to encourage the use of programmes which are likely to be effective and an evaluation strategy to see whether reductions in offending and other desirable changes actually result. This linked development and evaluation process is driven in the Probation Service by a series of 'pathfinders' or demonstration projects which are intended to build into a national curriculum of tested approaches to all the common forms of offending behaviour. This is linked to new investment in staffing and training to enable probation services to deliver the curriculum, and to numerical targets for the throughput of offenders in accredited programmes and for the anticipated reductions in reconviction rates (What Works Strategy Group 2000). The policy and research frameworks are consistent with those adopted for the government's wide-ranging Crime Reduction Programme (the research base of which was summarised in Goldblatt and Lewis 1998), and current pathfinder projects cover group programmes in probation orders, new approaches to Community Service, basic employment-related skills training for offenders, and the 'resettlement' of short-term prisoners.

Evaluative research on all these is under way at the moment, as has been summarised in the Introduction, so I do not need to elaborate. Accredited programmes, mainly using a cognitive-behavioural approach, already exist on quite a wide scale in the prison system, while some probation service programmes have recently achieved accredited status. Both prison and probation services have been set quite ambitious targets for the number of offenders completing accredited programmes (for example, the current target for probation services is 60,000 offenders completing accredited programmes in 2003–4), and this in itself will tend to increase the range of programmes developed, including programmes designed for individual rather than group delivery, and programmes based on community service as well as on probation orders. It is envisaged that half of the 60,000 target will be met through completions of accredited forms of Community Service, and discussions are already under way about how to identify and incorporate various possible components of effective practice into community service provision (Rex and Clark 2000).

As a member of the Joint Prisons and Probation Accreditation Panel I am finding this whole development process extremely interesting, not least because it is still based on quite a limited amount of evidence regarding the effectiveness of probation programmes in Britain (see, for example, Underdown 1998: chapter 9). I unreservedly welcome the official commitment to giving effective practice a chance and to a fully evaluated implementation process, even if the effects of some of this may be difficult to disentangle from other initiatives such as a much stricter approach to enforcement embodied in the new National Standards (Home Office 2000a). This stricter approach is meant to increase public confidence, but is based on a political perception rather than on research into likely positive or negative effects (see Ellis 2000). The principle of letting evidence guide policy clearly does not yet extend to all issues, but in the long run the evidence-based approach only makes sense if it is followed consistently rather than over-ridden by short-term political or presentational issues. However, for the purposes of this chapter I do not intend to attempt a detailed discussion of the nature and consequences of the 'What Works' initiative, but simply to explore two areas where it poses particular questions in relation to just deserts and proportionality: namely, the renewed popularity of the idea of flexible sentencing, and the impact of new forms of risk assessment.

The Home Office has recently announced a wide-ranging review of sentencing policy; one reason for this seems to be that the emergence of effective programmes is leading some people to think about a more flexible sentencing framework, in which the implementation of a sentence could reflect the offender's participation in approved pro-grammes or his or her response to them. This is related to the widely discussed possibility of a 'seamless sentence' for short-term prisoners, in which a period of custody will be combined with a period of supervised release, but the precise point of release may depend on various indi-vidual characteristics or behaviour or response to 'treatment'. According to the Home Office website, 'the review will identify and evaluate new more flexible frameworks for sentence decision-making and sentence management, which join up custodial and community sentences' (Home Office 2000b). There are several reasons why such flexible approaches to sentencing are beginning (again) to seem attractive, in addition to the restoration of some confidence in rehabilitative processes. The reasons include a penal environment in which, since 1992, much larger numbers of prisoners have been subject to compulsory post-release supervision and are in effect serving a mixed custodial and community-based sentence (Maguire and Raynor 1997); they may also include the dis-appointment of a generation of policy-makers and practitioners who hoped that the 'just deserts' framework embodied in the 1991 Criminal Justice Act would lead to long-term reductions in imprisonment.

The review may even contain traces of the traditional argument between executive and judiciary about who controls criminal justice. However, those who remember the consequences of social workers' unfettered discretion in the heavily custodial juvenile justice system of the 1970s (Morris and Giller 1983), or the perceived inequity of many parole decisions prior to the Carlisle Report (Home Office 1988), will be concerned (in my view rightly concerned) at the prospect of offenders having their sentences extended in order to be required to undertake programmes from which they might or might not benefit, or indeed having their sentences effectively shortened in response to some official judgement of 'good progress', with all the potential for arbitrariness and discrimination that such processes involve.

Another area of concern about justice is presented by the growing reliance on risk assessment and classification by risk to guide decision-making in criminal justice. Risk-based decision-making is widely seen as an important part of the new evidence-based approach and as a significant contributor to community safety; for example, the targeting of effective rehabilitative programmes is informed by the 'risk principle' that they are unlikely to have beneficial effects on low-risk offenders (Andrews *et al* 1990), while policing and crime prevention are also increasingly concentrated where assessed risks are high (see, for example, Cheney *et al* 1997). The 'What Works' movement in British probation has been associated with rapid development in risk assessment and prediction, first in the form of reconviction predictors based on 'static' risk factors (currently the Offender Group Reconviction Scale version 2: Taylor 1999) and later in the form of 'risk/need assessments' incorporating 'dynamic' risk factors. Static risk factors are characteristics of a person or his or her history which are related to the risk of offending but cannot be changed by intervention, e.g. age, sex and criminal record. Dynamic risk factors are those which are related to the risk of offending but are also potentially subject to change, such as problems of environment or resources, education, employment, associates, family life, attitudes, beliefs. These are also known as 'criminogenic needs', hence risk/need assessment, also known as third-generation risk assessment (Bonta 1996).

Interest in risk/need assessment in British probation services has concentrated mainly on three instruments: the established Canadian 'Level of Service Inventory – Revised' (LSI–R) (Andrews and Bonta 1995), the locally developed 'Assessment, Case Management and Evaluation' system (ACE) (Roberts *et al* 1996) and the Home Office's own instrument, still in development, the Offender Assessment System (OASys) (OASys Project Team 1999). LSI–R and ACE have been evaluated in their probation applications (Raynor *et al* 2000) and evaluation of OASys is awaited. The use of an effective risk/need assessment system is regarded as an essential underpinning for the 'What Works' developments in prisons and particularly probation, since it offers the possibility of matching programmes or supervision to offenders' assessed needs and can also be used on a repeated basis to produce at least approximate measurement of changes in risk during (or as a result of) supervision. However, serious concerns have also been expressed about the possible long-term impact of these new technologies of risk, not simply in terms of their contribution to a general preoccupation with risk in late modern society (Beck 1992) but also in relation to three specific issues. These concern the possible erosion of accepted standards of justice and civil rights; the possible misclassification of women offenders and of members of ethnic minorities; and the danger that because they identify adverse social and environmental factors as increasing the risk, they could lead to more severe punishment and coercive control for the poor simply because the poor already experience more disadvantages.

All of these criticisms raise serious concerns about justice. The first is particularly associated with the work of Feeley and Simon (1992), who point to the possibility of 'actuarial justice' in which the relative severity of penalties and level of surveillance or coercion is determined not by desert but by membership of groups with a low or high assessed risk of offending. Other critics have focussed on the application to women and ethnic minorities of predictive instruments based primarily on research about white male offenders (Shaw and Hannah-Moffat 2000). It is argued that this can lead to the overprediction of risk, the inclusion of irrelevant risk factors, or a failure to focus on significant needs of women or minorities which are less prevalent among white males. More generally, critical criminologists such as Hudson (1996) have argued that because indicators of risk include adverse social circumstances to which the poor are differentially exposed, the adoption of apparently 'scientific' and 'neutral' risk assessment methods can result simply in the increasing criminalisation and incarceration of the disadvantaged. It is difficult to give adequate weight and attention to all these important criticisms within the scope of a short chapter, but it is arguable that some of the research on risk/needs assessment offers some partial re-assurance, or at least points the way to some possible safeguards.

For example, the recent evaluative work in probation services suggests that risk/need assessment techniques are actually being used to support rehabilitation. In other words, identification of a need as a risk factor can actually increase the chance that somebody does something to address the need, and that offenders' lives improve as a result, together with a real reduction in their average risk of reconviction (Raynor *et al* 2000). Of course this happens only with assessment instruments which include dynamic factors. The implication is that provided they are used as designed to support decisions about rehabilitative services, the risk of an unwitting disservice to offenders may be reduced. For example, the LSI–R Manual (Andrews and Bonta 1995) points out that 'the instrument was designed to assist in the implementation of the least restrictive and least onerous interpretation of a criminal sanction, and to identify dynamic areas of risk/need that may be addressed by programming in order to reduce risk'; it was not designed to determine the appropriate sentence. In a society which is generally hostile to offenders we may have to relabel their needs as risk factors in order to persuade policy-makers to take their needs seriously. However, good intentions in the design and the manual need to be supported by continuing quality control in implementation. Also, such instruments are widely used in some countries to influence the level of security to which a prisoner is allocated, and there have been reports of the use of LSI–R in Britain to assist in decisions about which prisoners can safely be released on 'home detention curfew' (i.e. electronically tagged early release). These practices lie much closer to the territory of 'actuarial justice'.

The argument that models of risk assessment based on white male majorities in offending populations can disadvantage women and ethnic minorities is the subject of lively debate, which is reviewed by Loraine Gelsthorpe in chapter 8. There is also a limited amount of research which tends to support a degree of cross-cultural validity in well-designed assessment instruments (see, for example, Bonta 1993) but this tends to be concerned with broad predictive validity rather than with the fine detail of assessments. What is also clear is that both women offenders and ethnic minority offenders tend to experience patterns of disadvantage, discrimination or abuse which are likely to be different from those experienced by white male offenders, and are likely to be under-researched precisely because they affect a minority of the offending population available for research. This clearly runs the risk of reinforcing social injustice, also evident when, for example, effective programmes in a probation area are based on groupwork with men and are denied to women because there are never enough of them to form a group. (The emergence of effective programmes for individualized delivery may help, but the practice described still seems quite common.)

It is not feasible for criminal justice policies or practices to try to correct general inequalities in society which require a much broader approach, and the risk assessment methods which correctly identify the greater social difficulties faced by people in poverty are not responsible for creating those difficulties. It is questionable whether we would prefer decisions to be made without knowing anything about the social difficulties offenders face, and the practice of sentencing the poor as if they had the same opportunities as the rich to lead crime-free lives has been rightly criticised, sometimes by the same commentators who express reservations about risk assessment (for example, Hudson 1987). Risk/need assessment can open the way to effective help, not simply to graduated degrees of coercive control. However, it would be pointless to deny that the danger of 'actuarial justice' exists, and the possibility of basing sentences on likely future behaviour as well as past behaviour is one aspect of the new interest in 'flexible' sentencing.

In these circumstances it is salutary to remember the arguments which until very recently held almost undisputed sway in favour of 'just deserts' approaches to sentencing, with perhaps limited exceptions allowed (as in the 1991 Act) in respect of the demonstrably dangerous. A sense of legitimacy in sentencing depends partly on perceived fairness and compatibility with common-sense moral assumptions such as desert; the dangers inherent in unfettered flexibility and uncontrolled official discretion are no less important today than when pointed out by leading commentators over twenty years ago (for example Hood 1974, von Hirsch 1976). Even well-intentioned penalties should be limited to what the offence merits. These arguments still imply that it would be unjust to extend a sentence in order to require somebody to attend even an evidence-based programme, particularly as the evidence can never point to more than the probability that benefit might result. It does not guarantee the benefit in the individual case; nor does risk assessment provide accurate predictions of individual behaviour, only of the aggregate behaviour of groups of similar individuals. A more defensible approach is to see rehabilitative penalties as 'packages' which have both size and contents (Raynor 1993). The 'size' (i.e. the extent to which they restrict the liberty of the offender) should normally be determined by desert or, in 1991 Act language, by the seriousness of the offence. The 'contents' (i.e. the nature of the supervision programme, the work to be done by the offender, the skills to be acquired or problems to be addressed) should normally be determined by needs relevant to the offending behaviour, or in 1991 language 'suitability'. This kind of framework (see also Raynor and Vanstone 1994) would at least help to set some appropriate limits to enthusiastic intervention prompted by new evidence of potential effectiveness.

However, the very fact that policies such as flexible sentencing are again attracting serious attention is a measure of how the appeal of 'just deserts' arguments has been weakened by their perceived results. A framework which allows us to think about the rank ordering of penalties but offers little guidance about their absolute severity seems to have been vulnerable to a punitive drift in response to populist pressures in several countries, most notably the United States but also England and Wales. As we have already noted in the discussion of risk/need assessment above, just deserts theories have been criticised (for example by Hudson 1987, 1993) for underplaying relevant social factors and adding to the disadvantages of the poor, and also for ignoring differences between individuals or social groups in their opportunities to avoid crime, which should be relevant to a moral assessment of their blameworthiness if they commit crimes (Hudson 1998; Raynor 1980, 1997). Popular dissatisfaction with criminal justice reflects not just ignorance about it (Mattinson and Mirrlees-Black 2000) but a perception that it does not adequately respond to people's fears and needs, and does not reflect the 'community's' values and concerns about crime.

Although it seems probable that more general fears and insecurities resulting from broader social changes are helping to fuel public anger about crime, the perceived demand for greater severity and the consequent pressure on politicians and sentencers have not been successfully restrained by a sentencing framework which aims to deliver 'just deserts'. This suggests that the aim of developing a sentencing system which would be compatible with the 'community's' shared values and assumptions has not been achieved by 'just deserts', and we may need to consider other ways to enhance the perceived legitimacy of criminal justice processes. This brings me to my second question: can we find an alternative basis for fair penal practice and an alternative rationale for effective penalties in the cluster of ideas represented by 'community justice'?

Restoration, integration and the community ideal

'Community justice' and associated ideas such as restorative justice, reparation, relational justice and reintegrative shaming have been written about so widely and so persuasively, particularly by active reformers such as Braithwaite (1989), that it would be absurd and inappropriate to attempt any kind of comprehensive coverage here. Instead I will try to draw out some considerations that seem to be particularly relevant to thinking about community safety and community penalties. Restorative justice in particular seems to be an international focus for creative and optimistic thinking: at the recent United Nations Congress on the Prevention of Crime and the Treatment of Offenders in Vienna, restorative justice was by far the most discussed approach to sentencing, but the discussion centred more on its values and social purposes than on its beneficial results, which were largely taken for granted. To take just one example, the Friends World Committee for Consultation submitted a paper which argued that:

> The Quaker belief that there is intrinsic value in everyone calls for a vision of justice that maximizes the opportunities for trans-formation, forgiveness and reconciliation. Fundamental to these processes is healing of the damage that is both cause and effect of crimes … We believe that through restorative processes we can build stronger communities and peaceful societies.
>
> (Friends' World Committee 2000)

To take some other examples, Marshall's recent overview of restorative justice research for the Home Office (Marshall 1999) finds a good deal of evidence that participants in restorative processes usually (not always) welcome them and often rate them as more satisfactory than conventional criminal justice processes, but finds as yet much less evidence of a reductive impact on future offending. The reasons for advocating restorative justice approaches often seem to lie in their perceived moral appropriateness or presumed educative effects on participants, but some other claimed advantages are less clear: for example, as Haines pointedly asks, what exactly is restorative justice seeking to restore? (Haines 1998).

Some similar issues have arisen in respect of social reintegration in the current Home Office research on the 'resettlement' of short-term prisoners. The term 'resettlement' has been devised to replace the old-fashioned terms 'through-care' and 'after-care', apparently in obedience to a political belief that even if criminal justice services do care for offenders, this should not be advertised too openly. However, for many short-term prisoners 'resettlement' seems an inappropriate term, as they were not very settled in the first place: the aim can hardly be to restore them to a pre-sentence situation which was deprived, criminogenic and generally disadvantageous. A more appropriate strategy would be to seek to involve them in a new set of pro-social linkages, resources and opportunities; this is certainly a strategy for social integration or inclusion, but it is not resettlement or reintegration. Instead it is intervention to try to bring about a new and more constructive state of affairs. This is perhaps a clue to the meaning of 'community' in the network of reintegrative ideas surrounding 'community justice': community is being used in its ideal and aspirational sense, as in the Friends' statement quoted above. 'Community justice' is connected with the struggle to develop and improve communities, and to promote a better quality of community living with more cooperation, more mutual aid and more collective problem-solving. It points to an improved standard of social conduct and pro-social opportunities, and it promotes forms of criminal justice practice which are seen as consistent with these.

Real communities, on the other hand, may be divided, hostile, stratified, prejudiced, exclusive, in active internal conflict or simply not characterized by any high level of social interaction between their supposed 'members'. They may be candidates for improvement, but the improvement is still in the future. As Zedner and Lacey's research on the idea of community in British and German criminal justice policy has shown, even within criminal justice discourse the same word can carry a very different set of associations and assumptions, depending on culture, history and tradition: some concepts of 'community' may be much less welcoming to perceived 'outsiders' than others (Zedner and Lacey 1995). In many actual communities, justice under the control of the community is an unattractive option (the recent anti-paedophile riots have provided a graphic illustration of this). Instead, criminal justice processes perhaps need largely to remain under accountable professional control but also to act as a focus for communication with the 'community' or sections of it, with the aspiration that this may eventually lead to more appropriate community involvement in helping to handle the problems arising from crime. 'Community justice' involves a normative concept of community which is worth pursuing where possible for the sake of the values it represents, but whether restorative processes can really replace conventional criminal justice and move 'from margins to mainstream' (Restorative Justice Consortium 2000) seems to depend on the availability of a quality of community life which is far from universal.

Other formulations of a possible inclusive basis for criminal justice policy and practice have relied less on the questionable notion of 'community' and more on notions of interconnectedness or mutual concern. For example, Smith's discussion of socially inclusive approaches to social work with offenders (Smith 1998) points to the potential of 'peacemaking criminology' (Pepinsky and Quinney 1991) to inform the development of practical approaches to problem-solving and conflict-resolution which encourage dialogue, involvement and connectedness, and seek to promote social solidarity and social justice. This is not an argument that 'community' necessarily already exemplifies these qualities, but that we should look for practical opportunities to promote them.

In a similar vein, feminist commentators on criminal justice have pointed to different ways of doing justice: Heidensohn (1986) has written of 'Portia' and 'Persephone' models, in which the former represents an approach governed by formal rules and the latter is guided more by situational thinking, needs, relationships and an ethic of care (see also Masters and Smith 1998). Daly (1989) has pointed out that both these approaches clearly exist even within the current masculine-oriented criminal justice system, and are not straightforwardly identifiable simply as male and female ways of thinking: perhaps the practical problem is how to influence the balance of these approaches, as well as ensuring that those who are presently ill-served by criminal justice get a better deal. What these ideas have in common (put in a slightly different voice) is that they encourage pro-social approaches to resolving problems, drawing on positive forms of community involvement to do so. Pro-social orientations, processes and outcomes can be expected to reinforce pro-social learning and lead to more of the same. People are both individual subjects with individual moral responsibility, and social beings constructed by their group memberships, their relationships, their inclusion, their interdependency and their joint commitments. Just deserts concentrate on the first of these aspects, but community justice, like effective rehabilitation, needs to address the second. However, the pro-social values which lie at the heart of the community justice movement bring me straight to my third question: can we identify a moral basis and rationale for community penalties which could give them greater legitimacy and support?

Rehabilitating rehabilitation

The view that the public has 'lost confidence' in probation or community sentences has been repeated so often by politicians that it must be partly true by now, whether or not it was true originally. The same can be said of large parts of the criminal justice process. Various strategies have been advanced to correct this state of affairs, some of them highly damaging, like 'prison works' and populist punitiveness. More constructively, 'what works' and evidence-based practice have been identified as the central element in the rehabilitation of the Probation Service: the Chief Inspector of Probation has stated that 'there is no alternative to the pursuit and implementation of what works. It is no exaggeration to say the future health and existence of the Probation Service depends upon it' (HM Inspectorate of Probation 2000). I agree that it is of central importance, and represents a significant challenge to the Service. What is perhaps more doubtful is whether it will by itself quickly deliver a change in public perception. The target of a five per cent reduction in reconvictions of those supervised by the probation or prison services is estimated to represent approximately a one per cent fall in crime, which may well seem less dramatic to the public than it seems to professionals who know how difficult it is to achieve any improvement. Arguments in favour of community penalties also need to take account of the community safety implications of incapacitation (Pease 1999), which prison offers on a more reliable basis in the short term.

One possibility worth considering is that public support for effective rehabilitation and community sentences (in other words, a favourable context for delivering 'what works') depends on encouraging a perception that rehabilitation is not simply something for offenders, but has general value to the community in other ways. The vision of social possibilities and social solidarity which underpins the aspirations of 'community justice' actually suggests a number of ways in which the rationale of community penalties might be aligned with widely-shared notions of justice. Briefly, the moral ideas underlying restorative justice seem to have wide appeal as a potentially constructive way of dealing with a crime. While punishment inflicts disadvantages on the offender to cancel out the fact that he or she has taken an unfair advantage over the victim, restorative justice requires the offender to do some good as atonement for having done harm. Probation needs to find ways of realizing this vision on a large scale, not simply in a few experimental restorative justice projects but as a central and consistent theme of what it seeks to achieve on the community's behalf. The long-lasting and widespread appeal of Community Service confirms the attractiveness of the restorative principle. Community safety might conceivably be achieved, at least in the short term, by excluding and controlling offenders, but community justice would prefer to include and change them.

Instead of rehabilitative programmes being seen primarily as a benefit to offenders, and therefore arguably unfair to those facing similar difficulties who have not offended, we should try to understand rehabilitation as work that offenders undertake as a consequence of a crime: work which is directed to changing their own behaviour and attitudes in a more pro-social direction. A rehabilitative penalty can reflect the interests and values of the wider community and perhaps equip offenders with skills to maintain themselves more effectively and to contribute more to society. The notion of rehabilitation as offenders working to rehabilitate themselves may be better aligned with community values than the notion of offenders simply receiving help, and it may also be more constructive than the attempt to improve public confidence by more rigorous approaches to enforcement.

However, there is a risk that this conceptual shift, important though it is, may look simply like repackaging rather than rethinking, 'more spin than substance'. A more concrete way to embody these principles might be to seek to include an explicitly reparative element in every community sentence, or at least in all those which are substantial enough to warrant the delivery of an accredited programme. Community Service is already the most conspicuously restorative penalty, and the incorporation of reparative elements in other programmes might confer a greater perceived legitimacy on them. In a recent article Hans Toch has argued that the involvement of offenders in altruistic activities can be seen as a form of 'correctional treatment' in itself, offering 'a sense of accomplishment, grounded increments in self-esteem, meaningful purposiveness and obvious restorative implications. Altruistic activity can contribute to cognitive restructuring.... ' (Toch 2000). The reparative element need not be large in all cases, and although not resource-neutral it might not be hugely expensive, particularly in a context where probation service resources are once again growing rapidly. It might also be unnecessary in those cases where probation orders are still made for 'welfare' reasons. What is important is that it should be noticeable by those to whom it matters.

One possible way of achieving this might be to involve victims, if they wished, in the choice of rehabilitative work to be carried out by the offender. This seems more constructive than some other suggestions for involving victims, such as 'victim statements' which have limited influence and effect (Hoyle *et al* 1999). Tendencies to vindictiveness or unrealistic expectations could be controlled by offering a choice between possibilities which had already been assessed as suitable and feasible, and victims would be able to indicate which of the proposed alternatives offered, in their view, the most constructive reparation. Admittedly these proposals involve some blurring of distinctions between other community penalties and Community Service, but this is already happening through the importation of rehabilitative components and goals into community service; it should still be possible to distinguish between sentences which are primarily reparative and those in which reparation is an element in a wider rehabilitative process. Involving victims in selecting relevant reparation might also avoid offenders being set to work improving another neighbourhood when the victim's own neighbourhood needs the input more, or being avoidably allocated placements with voluntary bodies or church-based organisations of which the victim does not particularly approve. The central point, however, is to demonstrate that rehabilitation is itself fundamentally restorative and benefits the community as well as the offender.

The combination of visible reparation and effective programmes could bring together the community safety and community justice agendas in a particularly constructive way, and could underline the benefits to real communities which flow from the effective rehabilitation of their offenders. Some similar arguments have been advanced by Todd Clear and his colleagues in relation to reintegrative community justice initiatives in the USA (see, for example, Clear *et al* 2000) and they deserve attention both from those developing evidence-based practice and from those looking for a coherent and accessible value-base for the new Probation Service.

References

Andrews, D.A. and Bonta, J. (1995) *The Level of Service Inventory-Revised Manual.* Toronto: Multi-Health Systems Inc.

Andrews, D.A., Zinger, I., Hoge, R.D., Bonta, J., Gendreau, P. and Cullen, F.T. (1990) 'Does Correctional Treatment Work? A Clinically Relevant and Psychologically Informed Meta-analysis', *Criminology*, 28, 369–404.

Barclay, P. (Chair of the Working Party on the Role and Tasks of Social Workers) (1992) *Social Workers: their Role and Tasks.* London: Bedford Square Press.

Beck, U. (1992) *Risk Society.* London: Sage

Bonta, J. (1993) 'A Summary of Research Findings on the LSI'. Ottawa: unpublished.

Bonta, J. (1996) 'Risk-needs Assessment and Treatment', in A. Harland (ed.) *Choosing Correctional Options that Work.* London: Sage, 18–32.

Braithwaite, J. (1989) *Crime, Shame and Reintegration.* Cambridge: Cambridge University Press.

Chapman, T. and Hough, M. (1998) *Evidence Based Practice.* London: Home Office.

Cheney, S., Holt, J. and Pease, K. (1997) *Biting Back II: Reducing Repeat Victimisation in Huddersfield*, Crime Detection and Prevention Series Paper 82, Police Research Group. London: Home Office.

Clear, T., Karp, D. and Bruni, J. (2000) 'Evidence-based Practice: a Survey of Reintegrative Community Justice Initiatives in the USA', Paper Presented to the Probation 2000 Conference, London.

Daly, K. (1989) 'Criminal Justice Ideologies and Practices in Different Voices: some Feminist Questions about Justice', *International Journal of the Sociology of Law*, 17, 1–18.

Ellis, T. (2000) 'Enforcement Policy and Practice: Evidence-Based or Rhetoric-Based?', *Criminal Justice Matters*, 39, 6–8.

Feeley, M. and Simon, J. (1992) 'The New Penology: Notes on the Emerging Strategy of Corrections and its Implications', *Criminology*, 30, 449–474.

Friends World Committee for Consultation (2000) 'Offenders and Victims: Accountability and Fairness in the Justice Process', statement to United Nations Tenth Congress on the Prevention of Crime and the Treatment of Offenders, Vienna 2000.

Goldblatt, P. and Lewis, C. (eds) (1998) 'Reducing Offending', *Research Study No. 187*. London: Home Office.

HM Inspectorate of Probation (2000) *Annual Report 1999–2000*. London: Home Office.

Haines, K. (1998) 'Some Principled Objections to a Restorative Justice Approach to working with juvenile offenders', in L. Walgrave (ed.) *Restorative Justice for Juveniles*. Leuven: Leuven University Press.

Heidensohn, F. (1986) 'Models of justice: Portia or Persephone? Some Thoughts on Equality, Justice, Gender and Fairness in the Field of Criminal Justice', *International Journal of the Sociology of Law*, 14, 187–98.

Home Office (1988) *The Parole System in England and Wales: Report of the Review Committee*, Cmnd 532. London: HMSO.

Home Office (2000a) *The National Standards for the Supervision of Offenders in the Community*, 3rd version. London: Home Office.

Home Office (2000b) *A Review of the Sentencing Framework*. London: Home Office.

Hood, R. (1974) *Tolerance and the Tariff*. London: NACRO.

Hoyle, H., Morgan, R. and Sanders, A. (1999) *The Victim's Charter: an Evaluation of Pilot Projects*, Research Findings 107. London: Home Office.

Hudson, B. (1987) *Justice as Punishment*. Basingstoke: Macmillan.

Hudson, B. (1993) *Penal Policy and Social Justice*. Basingstoke: Macmillan.

Hudson, B. (1996) *Understanding Justice*. Buckingham: Open University Press.

Hudson, B. (1998) 'Doing Justice to Difference', in A. Ashworth and M. Wasik (eds) *Fundamentals of Sentencing Theory*. Oxford: Clarendon Press.

Maguire, M. and Raynor, P. (1997) 'The Revival of Throughcare: Rhetoric and Reality in Automatic Conditional Release', *British Journal of Criminology*, 37, (1), 1–14.

Marshall, T. (1999) *Restorative Justice: an Overview*. London: Home Office.

Masters G. and Smith D. (1998) 'Portia and Persephone Revisited: Thinking about Feeling in Criminal Justice', *Theoretical Criminology*, 2, (1), 5–27.

Mattinson, J. and Mirrlees-Black, C. (2000) *Attitudes to Crime and Criminal Justice: Findings from the 1998 British Crime Survey*, Research Study 200. London: Home Office.

Morris, A. and Giller, H. (eds) (1983) *Providing Criminal Justice for Children*. London: Edward Arnold.

OASys Project Team (1999) *The Offender Assessment System (OASys) Manual*. London: Home Office.

Pease, K. (1999) 'The Probation Career of Al Truism', *Howard Journal* 38 (1), 2–16.

Pepinsky, H. and Quinney, R. (eds) (1991) *Criminology as Peacemaking*. Bloomington: Indiana University Press.

Raynor, P. (1980) 'Is there any Sense in Social Inquiry Reports?', *Probation Journal*, 27, 78–94.

Raynor, P. (1993) *Social Work, Justice and Control*, second edition. London: Whiting and Birch.

Raynor, P. (1997) 'Some Observations on Rehabilitation and Justice', *Howard Journal*, 36, 248–262.

Raynor, P., Roberts, C., Kynch, J. and Merrington, M. (2000) 'Risk and Need Assessment in Probation Services: an Evaluation', *Home Office Research Study No. 211*. London: Home Office.

Raynor, P. and Vanstone, M. (1994) 'Probation Practice, Effectiveness and the Non-Treatment Paradigm', *British Journal of Social Work*, 24 (4), 387–404.

Restorative Justice Consortium (2000) *Restorative Justice from Margins to Mainstream*. London: Restorative Justice Consortium.

Rex, S. and Clark, D. (2000) 'Applying Accreditation Criteria to Community Service', Paper Presented to the Prison/Probation Services Joint Accreditation Panel, unpublished.

Roberts, C., Burnett, R., Kirby, A. and Hamill, H. (1996) *A System for Evaluating Probation Practice*, Probation Studies Unit Report 1. Oxford: Centre for Criminological Research.

Shaw, M. and Hannah-Moffatt, K. (2000) 'Gender, Diversity and Risk Assessment in Canadian Corrections', *Probation Journal* 47 (3), 163–172.

Smith, D. (1998) 'Social Work with Offenders: the Practice of Exclusion and the Potential for Inclusion', in M. Barry and C. Hallett (eds) *Social Exclusion and Social Work*. Lyme Regis: Russell House.

Taylor, R. (1999) *Predicting Reconvictions for Sexual and Violent Offences using the Revised Offender Group Reconviction Scale*, Research Findings 104. London: Home Office.

Toch, H. (2000) 'Altruistic Activity as Correctional Treatment', *International Journal of Offender Therapy and Comparative Criminology*, 44, 270–278.

Underdown, A. (1998) *Strategies for Effective Offender Supervision*. London: Home Office.

von Hirsch, A. (1976) *Doing Justice*. New York: Hill and Wang.

What Works Strategy Group (2000) *A Summary of the What Works Strategy for the Probation Service*. London: Home Office.

Zedner, L. and Lacey, N. (1995) 'Discourses of Community', *Journal of Law and Society*, 22, 301–325.

Chapter 11

What future for 'public safety' and 'restorative justice' in a system of community penalties?

Michael Smith

'Public safety' and 'restorative justice' are big, protean ideas. They have political value as well as substantive merit, which increasingly leads managers of community corrections agencies – and individual probation and parole agents – to try to operationalize and harmonize the ideas in their practice. History suggests that their operational capacity will fall short of what that ambition requires, but that their effort will move the field to a new, perhaps better, but still transitional condition.

To assess the relative merit of these ideas, and their likely futures as animating ideas for a system of community penalties, and to account for their emergence at roughly the same time in the US 'community corrections' field, I must first offer working definitions of them. Then, after examining some of the ways the ideas of public safety and restorative justice seem to conflict with and complement each other, I can speculate about their likely futures. As a preliminary matter, however, I need to explain what I understand a system of community penalties to be.

Some definitions and boundaries

What counts as a 'community penalty'?

At the heart of community penalty systems today, on both sides of the Atlantic, are the myriad conditions attached to sentencing courts' probation orders, and to special-purpose orders for community service, curfew and the like. Of course, a sentencing court imposing conditions of probation or of another community penalty may not believe or intend them to be subjectively or objectively punitive. The court may not be imposing a 'penalty' in that sense at all. In the United States, probation conditions are routinely imposed and executed without intention or expectation of exacting a penalty – they aim at securing treatment for the addiction, illiteracy, homelessness or other deficit the court thinks is causally linked to the offender's offending. And our probation orders defy the 'community penalties' label in other ways: many are served, in part, in custody rather than in the community, as they may require an initial period of local incarceration (more obviously for the punishment of confinement than for the community supervision that follows) and as they very often land the offender in prison for violation of the conditions imposed by the sentencing court. Nevertheless, the probation order – however various its contents, and whether it brings an offender misery or self-realization – is our archetypal 'community penalty' or 'intermediate punishment'.

Why the new terminology? US community corrections managers, and legislative staffers who hope to reduce courts' budget-breaking reliance on prison, have long worried that probation's value in the penal market place is drifting toward zero[1] and, as a consequence, they tend to highlight (and perhaps exaggerate) the penalizing burdens borne by probationers. Many of them are eager to attach the word 'punishment' or 'penalty' to probation programmes and practices, or to their agencies. The word suits retributive themes running strong in our politics today – a politics which has squeezed probation and parole budgets while allocating astonishing sums to the construction and staffing of penal institutions whose business is popularly and politically understood to be punishment.

US community corrections practice has kept pace with the new rhetoric in some places. And, very occasionally, the introduction of a punitive non-custodial sanction, effectively targeted at cases for which little but just deserts was sought by sentencing courts, has displaced from incarceration some (even many) who would otherwise receive routine custodial sentences (see note 4 below). But standard probation supervision in the United States is, in general, so passive and so reactive that claims of punitiveness in its administration cannot bear even casual scrutiny. In many probation areas, punishment is found mainly in the high rates of revocation and imprisonment flowing from such passive 'supervision.'[2]

Nevertheless, I will assume that 'community penalties' covers probation and the other non-financial non-custodial dispositions of successful criminal prosecution. What about parole? Is the post-confinement phase of a custodial sentence also a 'community penalty'? Even when it is styled 'after-care'? I say it is. To exclude it from the analysis obscures strategically important opportunities and dangers ahead.

In the United States, discussions about community corrections – its potential value and its potential demise – are shaped in part by the great variety of institutional arrangements we have for the exercise of non-custodial penal power. In some states, one state-wide agency is responsible for managing probation and parole supervision throughout the jurisdiction – and sometimes it manages the prisons as well. In others, these responsibilities are distributed to two or more state agencies, or to a state agency (for prisons and, perhaps, parole) and to a host of local or regional agencies (for all or some of probation super-vision and, usually, for gaols). These institutional differences seem to matter when states confront questions about how penal power might usefully be extended into communities, and how custodial and non-custodial penal measures ought to be balanced in penal policy. For example, in unified correctional systems such as Wisconsin's, where generic 'community corrections agents' supervise indiscriminately mixed caseloads of probationers and parolees, we tend to ignore the distinction when we ask how those agents might most fairly and effectively supervise offenders. There are two pretty good reasons why we do.

First, whatever operational capacity a community corrections agency has to advance its jurisdiction's interests in public safety, offender accountability, victim and community restoration, and the like, that operational capacity is not likely to differ by the legal status of the offender under its supervision.[3]

Second, if, in supervising parolees (or those released to post-confinement supervision of a different name), a community corrections agency were to discover more valuable ways to deploy its personnel and other resources – deployment that produces more public safety, for example – then shifts in sentencing patterns ought to follow. If post-con-finement supervision were sufficiently active and imaginative to eliminate (or, more likely, make more tolerable) the risk of harm to persons and property posed by some category of offenders recently released from imprisonment, the duration of their confinement and, perhaps, the desirability of it in the first place deserve re-examination – and might get it, given imprisonment's increasing share of the public purse. This point has more importance, of course, when pursuit of public safety figures prominently in the routine sentencing of the offenders in question than when retributive impulses trump any other purpose a sentencing court might have in applying penal measures to them. But I will argue that, for many cases in which retributive claims seem to explain the current custodial/non-custodial distribution of sentences or the length of the custodial sentences imposed, those retributive claims will yield with remarkable ease when a court becomes convinced that other important purposes can be achieved at sentencing.[4]

In any event, to make the points I wish to make, I must include parole supervision in the system of community penalties. While the supervision of parolees is legally and in some ways substantively different from the execution of probation orders and other non-custodial penal measures, they function together as the state's deployment of legal authority, personnel, and resources for constraining the liberty of the criminally convicted who are not incarcerated, and for effecting their return to community with as little harm as possible to us and to our property.

What is 'public safety' – and why does its definition require some care?

'Public safety' is one purpose toward which penal resources and legal authority might properly be applied, through penal strategies such as deterrence, incapacitation and rehabilitation. As a purpose for which penal power is exercised, public safety competes with, is trumped by, or is limited by another purpose: conforming penal measures to offenders' just deserts. Still, one might fairly ask, if we are to pursue public safety at all: What is it? Where is it found? What would have to be true if we are to have it?

In American public and political discourse – even in much of the legal academic literature – the phrase seems to mean 'a lower crime rate', 'more villains locked up', 'tougher sentences' or, in the community corrections business, 'reduced recidivism'.[5] These impoverished definitions endure, despite common experience in the 1990s of crime increasing in high-crime (and other) neighbourhoods even as prison populations rose, and of crime (as conventionally measured, i.e. offences recorded by the police) falling in neighbourhoods where potential victims felt (reasonably or not) too unsafe to venture forth or too dispirited to complain to the police when victimized. Public safety surely is not the same thing as a crime rate suppressed by the absence of crime targets in public spaces which adults have abandoned to unsupervised adolescents bent on mischief.

As an object of public policy, then, public safety would far better be conceived as: *a condition of a place at a time when one can be without fear of assault upon person and property there – and upon the persons and property of others – and be justified in that feeling* (see Dickey and Smith 1999).

As a condition of place (and of time),[6] public safety has multiple antecedents – and just as many vulnerabilities. It is at risk whenever a vulnerable person or unguarded property is in the same place as a potential offender at a time when the place, the potential victim or property, and the potential offender are all without 'guardians', when they come together in the absence of persons who are ordinarily in protective relationships with them (e.g. parents, wives, children, friends, employers, probation and parole agents, even security guards at the mall) (see generally Eck and Weisburd 1993). These naturally-occurring 'guardians' of people and places are abundant in safe places. When they are absent, there is no public safety. But they can be and are found in dangerous places too, and it is by invoking their guardianship, by finding them and enlisting their help, that effective police, probation and parole officers most effectively advance our interest in public safety.

Perhaps it is easier to illustrate than to define the difference between public safety properly conceived as a condition of place, and public safety as conventionally identified through criminal justice system input and output measures. Fortunately, illustrations abound in the literature documenting police experimentation with problem-solving community policing. Here is an example, from New York:

> Vincent Esposito [one of the first officers assigned to New York City's Community Patrol Officer Program in 1984] discovered a major problem location on his beat – a playground … [It] featured handball and basketball courts for adolescents, a sandbox, swings and seesaws for small children, and benches that lured senior citizens from the surrounding apartment buildings to sit in the sun. [But there were] no children in the park and no seniors sunning themselves – like too many locations of this type, the park was overrun with drug users and their dealers.…
>
> Residents of the surrounding apartment buildings told [Esposito] that police officers in radio cars frequently came by, causing the drug market to vanish, but that it returned as soon as the officers left the scene. He began to spend as much time as possible in the vicinity of the park. He would disperse the loiterers; when he actually observed drug sales, he made the arrests – and thereby removed the police presence from the park (and from the rest of his beat) for the balance of his tour while he processed the arrests. He knew the conventional police tactics were not solving the problem for the residents of this neighborhood, and that other neighborhoods have other problems, elsewhere in his beat. He couldn't just stand in the park and, by his presence, deter the trade.

[He convened] meetings of tenants in the apartment buildings overlooking the park. He told them he needed their help to solve the problem, and in time he recruited a number of homebound residents ... to watch the drug dealing from their windows and to observe where the dealers hid their stashes (as the dealers did not want drugs in their possession when Esposito paid one of his visits). The residents undertook to call [an answering machine Esposito installed at the stationhouse] and leave anonymous messages telling him where he could find the drugs... Armed with the information, he would enter the park and confiscate the drugs from each hiding place.... take the drugs to the precinct for vouchering as found property, and [return to] his beat.

Working this way, he was off patrol for only 20 to 30 minutes after each visit to the park. Some days, he would make five or six confiscation visits, some days none. But he quickly made the park an economically unbearable location for the dealers – who had to explain to their suppliers how they had parted with the drugs without being paid or arrested.... Before a month had passed the park was free of the drug users and the dealers who had controlled it for years .... [Seven years later, when last checked by research staff] children are playing, the swings are in use, teens are making baskets and playing handball – and the seniors are sunning themselves on the benches.

(NYPD and the Vera Institute of Justice 1993, 48–49)

Public safety, conceived as a condition of place, is only occasionally a plausible consequence of arresting, convicting and applying penal measures to an individual who has diminished it. It is not immediately apparent, therefore, what community penalties might have to do with it, either. There are, of course, crime problems in particular places (or in particular persons) which will yield temporarily or even durably to in-capacitating, deterring and/or rehabilitating penal strategies, through the individual application of custodial and non-custodial penal measures. (Zimring and Hawkins 1995; von Hirsch *et al* 1999). But neither the conditions necessary for these penal strategies to be effective, nor the infrequency with which those conditions occur, are obscure to today's correctional officials, who are also burdened by reasonable doubts about the suitability to those penal strategies of the penal measures at their disposal.

The idea of public safety as a condition of place cries out for substantial changes in the non-custodial supervision of offenders, about which I have more to say in the second main part of this paper. But why has this idea of public safety excited any interest at all in US community corrections agencies – whose offender-centred operating assumptions it directly challenges?

In the summer of 1998, at a national symposium on sentencing and corrections convened by the US Department of Justice, representatives of the judicial and correctional establishments of a majority of the states were shocked and a little excited, during the opening plenary panel, by the first words from the mouth of Dennis Maloney, Director of the Deschutes County (Oregon) Department of Community Justice (formerly, Department of Probation): 'Probation sucks.'

When order returned to the hall, Maloney made clear his view that if community corrections did not soon deliver something of value to taxpayers and voters, they would withdraw from probation and parole the token public investment that remained. For something of public value – something that might be generated by a redeployment of the legal authority, personnel and resources held by community corrections – he nominated first 'public safety' and then 'restorative justice' (see Maloney *et al* 1998, Maloney and Umbreit 1995). Maloney acknowledged positive contributions to probation practice from the 'What Works' literature, where plausible 'principles of effective intervention' have emerged from meta-analyses, but he mercilessly challenged the notion that dangerous places – some of which he described – could be made significantly safer through the 'statistically significant' treatment effects promised by What Works principles. 'Probation sucks' offended many in the hall, including Mario Paparozzi, president of the APPA (American Probation and Parole Association), but Maloney's principal offence was to make painfully public what the US probation and parole leadership had been saying privately for years.

In his opening remarks at a follow-up symposium in Washington, DC, in December 1998, that APPA president recalled Maloney's pithy indictment, thanked him for it, and introduced two days of strategic planning with this confession:

> It's been amazing to me that when you ask your probation and parole staff to give you examples of what they do that protects the public, they're baffled … [T]here's a malaise in the public about our business … but even more importantly there's a malaise in our own house, in the profession. I said to some of our folks recently, 'What would you do if you sat down with your townspeople and told them about your work?' and they said to me – and this is not uncommon, by the way – 'You mean, the truth?' And boy did that resonate with me, because we all know the party line and we all

know the truth. And, you know what? Other people outside of our business have figured that out too.

(Dickey and Smith 1999: 2)

In the discussions that followed, the community corrections officials were torn between conviction that their future claim on the resources necessary to create any value would require imaginative redeployment of what they have now, in ways that actually advance public safety, and deep doubts that they have the imagination and that their agencies have the operational capacity to do so. In that discussion, the competing idea was restorative justice.

What sort of justice is restorative?

The meaning of 'restorative justice' is up for grabs just as much as the meaning of 'public safety', and its advocates (including quite a few prominent corrections officials) use the phrase to include everything from family group conferencing to Native American sentencing circles, from victim–offender mediation to re-integrative shaming, from monetary restitution and community service orders to a smorgasbord of victims' rights within the ordinary criminal process. The roots of the restorative justice movement are also many, but the durable ones run deep – in religion, culture, political ideology, and spirituality, as well as in common sense. To its proponents, it is a new paradigm, a rejection of the criminal law's focus on culpability and retribution and an embrace of the idea that punitive responses aggravate the harm that flows from crime. In the new paradigm, justice's purposes are: restoration of the victim and the victim's intimates, who suffer the harm; restoration of the community whose fabric is torn by the crime; and restoration of the offender who, after all, will remain part of that community and, if unre-stored, a continuing threat to it. The key mechanisms appear to be respectful hearing of the story of the harm caused (as told directly by the victim and by those who support the victim in this process), voluntary acceptance of responsibility and making amends by the offender (also heard respectfully, lest stigmatization and self-loathing block his return to full membership in the community), and collaboration, consensus and caring all around in the fashioning of solutions.

John Braithwaite, whose accounts of restorative justice seem in-creasingly influential in the US,[7] resists greater specificity of definition than that 'restorative justice is about restoring victims, restoring of-fenders, and restoring communities' and is 'most commonly defined by what it is an alternative to [–] retribution and rehabilitation'. Definition is difficult because:

> [if] restorative justice is a process whereby all the parties with a stake in a particular offense come together to resolve collectively how to deal with the aftermath of the offense and its implications for the future, … stakeholder deliberation determines what restoration means in a specific context [though restoration is always about] healing rather than hurting, moral learning, community participation and community caring, respectful dialogue, forgiveness, responsibility, apology, and making amends [and a recognition that] those who have a 'stake in a particular offense' [are] primarily victims, offenders, and affected communities (which include the families of victims and offenders).
>
> (Braithwaite 1999: 5–6)

There are hundreds of US programmes attempting to apply these purposes and mechanisms to correctional practice – most of them small, but some state-wide; most of them operating outside or alongside the formal criminal justice process, but some of them elaborate attempts to weave restorative justice practices through the full range of agency operations. It is not necessary for me to describe or categorize them, daunted as I am by wonderful recent reviews of restorative justice programmes in all their variety (Braithwaite 1999, Marshall 1999). I want only to raise a few theoretical and practical features that are of particular relevance to my present task.

First, for the most part, restorative justice is understood by its advocates and practitioners not as a product (which might be produced, for example, by a new exercise of sentencing power or a new deployment pattern for correctional assets), but as a necessarily indeterminate process. One way to understand enthusiasm about restorative justice among US probation practitioners is that they see it, rightly or wrongly, as a better (or an attractive additional) process for delivering what has been required of them all along.

Second, it should be obvious that the consensual nature of restorative justice processes, and their need for offenders voluntarily to accept responsibility and make amends, are features not easily fused with a sentencing law concerned with authorizing and calibrating the use of state force to effect punishment.

Third, it could well be that bringing court process and correctional practice into line with restorative justice principles would advance public safety, as described above, better than any redeployment of probation and parole agents, authority and resources.

Are 'public safety' and 'restorative justice' conflicting or complementary ideas?

In my view, these ideas are not necessarily in conflict, their purchase on the future of the field probably depends on a satisfactory marriage being arranged between them, and in their most plausible relationship restorative justice processes are employed in production and maintenance of public safety – in part through the administration of non-custodial penal measures.

Ways in which the ideas are complementary

Political symbiosis
These ideas need each other politically – most obviously because neither could be implemented well without (a) major overhaul of sentencing law and practice and of the institutional arrangements within and between correctional agencies, and (b) substantial enlargement of these agencies' operating capacity, through re-deployment of their personnel, authority and resources and through formation of collaborative relationships with others who are positioned to advance or to frustrate public safety and restorative purposes.

Braithwaite, after reviewing accounts of every restorative justice programme for which an account can be had, does not think such transformations are at hand – he projects no easy victory of this 'third model' over the retributive and rehabilitative justice models which he sees giving shape and substance to sentencing and corrections today. To the contrary, 'if we take restorative justice seriously, it … means transformed foundations of criminal jurisprudence and of our notions of freedom, democracy, and community'. (Braithwaite 1999:2) Such sweeping transformations would be required even though, on Braithwaite's account, 'restorative justice has been the dominant model of criminal justice throughout most of human history for all the world's peoples.'

Similarly, although my colleague Walter Dickey and I are persuaded that there would be great public value in correctional agencies – particularly community corrections agencies – taking public safety seriously and redeploying personnel and resources accordingly, we argue that doing so would also require sentencing courts to make findings of relevant facts and to draw inferences from them, in order to decide what combination of penal measures would be most plausible to that purpose in individual cases (Smith 1998). In short, we too insist that daunting transformations of traditional criminal justice practices would be required. No correctional agency can take seriously the idea that advancing public safety is its primary purpose – or even a purpose for which it ought be held accountable in the execution of non-custodial penal measures – without taking a deep breath:

> [Such an agency] would have to develop capacities to do more than warehouse and case-work known offenders. It would have to develop knowledge about the great variety of public safety problems, in hundreds of neighborhoods, and it would deploy its resources to counter them.... Incremental investments in existing strategies and tinkering with current arrangement of institutional responsibility will not suffice. Radical restructuring is required – restructuring of our conception of the public safety problem, of the legal instruments aimed at it, of the strategies and penal measures employed against it, and of comfortable but ineffectual institutional arrangements in the criminal justice system.
>
> (Smith and Dickey 1998: 2, 26)

As organising ideas for community corrections, 'public safety' and 'restorative justice' are conceded by their proponents to require more sweeping contextual transformation than seems likely, but their purchase on the future of community corrections is likely to be stronger if they and the energy of their proponents can somehow be merged.

Conceptual overlap
Each idea already incorporates the essentials of the other.

The 'web of interdependency' on which restorative processes rely has much in common with the networks of 'naturally-occurring guardians' said to be essential to public safety.[8] Kay Pranis, since 1994 the full-time restorative justice planner of the Minnesota Department of Corrections, who has mounted restorative justice projects in diverse neighbourhoods around her state, expresses a view held by others working on similar reforms from inside other US correctional agencies:

> It has become clear that creating safe communities requires active citizen involvement. It calls for a re-engagement of all citizens in the process of determining shared norms, holding one another accountable to those norms and determining how best to resolve breaches of the norms in a way which does not increase risk in the community.
>
> (Pranis 2001)

My colleague Walter Dickey and I described the condition and the production of public safety in quite similar terms:

> Places [where public safety is found] would likely share the following characteristics:
>
> - A set of generally agreed-upon rules of behavior.
>
> - A shared appreciation that rule-breaking will be punished.
>
> - A further appreciation that playing by the rules will be rewarded.
>
> Viewed this way, creating and maintaining public safety requires teaching the lessons of responsibility and accountability and reinforcing them in raising children, supervising adolescents, and producing law-abiding young adults. These are tasks for parents, neighbors, schools, churches, athletic teams, community service groups, the labor market, and – on what needs to be relatively rare occasions – a local police, probation, or parole officer. This is not work that can safely be left to sentencing judges and correctional agencies. It will require imposing penal measures on convicted offenders but it cannot be achieved by that means.
>
> (Smith and Dickey 1999: 2)

John Braithwaite's most recent exploration of the advantages of adopting restorative justice processes makes explicit their instrumental relationships to public safety:

> Restorative justice can remove crime prevention from its marginal status in the criminal justice system, mainstreaming it into the enforcement process. It can deliver the motivation and widespread community participation crime prevention needs to work.
>
> (Braithwaite 1999: 55)

Braithwaite goes further. He attempts to show that deterrence and incapacitation are more likely to be effective strategies for reducing crime if they are grounded in restorative justice practices:

> Punishing crooks is a less efficient deterrence strategy than opening up discussion with a wide range of actors with preventive capabilities, some of whom might be motivated by a raised eyebrow to change their behavior in ways that prevent reoffending. [The strategy] is to keep expanding the number of players involved

in a restorative justice process until we find someone who surprises us by being influenced through the dialogue to mobilize some unforeseen preventive capability.

(*Ibid*: 59)

Braithwaite terms this 'benign general deterrence', but the argument is very like the argument Dickey and I have advanced for re-deploying community corrections agents to the places where public safety is most in disrepair – because there they can combine with 'naturally-occurring guardians' of the offenders under supervision, of the persons who are or might become vulnerable to them, and of the places where they might come together. Both ideas seek, and seek to create, circumstances where specific and general deterrent effects might plausibly be realized through the proper functioning of restored community, and both de-emphasize the role of the state in the mechanisms of deterrence. And both also cast the state in a back-up role in executing incapacitating strategies:

Intimates, in short, can incapacitate more intensively, more creatively, more sensitively, more consensually, and in a more dynamically responsive way than the criminal justice system.

(Braithwaite 1999: 68)

The dependent position of restorative justice
A major practical difficulty in trying to organise a system of community corrections (and certainly a system of community *penalties*) around the restorative justice idea arises from the restorative principle that offenders' acknowledgements of responsibility and making amends must be voluntary – or no more than shamed out of them by the pressure of the expectations of intimates gathered around the offender for that purpose (and, of course, for the purpose of making effective the offer of reintegration that should follow). It is not at all difficult to imagine (or to visit) restorative justice programmes operating as a kind of front door to the formal system. There, they might dispose informally and effectively of criminal matters in which consensual restoration proves possible, while passing the other matters along to an adversarial system of prosecution, criminal conviction, sentencing and corrections. Similarly, it is possible to imagine and visit programmes in which the threat of prosecution (or even non-custodial sentencing and a threat of revocation) accompanies referral from the formal criminal process to a restorative one. The last of these possibilities might be a 'non-custodial restorative justice sentence'. The rest seem something else. And the penal threat

which backs a court's order to participate in a restorative process seems both theoretically improper and quite likely to precipitate reactance in the offender and, thereby, failure of the restorative process itself.

Could probation and parole plausibly pursue the public safety purpose without attending to restorative justice principles? I suggest not, though my conclusion follows from the definition I have given 'public safety'.[9] It is just as clear, however, that restorative justice processes require back-up from an effective system of probation and parole supervision. When restorative processes do not work – when the propensity for further harm to victim and community is not diminished by engaging in those processes – the criminal justice system is the acknowledged fallback or default.[10]

Ways in which the ideas seem in conflict

If the ideas are not wholly incompatible, there are distinctions of importance that could easily lead the pursuit of one to undermine the other. At the simplest level,

- conventional community corrections is in the business of *normalizing offenders* (though, as noted above, it is often passive in that function but active in removing them from community to prison, for violating the conditions of probation or parole); but
- community corrections, if public safety were its purpose and animating idea, would be in the business of *normalizing places* – places where known offenders and those thought likely to become offenders (absent a change in circumstances) are found together with the rest of us; while
- community corrections would be in the business of *normalizing communities of 'interdependence'* (as repositories of community norms and engines of public safety), if it were animated by the restorative justice idea. (See Braithwaite 1999.)

Those eager to pursue restorative justice within community corrections often resist the idea that public safety ought to be accepted as the larger purpose, or even a worthy purpose best advanced by restorative justice principles and practices. Some are reluctant to accept it as a plausible purpose for non-custodial penal measures, period. The reluctance seems rooted in doubt that the idea of public safety will ever be understood as we have defined it – that it can ever be separated from the idea of arresting and imprisoning more villains, including those under correctional supervision in the community.

There is yet another dimension of conflict, one which has potential to sink any serious attempt to pursue both ideas from within the same agency. For a community corrections agency to advance public safety, its methods would have to be proactive. The active supervision of offenders, which would disperse its agents to the places where public safety is in disrepair, is desirable not only because offenders under supervision can be more appropriately supervised there, by agents and by naturally-occurring guardians, but also because the agency thereby extends itself into the place, and positions itself to gather information about local public safety problems and about those naturally-occurring forces with which it might combine to address them. A commitment to the restorative justice principles and methods seems to require none of that, and might be ill-served by an agency's reaching into community in this way.

In contrast, restorative justice processes, like conventional justice processes, are largely reactive. They are invoked after harm is done. Their problem-solving features – though more forward-looking than the conventional processes of adjudication, sentencing and corrections in criminal courts – are tied to particular conflicts and crimes rather than to the patterns of conflict and crime that would draw the problem-solving capacity of a community corrections agency committed to the public safety idea.

Some problems

The proponents of both ideas are regularly called upon to account for how one or another of the following problems could conceivably be overcome. The responses are often quite similar and, at the same time, revealing in their difference. Here are a few:

- the problem of victims
- the problem of offenders
- the problem of 'What Works'
- the problem of facts
- the problem of operational capacity

The problem of victims

It is dangerous to assume that victims of crime in general want any particular thing, or that any particular victim will want whatever it is that a system of justice has on offer (Davis *et al* 1980). But for restorative justice enthusiasts to have a problem of victims is a bit of an embarrassment. 'Restoring the victim' is a central objective and method of restorative justice, and victims' support of the idea is assumed by some proponents. There are, however, important segments of the US victims' movement opposed to many restorative justice ideas and initiatives. The problem has several sources:

1 At least in the hands of historically offender-centred courts and community corrections agencies, restorative justice processes can cast victims as props in a psycho-drama which is centred on the offender for the real purpose of restoring him (if only to render him less likely to offend again);

2 A victim comforted by the presence of intimates, feeling genuinely free to speak directly to his or her offender, may (and some do) press a blaming rather than restorative shaming agenda. The theory at least suggests that stigmatization of this kind (Braithwaite's 'disintegrative shaming') will make things worse.

3 The victims' movement focused for years on a perceived imbalance of 'rights' – the criminal process seemed to surround offenders with procedural rights (e.g. protection from having to acknowledge responsibility, a right to require proof beyond a reasonable doubt of the facts constituting the crime, freedom from the obligation to testify and, when the proof fails, protection from punishments they might deserve) while failing to extend victims any 'rights' at all. The movement's infrastructure grew along with the accumulation of 'victim rights' – rights to allocution at sentencing, to notice of plea offers, to notice and a right to be heard at parole release hearings, and (in some places) a right to be present at executions. To some in that movement, these are valuable gains, threatened by restorative justice processes, which require respectful listening to the offender's story, consensual dispositions, and acknowledgements of responsibility all around. These requirements can seem an affront to what may be felt to be rights of victims: a right to the status of 'victim', a right to insist on the offender being branded 'criminal', a right to blame and even harangue the offender, and a right not to be 'victimized all over again by the process'.

4 Some victims do want apology, if it is heartfelt and easy to get, but they may want even more to put the matter behind them, to get back the stolen property being held for possible use at trial, to be assured that the offender will receive the treatment he is thought to need if he

is not to victimize someone else, or to get any of the countless, unpredictable, individualized objectives victims reveal when asked (Davis *et al* 1980). While deliberative, consensual restorative justice processes are in theory well suited to discovery of a victim's objectives, it is by no means certain that a particular victim's objectives will be within the realm of the possible or, if they are, will win the day.

Plenty of individual victims and some important figures in the victims' movement disagree, of course, or see these problems as minor in light of the potential gains; restorative justice initiatives in community corrections agencies can usually claim the endorsement and involvement of some victim advocates. But restorative justice faces another, more serious problem of victims – indifference. The restorative process depends, case by case, on the active participation of victims, in a role likely to be emotionally more demanding than the role of complaining witness in a criminal prosecution – itself a role avoided by many, perhaps most victims. Their reasons for avoiding it are also many – and some of them (e.g., 'It's just not worth it to me', 'I've got to go to the job' or 'take care of the kids' or 'go to the football game') will render a victim equally unenthusiastic about being restored through respectful dialogue with the offender and his supporters.

The 'problem of victims' for public safety proponents is different, perhaps, but it seems just as serious and complex. It is hard to invoke naturally occurring guardians for a victim who either refuses to acknowledge the need for them or insists that the right and sufficient remedy is a substantial prison term for the offender. There is no shortage of illustrations. The retailer who cuts staff costs, neglects security in out-of-sight areas, and relies on prosecution, conviction and sentencing to deter a higher level of theft, might be unprepared to accept responsibility for securing his premises, even in the face of withdrawal by the criminal justice system, if the cost of prevention were greater than the cost of more theft. Public safety is served by neither position the retailer-victim is prepared to take. Tough questions arise: what, if anything, would warrant compelling victims' co-operation in pursuit of public safety, under such circumstances; and what form of compulsion would be permissible? It is not hard to foresee that the answers from traditional victim advocates would be: 'nothing' and 'none'.

The problem of offenders

Offenders also present a problem to both ideas, but most of the difficulty for restorative justice is individual to the offender (e.g., when he is unwilling or unable to participate in the process by acknowledging responsibility and making amends), while for the public safety idea the 'problem of offenders' is in the offender-centred habits of the criminal process and its correctional apparatus. The focus of community corrections agents on the offender and on the penal measures they are applying to him obscures their view and analysis of public safety problems of which the offender may be a part – but which could, at least, be observed and understood by agents if they were attentive to conditions in the places where offenders under their supervision are found. On the other hand, the 'problem' of focusing on offenders may serve as a saving constraint on what could easily be arbitrary and oppressive intrusions, by community corrections agents, into the life of communities and upon the autonomy of individuals in them who are *not* subject to correctional supervision but who are, for whatever reason, thought to be potential contributors to or detractors from public safety there. But perhaps the greatest problem for the public safety idea, under this heading, is that probation and parole agents might remain narrowly focused on individual offenders while taking to heart the idea that their mission is to advance a simplistic idea of 'public safety' (see, e.g., Corbett *et al* 1999). That combination could easily make supervision of offenders excessively costly, to liberty and to the public purse, while benefitting public safety, as we understand it, not at all.

The problem of 'What Works'

The prospect that correctional interventions will yield powerful rehabilitative effects if they follow the 'what works' principles drawn in recent years from meta-analyses has excited practitioners everywhere (see, for example, Gendreau and Andrews 1990; Gendreau 1996). But commitment of the field to the new recipe for efficacy is a problem both for the public safety idea and for restorative justice – most obviously for the latter. The new principles of effective intervention require that offenders be matched to services on the basis of risk classification, criminogenic needs and individual characteristics derived from meta-analysis, and that the intervention be grounded principally in cognitive-behavioural treatment models. Public safety could of course be the purpose for application of non-custodial penal measures and for a community corrections agency's deployment of legal authority, personnel and resources, without diluting that agency's preference for cognitive-behavioural interventions and for schemes for matching individual offenders to particular programmes. The problem for public safety, then, is only that commitment to the 'What Works' principles intensifies a focus on the offender when public safety is really a condition of place. For restorative justice, which is less a purpose than a process, the question inevitably arises whether that process is consistent with 'what works' principles:

> As currently implemented, most restorative justice programs fail to incorporate the principles of effective intervention, particularly as they relate to the risk, need, and responsivity principles ... Restorative justice programs run the dual risks of producing an interaction effect in low-risk offenders and of underservicing high-risk offenders.
>
> (Levrant *et al* 1999: 19)

The problem of facts

Facts are a problem because they are difficult to agree upon, they change over time, and it is often difficult to decide what facts are relevant – relevant to decisions about disposition and to decisions that must be made in the course of community supervision. A public safety purpose demands reliable fact-finding – at sentencing, during the execution of sentence, and in support of decisions about where and how to allocate non-custodial correctional personnel and resources. Without overhaul of fact-finding in sentencing courts and correctional agencies, there is great danger that, in a public safety regime, penal authority and resources would be deployed as they are now, but in greater measure and indiscriminately – every case a simultaneous pursuit of all penal strategies, by every authorized penal measure, without regard to the plausibility of any. The result would quickly become simply and unbearably harsh (pursuit of public safety through incapacitation and deterrence, by application of particularly burdensome non-custodial penal measures), oppressive (through overuse of incapacitating conditions of community supervision), and wasteful (as when corrections' treatment resources and coercive legal authority are combined in an effort to reform an offender for his own sake rather than for ours).

For this reason, if public safety were taken seriously as the primary purpose at sentencing, the decision-making of sentencing courts and correctional agencies would need re-framing, to conform them to the fact-finding methods and inferential reasoning that characterize the rule of law in virtually every legal field but this one.[11]

In contrast, although the restorative justice idea attends to what happened and why, and requires some specification of the resulting harms and paths to restoration for each party having a stake in the crime, reliability of the facts used in the process may be less important than their agreeability, as they are not so much relied upon to support inferential reasoning as to precipitate and test the strength of individuals' feelings. Greater fact-finding rigour, and a legal style of reasoning to disposition from facts found, would probably not suit the restorative justice idea well.

The problem of operational capacity

I doubt that any community corrections agency today has the operational capacity to pursue either of these ideas effectively. That is in part because their personnel lack many of the necessary skills and have for years been deployed in ways incompatible with public safety purposes or restorative justice practices. But it is even more because neither of these ideas is within the plausible capacity of a community corrections agency, except one that has enlarged its operational capacity by integration with naturally occurring forces for social control in communities where the work must be done.

Some futures

The public safety and the restorative justice ideas are already strong in US discussions of community corrections policy and practice (Kurki 1999); they are also complicating the lives of community corrections officials in an (unknowable) number of US jurisdictions. The ideas are not going away. Minnesota's Department of Corrections sports a full-time Restorative Justice Coordinator, Vermont's Corrections Commissioner is methodically trying to turn his agency from what he characterizes as valueless execution of retributive sanctions imposed by courts to partnership with informal community boards ('reparative boards') engaged in restoring victims, offenders and communities. The (many-times elected) District Attorney of Austin Texas preaches that the purpose of sentencing and corrections (and of prosecution and conviction) is a 'reweaving of the community'. Until last year, Washington State had a thoroughgoing desert-only statutory scheme for sentencing, and a correctional regime almost exclusively concerned with exacting deserved punishment and preventing repetition of the crime of conviction. The scheme was amended, at the Governor's request, to require deployment of probation agents in response to place-specific public safety problems and to direct that they supervise offenders in ways likely to increase public safety in the places where the offenders are found. And two probation regions in Wisconsin (Dane and Racine counties) have redeployed agents and resources along lines we have suggested public safety requires.

Much more common, however, is the use of these ideas as rhetorical cover for business-as-usual. Promising 'offender accountability' and 'victim restoration' looks a promising strategy to corrections managers who think they are without a market for 'offender rehabilitation'. Embracing 'public safety' seems smart in these risk-averse times, when the public's experience of less crime-in-fact seems to leave fear of crime in place. I once thought this phenomenon dangerous to the survival of good ideas, but it is no fault of scripture that the devil can read it. Concepts *are* a bit tarnished by political exploitation, but their substantive value is not affected. The 'malaise' to which the president of APPA referred is real – in the public and in the community corrections field. It will not be dissipated by slapping feel-good labels on impoverished correctional practices, but it will motivate a continuing search for something more plausible than probation as we know it. The need will remain for strategic re-direction of community corrections, for redeployment of its legal authority and resources, and for transformation of sentencing law to authorize and support a different array of correctional purposes and techniques. The systems of community penalties with which I have familiarity are in search of value. My guess is that both 'public safety' and 'restorative justice' have merit, as ideas around which the future of community corrections might form – and that the ideas competing with them do not.

Notes

1 See Dickey and Smith (1999). In Wisconsin, the Governor's Task Force on Sentencing and Corrections recommended abolishing 'probation' as a legal status and as a term describing a style of community corrections; it urged the introduction of 'Community Confinement and Control' (CCC) as a legal status to which an offender might be sentenced directly, into which imprisoned offenders would have to be released before discharge, from which offenders would ordinarily be paroled before discharge, and through which all felons not sentenced to conditional discharge would be required to pass at some point. The Task Force detailed the redeployment of community corrections agents and resources that it thought necessary, for CCC to deliver 'active supervision' of offenders, in a way responsive to public safety problems which were found to vary from place to place and from time to time (Smith and Dickey 1998). The Task Force chose this course, rather than

trying to 'fix' the state's rather conventional community correctional apparatus, in part because the officials responsible for administering probation in Wisconsin joined a judicial and legislative consensus that 'probation' has become a dispositional category rather than a set of community supervision techniques which might be wisely imposed and seriously enforced.

2 There are many ways to illustrate this, none better than to point to the substantial portion of probationers carried in 'absconder status' on the books of probation agencies. Arrest warrants may or may not have been issued, but the absconders are quietly retained in the caseloads without any attempt to find them – without even a phone call to the last known residences – until they show up for initial appearance on new charges. See Corbett *et al* 1999, page 2 ('By the end of 1996, of the 3.2 million offenders on probation, some 288,000 were on absconder status, out of contact with probation, out of compliance with court orders and out from under any control or monitoring.')

3 It would be odd if probation were different from parole, given the frequency with which offenders move back and forth between the categories. Often unnoticed in policy discussions is the increasing frequency with which sentences to 'probation' (or, as in Wisconsin, commitment to probation with 'sentence withheld' until such time as the need for it might become apparent) are in due course transformed into prison sentences from which, in due course, the offender emerges on parole (or, as in Wisconsin after 1 January 2000, on 'extended supervision'). The high and increasing percentages of US probationers now being revoked and imprisoned, only to be returned to community supervision by discretionary parole or statutorily mandated conditional release, makes it even more obvious that community supervision in lieu of penal confinement raises most of the same problems and opportunities as community supervision upon release from penal confinement. (See Simon 1993: 203–229; Smith and Dickey 1998.)

4 Examples of the contingent nature of desert abound. It surfaced, for example, in a number of Vera Institute initiatives aimed at revising normal sentences in categories of cases that usually drew incarceration from New York City judges. Short jail terms routinely imposed on petty recidivists were displaced, upon it being demonstrated that a (subjectively less punitive) community service order benefitting service-deprived areas of the city would in fact be enforced if imposed; similarly, felony prison terms for young robbers were displaced by enforced full-time participation in a programme of education, drug treatment and employment, which was found by many judges sufficiently incapacitating in the short run and likely to be sufficiently socializing in the long run to warrant trading several years otherwise deserved imprisonment for it. (See McDonald 1986; Smith 1983–84, 1998.) The mutability of desert norms, when competing values appear to be within the reach of a sentencing court's power, is also evident in reports of deliberative public opinion polling and focus groups. (See Hough and Roberts 1998: 27–30; John Doble Associates 1989, 1991.)

5 It is sometimes said, by people with experience as politically accountable officials in charge of these agencies, that 'public safety' can come to mean: 'None of the awful things done last night and reported in this morning's newspaper was done by one of ours!'

6 'Time' is added to the dominant 'place' dimension because some places may seem safe at some times (e.g. noon), but unsafe at others (e.g. at night when certain people begin to gather there).

7 Mark Umbreit and Howard Zehr are disturbed about this, lamenting the rapid US take-up of the Australian version of family group conferencing associated with Braithwaite, rather than the New Zealand original; they suggest at one point that Braithwaite's theory of 're-integrative shaming' (Braithwaite 1989), which informs a host of other US restorative justice initiatives in community corrections, is inconsistent with restorative justice principles (Umbreit and Zehr 1996).

8 See Smith and Dickey 1998. For probation views of this kind, see Maloney *et al* 1998. A few outspoken prosecutors advocate what they believe to be restorative dispositions in criminal cases, seeing them as useful for 'reweaving the fabric of community' upon which public safety rests. Most prominent is Ronnie Earle, the District Attorney for Austin, Texas:

> The most powerful way to realistically affect crime is to strengthen the community. We can best do that by reweaving the fabric of community, which consists of family, extended family, neighborhood, church, school, workplace – that matrix of threads carefully woven over the years that gives meaning to our lives. It is that web of relationships – the ethics infrastructure – that regulates behavior, not the law.
>
> (Earle 1997)

9 Of course there are many in the US community corrections who embrace 'public safety', but understand it in the more conventional way – 'tough on crime' and more imprisonment. For them, the idea of restorative justice and the restorative process that can foster public safety are afterthoughts; they emphasise strict conditions of supervision and strict enforcement of them, more certain revocations and partnering with police rather than with naturally occurring guardians. The idea becomes: 'Tail 'em, Nail 'em, Jail 'em.' For examples of this manifestation of the public safety idea in probation, see generally Corbett *et al* 1999; Beto *et al* 2000.

10 Braithwaite makes this explicit:

> There are good preliminary theoretical and empirical grounds for anticipating that well-designed restorative process will restore victims, offenders, and communities better than existing criminal justice practices. More counter-intuitively, a restorative justice system may deter, incapacitate, and rehabilitate more effectively than a punitive system. This will be especially so if restorative justice is embedded in a responsive regulatory framework that opts for deterrence when restoration repeatedly fails and incapacitation when escalated deter-

rence fails. We find active deterrence under a dynamic regulatory pyramid to be more powerful than passive deterrence in a sentencing grid; community incapacitation is more variegated and contextually attuned than clumsy carceral incapacitation.

(Braithwaite 1999: 104–5)

See also Umbreit and Carey 1995.

11 This problem is part of another: the problem of (not enough) time. In discussions with judges and correctional officials about the fact-finding challenges of a public safety-centred system, I have found them accepting of the idea that more and better fact-finding is needed but inclined to dismiss the possibility of it – 'We just don't have the time.' But I have also found that some judges (and more experienced advocates) go on to remember how much time of court and counsel is taken up with fact-finding in all sorts of litigation where much less is at stake than in criminal sentencing; they also come to remember that, if they are qualified to contribute to the sentencing decision, it is as lawyers not as philosopher-kings. For those who get to that point, it is a short way to imagining rule-of-law fact-finding: about the public safety problems arising from an offender's presence in particular places, and about the plausibility of whatever deployments of correctional resources and authority is proposed for addressing them.

References

Beto, D.R., Corbett, R.P., Jr. and DiIulio, J.J., Jr. (2000) 'Getting Serious about Probation and the Crime Problem', *Corrections Management Quarterly* 4 (2), 1–8.

Braithwaite, J. (1989) *Crime, Shame and Reintegration*. Cambridge: Cambridge University Press.

Braithwaite, J. (1999) 'Restorative Justice: Assessing Optimistic and Pessimistic Accounts', in M. Tonry (ed.) *Crime and Justice, A Review of Research*, 25, 1–126. Chicago: University of Chicago Press.

Corbett, R.P., Jr., Beto, D.R., Coen, B., DiIulio, J.J., Jr., Faulkner, J.R., Jr., Fitzgerald, B.L., Gregg, I., Helber, N., Hinzman, G.R., Malvestuto, R., Papaozzi, M., Perry, J., Pozzi, R. and Rhine, E.E. [the 'Reinventing Probation Council'] (1999) '"Broken Windows" Probation: The Next Step in Fighting Crime', *Manhattan Institute Civic Report*, 7, 1–13.

Davis, R.S., Russell, V. and Kunreuther, F. (1980) *The Role of the Complaining Witness in an Urban Criminal Court*. New York: Vera Institute and Victim Services Agency.

Dickey, W.J. and Smith, M.E. (1999) 'Five Futures for Community Corrections', in *Rethinking Probation: Report of the Focus Group*. Washington, D.C.: Department of Justice, Office of Justice Programs.

Earle, R. (1997) 'Reweaving the Tapestry of Ethics Infrastructure', *Austin American Statesman*, 7 April 1997, at A11.

Eck, J.E. and Weisburd, D. (1993) 'Crime Places in Crime Theory', in J. E. Eck and D. Weisburd (eds), *Crime and Place*. New Brunswick, NJ: Rutgers University Press.

Gendreau, P. (1996) 'The Principles of Effective Intervention With Offenders', in Alan T. Harland (ed.) *Choosing Correctional Options That Work*. California: Sage Publications.

Gendreau, P. and Andrews, D.A. (1990) 'Tertiary Prevention: What the Meta-Analyses of the Offender Treatment Literature Tell Us About What Works', *Canadian Journal of Criminology*, 32, 173–184.

Hough, M. and Roberts, J. (1998) *Attitudes to Punishment: Findings from the British Crime Survey*. Home Office Research Study No. 179. London: Home Office.

John Doble Associates (1989) *Punishing Criminals: An Alabama Survey*. New York: Edna McConnell Clark Foundation.

John Doble Associates (1991) *Punishing Criminals: The People of Delaware Consider the Options*. New York: Edna McConnell Clark Foundation.

Kurki, L. (1999) 'Incorporating Restorative and Community Justice into American Sentencing and Corrections', *Sentencing and Corrections: Issues for the 21st Century*, 3. Washington: US Department of Justice, Office of Justice Programs.

Levrant, S., Cullen, F.T., Fulton, B. and Wozniak, J.F. (1999) 'Reconsidering Restorative Justice: The Corruption of Benevolence Revisited?', *Crime and Delinquency*, 45 (1), 3–27.

McDonald, D.C. (1986) *Punishment without Walls: Community Service Sentences in New York City*. New Brunswick, NJ: Rutgers University Press.

Maloney, D., Romig, D. and Armstrong, T. (1998) *Juvenile Probation: The Balanced Approach*. Reno, Nevada: National Council of Juvenile and Family Court Judges.

Maloney, D.M. and Umbreit, M.S. (1995) 'Managing Change: Toward a Balanced and Restorative Justice Model', *Perspectives*, 19 (2), 43–46.

Marshall, T.F. (1999) *Restorative Justice: An Overview*. London: Home Office Research Development and Statistics Directorate.

New York City Police Department (NYPD) and the Vera Institute of Justice (1993) *Problem-Solving Annual for Community Police Officers and Supervisors*.

Pranis, K. (2001) 'Restorative Justice, Social Justice, and the Empowerment of Marginalized Populations', in G. Bazemore and M. Schiff (eds) *Restorative Community Justice: Repairing Harm and Transforming Communities*. Cincinnati: Anderson (forthcoming).

Simon, J. (1993) *Poor Discipline: Parole and the Social Control of the Underclass, 1890–1990*. Chicago: University of Chicago Press.

Smith, M.E. (1983–84) 'Will the Real Alternatives Please Stand Up?', *New York University Review of Law and Social Change*, 12, 171–197.

Smith, M.E. (1998) 'Let Specificity and Parsimony of Purpose Be Our Guide', *Law and Policy* 20 (4), 491–525.

Smith, M.E. and Dickey, W.J. (1998) 'What if Corrections Were Serious About Public Safety?', *Corrections Management Quarterly* 2 (3), 12–30.

Smith, M.E. and Dickey, W.J. (1999) 'Reforming Sentencing and Corrections for Just Punishment and Public Safety', *Sentencing and Corrections: Issues for the 21ˢᵗ Century*, 4. Washington: US Department of Justice, Office of Justice Programs.

Umbreit, M. and Carey, M. (1995) 'Restorative Justice: Implications for Organizational Change', *Federal Probation*, 59, 47–53.

Umbreit, M. and Zehr, H. (1996) 'Restorative Family Group Conferences: Differing Models and Guidelines for Practice', *Federal Probation*, 60, 24–26.

von Hirsch, A., Bottoms, A.E., Burney, E., Wikström, P-O. (1999) *Criminal Deterrence and Sentence Severity: An Analysis of Recent Research.* Oxford: Hart Publishing.

Zimring, F.E. and Hawkins, G. (1995) *Incapacitation: Penal Confinement and the Restraint of Crime.* New York: Oxford University Press.

Chapter 12

Concluding reflections

The Editors

Editors of books originating as conference proceedings always have to decide how closely the final volume should resemble 'the book of the conference'. We have chosen not to approach this concluding chapter in that manner, though equally we remain committed to the origins of this book in the Cropwood Conference of 2000 (see Preface).

Some weeks after the Cropwood Conference, a summary of the 'Key Conclusions' arising out of the conference discussions was distributed widely to interested parties. That summary is included here as an Appendix, and we venture to suggest that many of the points listed in the Appendix remain extremely pertinent to policy and practice in the field of community penalties.

We shall return to one of the 'Key Conclusions' of the conference towards the end of this final chapter. Prior to that, however, we propose to offer some reflections that are structured around five 'dimensions' or 'themes'. Each of these reflections takes as its starting point an event that has occurred since the Cropwood Conference, and some of those events are not directly connected with community penalties. Each event has, however, caused us to reflect on, or reconsider, some aspect of the recent development of community penalties, or their future direction; and, together, they cover five themes that we judge to be of great importance for the future of community penalties – namely, (i) the macro-political dimension, (ii) the research dimension, (iii) the public safety dimension, (iv) the procedural dimension, and (v) the social dimension.

Theme 1: the macro-political dimension

On Wednesday 31 January 2001, just as this volume was being finally prepared for the press, two important speeches were made in London. One, by the Lord Chief Justice of England and Wales (Lord Woolf) was delivered to the Prison Reform Trust, ten years to the day after Lord Woolf had submitted his major report on prisons to the then Home Secretary (see Woolf 1991, 2001). The other speech was delivered by the present Home Secretary, Mr Jack Straw, to the Social Market Foundation: it drew attention to the main policies in the field of criminal justice that the Labour government had put in place since its election in 1997, and it looked forward to future policy initiatives planned by the government (Straw 2001).

Neither speech focussed principally upon the theme of community penalties, but both included some mention of them. Lord Woolf stated, in his conclusions, that 'the credibility and effectiveness of community sentences has to be increased'. He went on:

> It should be generally accepted that any initiative to tackle offending that can be achieved in custody can be achieved even more effectively in the community. Judges and magistrates already contend, with some justification, that they only use custody as a last resort. But offenders may receive custodial sentences because the judiciary does not believe there is any credible community alternative. What has to be realised (and I include the Government here) is that a short custodial sentence is a very poor alternative to a sentence to be served in the community. ... It should be regarded as being no more than a necessary evil whose primary purpose is to obtain compliance with court orders. Prisons and young offender institutions find it almost impossible to do anything constructive during a short sentence, so they do nothing. The result is that a short sentence is a soft option. It is much more challenging for the offender to have to complete a community punishment.

Lord Woolf also added a comment on the enforcement of community penalties. Noting the new provisions of the Criminal Justice and Court Services Act 2000 in this area, the Lord Chief Justice described them as 'a variant on two strikes and you're out'.[1] These new provisions he considered to be 'a retrograde step likely to increase the prison population'; a preferable approach, he suggested, would be that the offender should be given an additional punishment for the breach of his order, 'but he should still usually have to finish his community sentence'.

In his speech on the same day, the Home Secretary explicitly stated his agreement with Lord Woolf 'that it is essential that we improve the effectiveness and scope of community sentences'; and he emphasised that 'more effective community sentences should turn more offenders away from crime *before they are sent to prison*' (emphasis added). But a main focus of Mr Straw's speech was the troublesome core group of persistent offenders – estimated in preliminary Home Office research to constitute 100,000 people at any one time, though with a constantly changing membership.[2] The Home Secretary was at pains to point out that 'almost without exception, every persistent offender sentenced to custody has been through the mill of community sentences and has still re-offended'. He also regretted the fact that, as they are convicted and reconvicted, 'persistent offenders see little increase in the length of sentence they receive, so the deterrence value of the punishments they receive is correspondingly less'. The implication of these remarks appeared to be that community penalties should be imposed only (or at any rate, very predominantly) on those who have not yet been given a custodial sentence. Once an offender has been to prison, then in successive convictions (unless there is a long gap between them) the custodial term must become progressively longer – though the Home Secretary also expressed the view that better links needed to be developed 'between the supervision provided in custody and that provided in the community' after release from prison.

In these speeches, there is explicit agreement between Lord Woolf and the Home Secretary about the need to develop more effective community penalties. But that consensus should not deceive us. In other respects, the two speeches reveal significantly different underlying understandings of the nature, the purpose and the promise of such community penalties. For the Lord Chief Justice, in an ingenious reversal of traditional language about community penalties being 'alternatives to custody', short custodial sentences are 'a very poor alternative' to community sanctions. More people, he suggests, need to realise this – and that includes the government. For the Home Secretary, community penalties need to be developed to provide more effective rehabilitation early in a criminal career, but beyond that they have little purchase, except for the purposes of post-custodial licences. There is, in the Home Secretary's tone, little positive enthusiasm for what community penalties can deliver, particularly in relation to persistent offenders. By contrast, Lord Woolf emphasises that community penalties, properly developed and delivered, can be 'much more challenging' for offenders than short custodial sentences; and he explicitly questions the value of the government's newly enacted policy that makes imprisonment the

normally expected sanction for a second unjustified breach of requirement in a community order.

We shall not here attempt any thorough analysis of the claims of these
two distinguished speakers. It is enough for our purposes to note the
obvious contrast between their approaches, a contrast that clearly also
has links to wider debates about sentencing. It is quite clear from the
speeches that the appropriate future role and nature of community
penalties can be, and is likely to be, the subject of political contestation at
the highest levels. Whatever might once have been the case, in twenty-
first century Britain the future of community penalties is not simply a
technical matter, and anyone seeking to contribute to policy debates on
this topic is necessarily entering a politically highly-charged arena.

Theme 2: the research dimension

In December 2000, the Australian National University's Research School
of Social Sciences released the first research results on recidivism
patterns arising from the so-called Reintegrative Shaming Experiments
(RISE) that had taken place in Canberra. In these experiments, the aim
has been to compare the effects of standard court processing with the
effects of a restorative justice 'conferencing' approach, by randomly
allocating cases to 'court' or 'conference', and then measuring comparative re-offending rates. The experiments have been conducted with
four different samples of offenders, namely those convicted of: (a) drink-
driving (offenders of any age); (b) violence (offenders aged under 30);
(c) shoplifting (juvenile offenders under 18); and (d) property offences
involving a personal rather than an organisational victim (juvenile
offenders under 18).

It is safe to say that no-one could have correctly predicted the actual
pattern of results. While all results are at this stage provisional, basically
the violence sample showed a large difference in favour of the crime-
reductive effectiveness of conferences; the two samples of juvenile
property offenders produced a nil result as between the two approaches;
while for drink-driving there was a very small (but still statistically
significant) advantage for the court sample (Sherman *et al* 2000).

For present purposes, two central messages can be derived from these
findings. One arises out of the substantive results of the study, and the
other concerns the role of research in the future development of
community penalties.

Those who set up the RISE study constructed as a central hypothesis
the proposition that 'there will be less repeat offending after a conference

than after court'. The expectation was that the process of engagement with the victim (and their supporters) in a restorative justice (RJ) forum would require offenders to confront the consequences of their actions more fully than does a traditional, formal court appearance; moreover, the hope was that those involved in the RJ forum would set up post-conference arrangements of formal and informal social control that would be significantly more effective in preventing re-offending than is the traditional armoury of court penalties. So stated, in the language of compliance theory (see chapter 5), it is clear that the expectation was that RJ is likely to be more effective than court processing because it will produce a greater *normative engagement* on the part of the offender, and a subsequent (predominantly) *normatively-based adjustment* in their behaviour.

These expectations seem to have been very clearly met in the case of the violence sample in the RISE experiment. But what about the most obviously different result, i.e. that among drink-driving cases, where court processing actually produced slightly lower re-offending (including lower subsequent drink-driving) than did experience of an RJ forum?[3]

On this question, a preliminary examination of the details of the drink-driving results (in terms of number of subsequent offences, and the timing of those offences[4]) has led the researchers to the interpretation (to be more fully tested and explored in later analyses) that *'it is licence suspensions which help court to prevent re-offending'* (emphasis added). This effect arose, it seemed, because in the drink-driving sample courts routinely imposed licence suspensions, but in the Canberra experiments RJ fora did not have the power to suspend the offender's licence.

For those interested in community penalties, these results have considerable implications. They suggest, principally, that re-offending in community settings can be reduced by more than one social mechanism – in this case, in different contexts both the normatively-oriented mechanisms of RJ, and the incapacitative/deterrent mechanisms of licence suspension seem to have been effective to some extent within the overall study. Thus, the preliminary results of the RISE study are highly congruent with one of the main messages to emerge from the papers at the Cropwood Conference – that is, that in the search for effective community penalties, we should not restrict ourselves to just one approach (such as the cognitive-behavioural approach, important and promising though that clearly is), but rather we should be open to the possibilities offered by several different approaches (see chapter 4).

The second main conclusion to be drawn from the RISE results (at any rate in the present context) concerns the role of research itself. As previously indicated, the diverse pattern of results from RISE could have been predicted by no-one. That is the nature of empirical research – sometimes it produces results that seem obvious, at other times it greatly surprises us. Moreover, we should not treat the RISE results as certain to be replicated in all RJ experiments – for, as previous replication studies in criminology have shown, sometimes in a different community context, or with some adjustment to the intervention method being tested, or with different research methods, very different results from those found in the original study can emerge.[5] In this regard, it is important to bear in mind, at the present time, that research into the effectiveness of community penalties is still in its infancy. Only 20 years ago, the research consensus – subscribed to by some very able researchers – was that there was little to choose between the effectiveness of most penalties (custodial or non-custodial) in preventing re-offending. We have clearly moved on from that point, to a better, and more nuanced, understanding of the field. But it is likely that our current best understandings will need to be revised in the decade ahead. Some (though not all) aspects of contemporary British policy on community penalties claim – with much justification – to be 'evidence-led'. But committing oneself to an evidence-led approach is certainly not a guarantee of a quiet or a settled life. It is highly probable that fresh evidence will soon emerge that will question some of our existing policies and practices. We need a mind-frame, and organisational practices, that can accommodate and adapt to such changes.

Theme 3: the public safety dimension

On 5 May 2000, seven weeks before the Cropwood Conference, the Governor of Blantyre House Prison, a resettlement prison in Kent, was abruptly removed from his post. That evening, 84 prison officers from other prisons were sent into Blantyre House to conduct a full, overnight search for drugs, contraband, and evidence of criminal activity. Very little was found.

The events at Blantyre received limited publicity at the time, and they were not discussed formally or informally by the participants at the Cropwood Conference. Since that time, however, the Blantyre search has moved more prominently into the public domain, particularly because of the decision of the House of Commons Home Affairs Committee to conduct a full inquiry into it; their report was published in November 2000 (House of Commons 2000). One of the Committee's main conclusions was that, on the available evidence, neither the extensive search, nor the way in which it was carried out, was justified (para 37).

Why are these events relevant to community penalties? Blantyre House is one of the Prison Service's three 'resettlement prisons'. It prepares longer-term prisoners for release into the community, with a special focus on education programmes and a scheme whereby selected prisoners are given day release to work with employers in the surrounding area. The goal of the prison is that, by pursuing such programmes, prisoners will be enabled to prepare more effectively – during the last portion of their period in custody – for the challenges that will face them after release. Thus, Blantyre is firmly focussed on the reduction of re-offending, to be achieved (it is hoped) by improved resettlement programmes. This approach could be reasonably described as evidence-led, since there is significant research evidence that this strategy does constitute a potentially promising approach to the reduction of recidivism, even if the research evidence is still to an extent tentative (for a relevant review of research, see Haines 1990; see also Sampson and Laub 1993).

The evidence before the Home Affairs Committee suggested that the re-offending rates of prisoners released from Blantyre House were, consistently, very much lower than were the equivalent rates for other Category C prisoners (for example, among 1996 releasees, 8 per cent were reconvicted within two years, by comparison with 55 per cent among all Category C releasees – see House of Commons 2000: vii–viii). As the Committee noted (p. vii), this marked difference might result from the regime at Blantyre (a 'regime effect'), or it might arise 'because Blantyre House takes selected prisoners – from among volunteers – who are the most motivated not to re-offend' (a 'selection effect'). From the data currently in the public domain, one cannot be certain which interpretation is more likely to be correct, but it seems clear that on present evidence the possibility of a regime effect interpretation certainly cannot be ruled out.

One might expect the Prison Service to be enthusiastic about this possibility, but the bulk of the evidence in the Home Affairs Committee's report suggests otherwise. One particularly telling comment came from Mr Colin Allen, HM Deputy Chief Inspector of Prisons:

I think I would be very doubtful about whether, if Blantyre House did not exist, it would be created in the climate of today's Prison Service. The reason for this is the aftermath of the escapes at Whitemoor and Parkhurst, the ramifications of which with regard to physical security and preventing escapes are still very heavy with the Prison Service .… At the end of the day, I think governors are quite clear, and certainly senior Prison Service personnel are quite clear, *that it is losing prisoners or losing control of prisoners that is the thing by which they will be judged, not whether prisoners commit offences after release.*

(House of Commons 2000: 29, emphasis added)

What Mr Allen is saying here is of huge importance. Whether or not the remarks are justified in the particular context of Blantyre House, they do very valuably draw attention to a pattern of thinking that is certainly not unknown in today's penal climate, in Britain and elsewhere (see for example, Michael Smith on the United States in chapter 11). That pattern of thinking is: take no risks; concentrate on security and safety; deliver that security and safety by physical restrictions and constant checks on offenders. The danger with such an approach, if pursued as an exclusive goal, is that it can – as Mr Allen suggested – lose sight of longer-term objectives such as the rehabilitation of ex-prisoners (for example, fewer risks with immediate security will arise if the Prison Service immediately stops all schemes of day release to work with outside employers, but that might well reduce prisoners' longer-term prospects of rehabilitation). As the Rev. John Bourne, a part-time chaplain at Blantyre House, put it:

[The prison] needs a proper balance between security and trust, and that is the big issue that the Prison Service is wrestling with and is so frightened of making a mistake.

(House of Commons 2000: 14)

These issues are highly relevant to community penalties in the modern era. As discussed by George Mair (chapter 9), modern technology, in particular, now allows a more constant surveillance of offenders in the community than was the case in the past, and we can envision its further development in the future. Used sensibly and appropriately, such technology can constitute an important check on offenders' actions, and can therefore play an important role in maximising public safety. But there is a danger, of a kind directly analogous to that described by Mr Allen, whereby an organisation or a government might become so preoccupied with physical security, the constant checking of offenders, and immediate control, that it loses sight of longer-term objectives of rehabilitation. In much the same way, Michael Smith in his chapter (chapter 11) points out that in the United States there are now two principal visions of so-called 'public safety' policies. One concentrates on physical restrictions on offenders, while the other tries to focus on what is required to make specific locations feel safe for those who want to use them peaceably.

The general lesson to be derived from this discussion is that policies and practice in the field of community penalties, if they are to remain constructive, cannot properly be exclusively risk-aversive. Also, an exclusive focus on physical constraints might easily overshadow the processes by which longer-term normative compliance might be secured.

Theme 4: the procedural dimension

In the contemporary world of community penalties, assessments of the potential risks posed by offenders play a significant part, and increasingly those assessments are made using formal instruments. But what should be the relationship between formal and less formal assessments of risk?

A salutary warning is provided by very recent research in the context of imprisonment. David Price, a Ph.D. student at the Cambridge Institute of Criminology, was very generously allowed access to the deliberations of the Category A Committee, a Prison Service body that meets from time to time to consider whether the highest-security prisoners (those in 'Category A') should or should not be downgraded to Category B. The criterion for retention in Category A is not that the prisoner is thought likely to escape, but rather whether, *if* he were to escape, he would pose a substantial risk or danger to the public. The offender's likely future re-offending is, therefore, crucially linked to his current security classification.

David Price (2000) carried out a multivariate statistical analysis on the factors associated with the decisions of the Category A Committee whether or not to downgrade.[6] Two factors were dominant, namely, the advice of the Police Advisor, and whether or not the prisoner had completed a formal offending behaviour course. It is the second factor that is of interest for present purposes, especially because other recent research reports by Hood and Shute (2000) on parole decisions, and by Padfield and Liebling (2000) on the work of 'discretionary lifer panels' (DLPs), have similarly pointed to the very great importance now attached, in various decision-making contexts, to the formal completion by prisoners of accredited offender behaviour courses.

But Price's research also pointed out two other things. First, formal offending behaviour courses are not in fact available for all the kinds of offences that might be committed by Category A prisoners. Secondly, even where courses are available, waiting lists can be long. Many Category A prisoners, therefore, have had no opportunity to attend an offending behaviour course.

Prison staff always supply the Category A Committee with their assessments of the prisoner's attitude, behaviour, and likely prospects. The evidence is, however, that assessments of this sort carry little weight with the Committee – even where the prisoner has, through no fault of his own, been unable to attend an offending behaviour course. Attendance at courses, it seems, has in practice become completely dominant over informal assessments in the Committee's decision-making; and prisoners themselves have gradually become aware of this, albeit necessarily less clearly than is now apparent from Price's statistical analysis. Not surprisingly, David Price found clear evidence of anger from prisoners about the fact that the opinions of those who knew them best (the wing staff in their prison) seemed to count for nothing in the downgrading process.

It is not difficult to imagine that, as accreditation processes accelerate in the Probation Service context, essentially similar issues could arise in the context of community penalties – that is to say, only accredited programmes will carry any real credibility with probation managers and Ministers. The lesson that we draw from this fourth theme is therefore that, while accreditation is a sensible policy, there is a significant danger that it might become a procedural neo-orthodoxy. The formalisation of accreditation could have the unintended consequence that other potentially valuable approaches to crime reduction could be systematically neglected, or even (at worst) denigrated. There are also implications here for the future role of the case manager in probation supervision. Ideally, he or she could develop an in-depth understanding of the offender, and his or her criminogenic needs; and the relationship thus developed between officer and offender could form the basis for normative attachment (chapter 5), within which what the offender has gained from an accredited programme or other intervention could be properly assessed and built upon. The worst-case alternative is that the case manager's views could be simply ignored at key moments, as those of prison staff seem to be in the Category A decision-making process.

Theme 5: the social dimension

For our final theme, we return to the Home Secretary's 31 January speech at the Social Market Foundation. Describing the estimated 100,000-

strong group of persistent offenders, Mr Straw said:

> This group looks very different to the population as a whole. Half
> are under 21. Nearly two-thirds are hard drug users. More than a
> third were in care as children. Half have no qualifications at all.
> And three-quarters have no work and little or no legal income.

In other words, this group of persistent offenders contains a wholly dis-
proportionate share of people who have grown up in troubled families
(to the point of having been received into local authority care). It also has
more than its share of educational failures (people with no qualifications). And, since both admission to local authority care and
educational failure have been found to occur disproportionately among
those from the lowest socio-economic groups, we can be pretty sure also
that the cadre of 100,000 persistent offenders is recruited, to a significant
extent, from among those who have grown up in very socially
disadvantaged communities or circumstances.

Of course, none of this excuses their persistent lawbreaking, and there
are other people (especially females) who have grown up in similarly
disadvantaged circumstances, yet who have not become persistent
offenders. Nevertheless, viewed dispassionately, there can be little
doubt that concentrated social disadvantage is part of the *causal
explanation* of high offending rates (see for example, Wikström and
Loeber 2000; Sampson, Raudenbush and Earls 1997). Regardless of one's
party political affiliation, there is a very good case for saying that policies
for crime reduction should indeed be 'tough on crime, and tough on the
causes of crime'. The problem – and it is a serious one – is that it is much
easier to construct policies that are 'tough on crime' than it is to develop
strategies to tackle some of the deep-seated causes of crime.

An example of exactly this problem was manifested in Mr Straw's
31 January speech. Having, in the paragraph quoted above, drawn
attention to the social backgrounds of the group of persistent offenders,
Mr Straw made no further reference to this aspect of their lives. The
overwhelming thrust of his policy proposals was focussed on
adjustments to the criminal justice system, for example:

> We need to raise the game against these criminals by the twin
> process of investment and reforms, at each stage of the criminal
> justice process – catching, prosecuting and convicting more of
> them, and then ensuring they are more effectively punished and
> deterred from crime.

Certainly, the Home Secretary is on solid ground in his emphasis on 'catching, prosecuting and convicting more' offenders, since there is good evidence that enhanced certainty of apprehension and conviction is linked to reduced crime, in a process of general deterrence (see von Hirsch *et al* 1999). But policies of this kind, if pursued in isolation, do not attend to what can reasonably be called the 'social dimension' of crime.

The Probation Service, in its work, cannot ignore this social dimension, because its officers are confronted with it, day in day out, in the lives of the offenders with whom they have to deal. This theme therefore arose with some prominence in the discussions at the Cropwood Conference, with a particular focus on the need to avoid perpetuating social exclusion, and to accommodate social difference, in the future development of community penalties (see, for example, chapter 8). These concerns also brought the theme of *Citizenship* to the fore at the Conference (see Appendix, especially Key Conclusion B2). Citizenship, of course, is a concept that embraces the obligation of citizens to obey the law. However, it also places obligations upon the state itself: for example, an obligation not to enact laws that degrade or oppress its citizens; an obligation to treat citizens with respect even when they break the law; and an obligation on the part of those placed in authority by the state (including police, probation officers and prison staff) to act fairly and responsibly in the exercise of that authority. All this, however, lies essentially in the realm of law and of formal authority, and citizenship – if it is to be a meaningful concept – must have a social as well as a legal dimension. This key point was very well put by Anatole France (1844–1924) in his biting caricature of 'the majestic egalitarianism of the law, which forbids rich and poor alike to sleep under bridges, to beg in the streets, and to steal bread'.

The importance of this social dimension led probation service partici-pants at the Cropwood Conference particularly to press the conclusion that, in the actual delivery of community penalties, 'implicit in the notion of citizenship is that accountability to local communities, and their sense of responsibility and ownership, will be crucial for success in the work of the Probation Service' (see Appendix, Key Conclusion B2). That 'sense of responsibility and ownership' must necessarily involve many people and organisations in local communities, including for example organisations such as schools and businesses which will have among their members not only victims, and potential victims, but also offenders. It will also, as in the very promising multi-agency Youth Offending Teams, bring agencies that deal with (for example) mental health or housing into much closer and more creative partnerships with criminal justice agencies than has typically been the case in the past.

237

Finally ...

We hope that the discussion in this concluding chapter has demonstrated that the coherent development of community penalties into the future must take account of the following six imperatives

- awareness of the broader political context;

- awareness that re-offending can be reduced by more than one social mechanism;

- responsiveness to new research findings;

- the constructive pursuit of public safety;

- accommodation of properly informed assessments of offenders in decision-making procedures, including assessments by those who know them best; and

- an understanding of offenders as citizens who live in particular social environments, often of a disadvantaged character.

Mike Nellis, in his historical overview (chapter 2) sees the then Conservative government's 'punishment in the community' initiative of 1988–92 (and especially the community penalties provisions of the Criminal Justice Act 1991) as, in retrospect, 'the last phase of post-war penal reductionist thinking'. Those policies have been replaced, he suggests, by a new penal context in which, among other things, new technology, risk management, attention to the voice of victims, and populist punitiveness all play their part. It is probably still too early for all the features of this new penal context to be fully understood, but it is surely clear that, in this shift of policies, there are major implications for the development and delivery of community penalties. Moreover, in our judgement at least, it is pointless to try to turn the clock back: many aspects of the new penal context are here to stay. But within such a general framework, there remain various different ways in which detailed policies and practices can be pursued, and in these concluding reflections we have, for example, suggested that there are both less and more constructive ways of focusing upon matters such as public safety and procedures for risk assessment. Moreover, perhaps one of the most important messages to emerge from this book is that the effective pursuit of penal policy in relation to community-based sanctions needs to engage with the reality of the social lives of offenders, and the communities in which they live.

Notes

1 The reference is to the provision whereby, on a second unjustified breach of requirement in a community order, the court is normally expected to pass a sentence of imprisonment: see Criminal Justice and Court Services Act 2000, s.53.
2 This research is briefly described in a note entitled 'Estimating the Active Offender Population' prepared by the Home Office Research, Development and Statistics Directorate, and published on 31 January 2001 in the Home Office News Release relating to the Home Secretary's speech to the Social Market Foundation (Home Office 2000).
3 For reasons of space, we leave aside here the nil results obtained with the two samples of juvenile property offences.
4 An important factor in the interpretation reached by the researchers on the results in this sample has been, in court cases, the timing of re-offending relative to the length of licence suspension awarded.
5 For an important example in the criminological literature of a set of replication studies which produced diverse results, see the random allocation studies of responses to domestic violence in various sites in the United States, summarised and synthesised in Sherman (1992).
6 We are grateful to David Price for permission to summarise his unpublished results.

References

Haines, K. (1990) *After-Care Services for Released Prisoners: A Review of the Literature*. London: Home Office.

Home Office (2001) *Tackling Persistent Offenders is Key to Improving Effectiveness in the Criminal Justice System*, Home Office News Release 024/2001, 31 January 2001.

Hood, R. and Shute, S. (2000) *The Parole System at Work: A Study of Risk-Based Decision-Making*, Home Office Research Study No. 202. London: Home Office.

House of Commons (2000) *Blantyre House Prison*, Fourth Report of the Home Affairs Committee, Session 1999–2000. London: HMSO.

Padfield, N. and Liebling, A. (2000) *An Exploration of Decision-Making at Discretionary Lifer Panels*, Home Office Research Study No. 213. London: Home Office.

Price, D.E. (2000) *Security Categorisation in the English Prison System*, unpublished Ph.D thesis, University of Cambridge.

Sampson, R.J. and Laub, J.H. (1993) *Crime in the Making: Pathways and Turning Points Through Life*. Cambridge, Mass.: Harvard University Press.

Sampson, R.J., Raudenbush, S.W. and Earls, F. (1997) 'Neighborhoods and Violent Crime: a Multi-level Study of Collective Efficacy', *Science*, 227, 918–924.

Sherman, L.W. (1992) *Policing Domestic Violence*. New York: Free Press.

Sherman, L.W., Strang, H. and Woods, D.J. (2000) *Recidivism Patterns in the Canberra Reintegrative Shaming Experiments (RISE)*, Report posted on the website of the Australian Institute of Criminology, Canberra (http://www.aic.gov.au/rjustice/rise/recidivism).

Straw, J. (2001) 'Next Steps in Criminal Justice Reform', Speech to the Social Market Foundation, 31 January 2001 (unpublished).

von Hirsch, A., Bottoms, A.E., Burney, E. and Wikström, P-O. (1999) *Criminal Deterrence and Sentence Severity: An Analysis of Recent Research*. Oxford: Hart Publishing.

Wikström, P-O. and Loeber, R. (2000) 'Do Disadvantaged Neighborhoods Cause Well-adjusted Children to Become Adolescent Delinquents? A Study of Male Juvenile Serious Offending, Individual Risk and Protective Factors, and Neighborhood Context', *Criminology*, 38, 1201–1233.

Woolf, Lord Justice (1991) *Prison Disturbances April 1990*. Cmnd. 1456. London: HMSO.

Woolf, Lord Justice (2001) 'The Woolf Report: A Decade of Change?', Address to the Prison Reform Trust, 31 January 2001 (unpublished).

Appendix: Key conclusions

The University of Cambridge Institute of Criminology recently convened a small Round-Table Conference, financed by the Barrow Cadbury Trust, to discuss 'The Future of Community Penalties'. This subject seemed particularly important at the present time for a variety of reasons:

- There have been a number of new community penalties introduced in the last decade, including the curfew order with electronic monitoring and the drug treatment and testing order. National Standards have also prescribed tighter enforcement procedures for existing orders. The overall nature of community penalties is therefore changing.

- The courts have been making increasing use of imprisonment (and other custodial sentences) since 1993. This is financially expensive, but successive governments have been willing to find the necessary resources, clearly backed by public opinion. Sometimes, governments and public opinion have also seemed doubtful about the adequacy of the public protection that community penalties can provide. Constructive thinking about the future of community penalties in such a context is therefore of great importance.

- There have been significant gains during the last decade in our research-based understanding about the kinds of intervention with offenders that are most promising for the reduction of re-offending. Some, but not all, of this research has strongly influenced probation practice. There is a clear need for dialogue between researchers and practice managers in such a context.

- Legislation currently going through Parliament will establish for the first time a National Probation Service for England and Wales, creating a new organisational framework for the lead agency in the delivery of community penalties.

This [Appendix] summarises some of the most important conclusions to arise from the discussions at the Conference. The primary focus of the conference was on the delivery of community penalties by the Probation Service, though it was fully recognised that other agencies and bodies play an important role.

A Contributing to the public debate about crime

A1 A clear sense of priorities is crucial if the Probation Service is to convince the public, and victims, of the value of community penalties, and to secure the involvement of local communities. Creative strategies are also needed for communicating ideas to other players in the criminal justice system.

A2 Convincing policies to deal with offenders in the community need to be developed, recognising that the political context is one of intolerance towards crime and a willingness to see further rises in the prison population.

A3 But experience has shown that apparently attractive short-term measures, which may attract initial public support, often fail to secure the longer-term aims of reducing crime and protecting the public. In this climate, the readiness shown by the Home Secretary to wait for the outcome of research on what works in evidence-based practice is impressive and welcome.

A4 The demand that 'something should be done' produced by public anger and fear about crime offers the prospect that people will be prepared to support initiatives to develop constructive solutions. Policies that seem to have as their driving force simply the avoidance of imprisonment are unlikely to attract support. What is needed is a long-term strategy to develop demonstrably constructive and effective methods of dealing with offenders in the community, so that the public begins to prefer these measures to custody.

B Responding to diversity and local needs

B1 The principle of social inclusion means respecting diversity and individuality, while in no way condoning offending behaviour. An important challenge for criminal justice agencies and local authorities is to reach members of the community who are amongst the most marginalised, including young people coming out of care at the age of 18 or 19, those outside the benefits system, and those trapped on disintegrating urban estates – all of whom have an enhanced risk of offending. The development of approaches in which such people will have a stake relies upon an ability to communicate effectively with them, and to understand their experiences.

B2 The concept of *Citizenship* seems to have particular potential as an organising principle for the probation service, because it not only encompasses social inclusion but also emphasises both the rights *and* the duties of different citizens. Promoting good citizenship obviously means upholding the law, but it also means recognising social diversity, and realising that the long-term objective of reintegrating offenders as citizens will be undermined by demands for offenders to forfeit rights. Implicit in the notion of citizenship is that accountability to local communities, and their sense of responsibility and ownership, will be crucial for success in the work of the Probation Service.

B3 Effective work to reduce offending and to increase public safety has to be based on the incontrovertible fact that offenders, victims and small communities are (especially in disadvantaged areas) linked in a network of relationships based on need and obligation. This raises very practical questions about how a national Probation Service can serve local communities in what is becoming an increasingly complex contemporary social environment. Careful thought is needed as to how to structure the Probation Service nationally and locally so that it supports linkages with effective practice, e.g. through crime and disorder partnerships, and through links with other service providers such as Youth Offending Teams and the voluntary and private sectors.

B4 Strong community and professional leadership, capable of generating in local communities a sense of ownership in dealing with problems of crime, can help to prevent the public's appropriate demand for effective measures from becoming automatically a demand for more imprisonment.

B5 Some local initiatives have shown that there is a wealth of knowledge and experience in developing coherent partnership work in some extremely difficult and tense situations. Yet exciting projects like Kirkholt, which resulted in the restoration of vandalised and burglarised houses and apartments, have received too little attention in the local and national media. More could be done to record and transmit such experiences.

B6 US experience also shows that initiatives that engage local resources in pursuit of public safety can produce a quite dramatic political response. Harnessing state resources to local forces that might produce more safety and more justice can produce very positive community responses. This 'public safety' concept seems to have a significant value in considering the future work of the Probation Service, addressing as it does the need to make particular places and situations non-threatening to victims and potential victims, through a combination of types of intervention.

B7 An important opportunity is presented by developments in youth justice. By the year 2002, the majority of offenders making their first appearance at the Youth Court (i.e. thousands of people) will be referred to an informal Youth Offender Panel that will be seeking to implement restorative processes. The full use of this opportunity calls for radical thinking about whom to include on the panels, so that they involve people from different social backgrounds and different local and cultural communities, including some who may have experienced victimisation, or who have overcome their own difficulties in poor urban areas.

C Developing 'What Works?'

C1 A sharp divide between the worlds of research and practice will not promote the critical environment that is needed to develop effective practice in the field of community penalties. A revival of links between the Probation Service and the universities, and the re-development of a strong practitioner-oriented academic literature will help to foster such a climate. It is essential to sustain and revitalise intellectual life in the probation service if research-based ideas are to be fruitfully developed in practice.

C2 The expectation for the future is for a more coherent evidence base for practice, capable of withstanding the test of public scrutiny to which all public sector agencies are now exposed. This challenges both academics and practitioners to produce ideas that can be translated into practice, and then to apply these ideas effectively in local communities.

C3 The major emphasis in the 'What Works?' initiative has so far relied primarily upon a relatively narrow range of research evidence, and a narrow approach to what counts as effective. There are a variety of ways in which community sentences might be effective, and a variety of stakeholders that might be satisfied by different modes of success. Links with a much wider body of literature, for example on effective social work practice, will assist probation officers who are looking for ideas about inter-personal effectiveness in work with offenders, and who want to integrate the treatment manager and case manager roles.

C4 A rounded understanding of effective work with offenders en-compasses the proper implementation of probation cognitive-behavioural programmes, accompanied by intervention aimed at helping offenders to improve their social environments (par-ticularly by overcoming problems of drugs misuse, accommodation and employment) and developing the normative processes associated with taking non-offending choices. There is evidence that offenders achieve more social change if they participate in programmes that improve their problem-solving skills rather than having practitioners solve their problems for them.

C5 The Community Service Order (soon to be renamed the 'Community Punishment Order') seems, at least on some research evidence, to be particularly successful in preventing recidivism. This might be because of the opportunities it offers to influence offenders' attitudes and promote their normative development, as well as to improve their position in the social environment in practical ways through gaining skills and the belief that they have something useful to offer the community. In order to understand what CS might offer, evaluations need adequately to take account of dynamic risk factors as well as the static risk factors on which studies have traditionally relied (a methodology now made possible by the development of risk-need tools such as ACE and LSIR, and ultimately OASys).

C6 Pro-social modelling, intended to assist the normative processes leading to non-offending, is an important idea that sounds straightforward in theory but is very challenging to deliver in practice. Its effective use involves close attention to how to sustain the specific, detailed practices needed to maintain a pro-social influence, especially given the diverse interpretations of what pro-social behaviour means in our society. There are obvious links here to the idea of 'citizenship' as an organising principle (see B4 above).

C7 There is quite high current interest in the principles of restorative justice, with important and innovative programmes in areas such as Thames Valley and Hampshire. Theoretically, restorative justice programmes seem to have much potential for crime reduction, but the empirical evidence on this point is at present limited. There is therefore a need to take practice forward in this area hand-in-hand with rigorous research.

C8 In the delivery of programmes, principles of legitimacy (see further D2 below) create the expectation that we should be capable of responding to gender, ethnic and other forms of social diversity without creating stereotypes. Unfortunately, some recent developments create a countervailing tendency to treat people primarily as members of groups who are dealt with according to their statistical probabilities. Statistical probabilities have to be taken into account if public safety is to be delivered, but the individuality of particular offenders, and their capacity to change and develop, must also be recognised. In order to facilitate this, there is a need to ensure that offenders play a more active role in decisions about the kinds of interventions that are likely to have an impact on their offending.

C9 Sensitivity is needed in the delivery of programmes – balancing, for example, the need to avoid exposure of a black offender to a group work programme where he or she feels uncomfortable, whilst also avoiding discriminatory assumptions that black people are unsuitable for group work because of intrinsic differences from white people. Attention to the particular experiences and needs of black and female offenders is vital, not least because the research evidence suggests that re-offending outcomes for particular programmes are not always the same for them as for white males. But this should not lead to the complacent inference that the Probation Service is now effective in its practice with white male offenders – some issues that become identified as important to develop in relation to female or black offenders may well have relevance for white male offenders as well.

C10 Some major recent developments in policy and practice have been under-theorised. An obvious example is electronic monitoring, now being implemented in a way that has outpaced current capacity to understand its implications and consequences. The development of ideas about electronic monitoring needs to match the development of its actual use. Another priority is to evaluate the way that the Probation Service has developed its assessment and management of risk, and high-risk offenders, practices that are now absorbing very considerable resources.

D Compliance and participation

D1 In recent years, the Probation Service has, through the application of National Standards, devoted increasing attention to ensuring that offenders comply with the requirements of court orders (short-term compliance); it has also (especially through the 'What Works?' initiative) focused more fully on delivering programmes that will secure long-term avoidance of crime. However, these two developments have occurred largely separately, and in some respects with different underlying assumptions about behaviour. There is a need to develop closer links, at both a theoretical and a practice level, between policies aimed at securing short-term and longer-term compliance.

D2 The Probation Service can learn from applying principles of *legitimacy* both to promote short-term compliance and to make a lasting impact on offenders' attitudes and behaviour. (Where compliance results from 'legitimacy', a primary reason for the compliance is that the law is being enforced by a legal or social authority recognised by the subject as holding office legitimately, and as acting appropriately in the performance of his/her/their duties). There is a developed criminological and theoretical literature on the importance of *fairness* in authority figures as a factor influencing people's motivation to offend or not. What is known about why people form social bonds, and what makes them respect the laws of society, chimes with recent literature on the impact of legitimacy in securing compliance.

D3 Finding space for social diversity may be fundamental to normative development and motivation away from crime. It is intrinsic to treating people with respect, an element in legitimacy that appears (from the research evidence) to promote normative development.

These ideas link strongly with the agenda on citizenship (see B2 above).

D4 Current practice relies predominantly on deterrent-based approaches for securing short-term compliance (compliance with requirements of orders). Such approaches do not necessarily get an offender out of bed and on the right bus to attend a programme in the community. A more imaginative, incentives-based and encouragement-based approach might be more effective. This would rely on realistic incentives beyond the early discharge of an order. It might be fruitful to focus on the offender as a citizen, based on an understanding of what motivates people to adopt law-abiding choices and lifestyles.

D5 Simple strategies, such as 'Big Breakfast' in Teesside (providing breakfast for offenders before attendance at a community programme), or making telephone calls to remind offenders about the programme they are due to attend, can be used to demonstrate respect and encouragement for offenders, as well as delivering desirable social outcomes. This kind of approach also informs the philosophy behind the new Youth Offender Panels, i.e. that people are more likely to co-operate if they have had a say in designing the requirements imposed on them.

D6 Current national-level political strategies for the development of community penalties depend upon securing higher levels of attendance and completion, and lower levels of acceptable and unacceptable absences, than are now achieved. There is a need to monitor the consequences of more rigorous enforcement, not just for offenders' compliance, but in addressing their lifestyles and their outlook, and in enabling promising programmes to work in the way that is intended. The goal of securing short-term compliance should not be conducted in such a manner as to undermine offenders' likelihood of longer-term compliance with the law.

Index

Action Plan Order 2

Alcohol use
  abstinence order 128
  drink-driving 229–230
  harm minimisation 129
  offenders 22, 81, 120
  reduction 88, 89

Anti-social behaviour 47
  anti-social behaviour orders 48
  community safety 47, 57
  partnership arrangements 52

Attendance centres 1, 2, 16, 20, 31
  junior 22

Bail
  electronic tagging 170, 177

Binding over 20

CCTV 107, 174, 180

Child abuse 133

Children's departments 21

Citizenship 161, 237, 243

Combination Order 2, 5, 28, 79, 179
  see also Community Punishment
    and Rehabilitation Order
  attendance 120
  breach of 120

Communities

  harm to 133
  leadership 243
  meaning of 183–184

Community justice 183–184, 191, 193
  pro-social solutions 194

Community penalties 17–19, 27
  as an alternative to custody 19
  breach of 98, 100, 120
  compliance 87–117
  definition 200–201
  effectiveness of 31, 60
  enforcement 227
  harm minimisation 131
  holidays 48
  human rights 148
  incentives 120
  legitimacy of authority 103
  national standards 27
  probation 19
  value of 242
  versus imprisonment 131

Community Punishment and
  Rehabilitation Order 2
  see Combination Order

Community Punishment Order 2
  see Community Service Order

Community Rehabilitation Order 2
  see Probation Order

Community safety 12, 42–49, 200–225,
242
anti-social behaviour 47
conditions of 204, 211–212, 219–220
correctional agencies 210, 220
definition 44–45, 203–207
fear of crime 46–47
local government strategies 46
partnership arrangements 48, 55, 57
Probation Service 46
restorative justice 209–211
urban regeneration 46
Community Service 16, 30, 31, 77, 179
accredited 185
compliance 88
legitimacy of authority 103
offending 77
pro-social modelling 79
versus custody 78
Community Service Orders 4, 245
as alternatives to custody 24
conditions of 2
breach of 3
effectiveness of 22
re-offending 150
Community supervision 3
national standards 3
Compliance 87–121, 247–248
access restriction 93
alcohol use 89
community-based programmes 97
compliance theory 12
compliant behaviour 88, 90
constraint-based 92, 112
drug testing 93
electronic tagging 93
habit-based 93–94, 97
hostels 95–96
interaction effects 104–107
legitimacy of authority 92, 100–104
normative compliance 91, 98, 104
prisons 100, 105–106
programme attendance 119
rates of 121
scientific positivism 98–99

social relationships 90–92, 96, 105
subjectivity 99–100
Correctional agencies 201–202, 206,
209–210, 219
Correctional policy framework 3, 5
Counselling 1
Crime prevention 42–49, 242
and community safety 57
community-based measures 46
community life 58
community safety units 44
community service 77–78
conviction 237
Costs of Crime Report 44
Crack Crime Campaign 44
Crime Prevention Agency 47
defensive strategies 107
education 108
environments of trust 108–110
fear of crime 46–47, 57
Fear of Crime Report 44
guardianship 107
histories of 43
monitoring 107
neighbourhood renewal 48
partnership arrangements 50–52, 55
'private public space' 58
'Probation Service' 43, 46, 62, 185
shopping malls 58
situational crime prevention 43
social exclusion 48
social order 108
Standing Committee on 43
theories of crime 42
urban regeneration 46
Crime reduction
see crime prevention
Curfew order 2, 5, 179, 189, 241
electronic monitoring 2, 5, 28, 30,
171, 177, 241
experimental schemes 30, 171
Custody 117
alternatives to 1, 3
intermittent 22, 23, 27
level of use of 2–3, 29, 44, 138, 241

replacement of 4, 17
suspended sentences 4

Day centres 2, 22, 26
Deferred sentences 22
Desert-based sentencing 2
    desert model 4
Detention and Training Order 60
Detention centres 20, 25, 113
Disqualification 22, 32
    see also forfeiture
    benefits 32
    driving 30
Domestic violence 103
Drugs
    dealers 204–205
    Drug Abstinence Order 2
    Drug Treatment and Testing Order
    2, 5, 120, 127, 241
    HIV 128
    partnership arrangements 49
    re-offending 71
    testing 176
    use of 22, 81, 120, 128, 129, 134

Economic regeneration 46
    see also urban regeneration
    partnership arrangements 49
    quangos 54
Effective Practice Initiative 7
Electronic monitoring
    see electronic tagging
Electronic tagging 1, 27, 33, 103, 169–
    172, 247
    see also curfew orders
    community orders 2, 5, 97
    curfew 241
    human rights 148
    private sector 171
Ethnic minorities 69
European Convention on Human
    Rights 147
Exclusion Order 2

Fines 22

default 30, 171
electronic tagging 171
unit fines 28, 29, 117
Forfeiture 22, 32
    drug profits 32
    football supporters 32

Gender differences 149–150
    see also women
    pro-social modelling 152
Government
    local 49
    national 53
    quangos 54

Hostels 20
    approved probation 95
Howard Houses
    see attendance centres and
    detention centres
Human rights 11, 161

Intermediate punishment 201
Intermediate sanctions 18
Intermediate treatment 21, 25
    see also community penalties
    centres 26

Joint Prison Probation Accreditation
    Panel 178
'justice model' terminology 26
Juveniles
    see young offenders

Legitimacy of authority 101–102

Magistrates 16, 30, 31
Managerialism 33, 51, 59
May Enquiry 24
Mentally disturbed offenders 21
Morgan Report 44, 48, 50
Motivational interviewing 121
Multi-agency working
    see partnership arrangements

Neighbour nuisance
  see anti-social behaviour
'Nothing works' 4, 7, 67, 68

Offenders
  accountability 146
  community safety 217
  crimogenic needs 79
  damage to 129
  female 21, 155–156
  human rights 147
  in communities 135–136
  persistent 227–228, 236
  pro-social modelling 152
  reasoning skills 68
  rehabilitation 137
  restorative justice 216
  risk reduction 137
  social environment 70, 236
  supervision of 217
  victims relation to 135–137
Offending 42–49
  behaviour 69, 153, 185
  cognitive-behavioural programmes
  67
  harm due to 129–130

Parents
  parenting orders 158–160
  support for 160
Parole 19, 201–203
  community safety 213
Partnership arrangements 10, 42, 44,
  45, 49–51
  community safety 48
  economic regeneration 49
  efficiency 51
  evaluation of 50–51
  funding 49
  local authorities and the police 48
  local government 49
  managerialism 54, 61
  probation and prison services 59–60
  quangos 49
Policing

zero tolerance 48
Prisoners
  assessment of 234–235
  compliance 100
  harm to 130–131
  re-offending 233
  resettlement 71, 111, 185, 192, 232
Prison population 4, 24, 26–27
Prison reform 227
Prisons
  disorder 101
  incentives and earned privileges
  105
  legitimacy of authority 103
  offender behaviour courses 234–235
  technology 169
Prison service 3, 12
  accredited programmes 185
Probation
  accommodation 122
  accredited probation programmes
  68, 97
  community safety 46, 126, 139, 213,
  244
  completion of programmes 118–119
  crime prevention 43, 46, 126
  employment 122
  history 16, 17, 19–35, 169, 238
  intensive probation schemes 29
  in the USA 201
  programme accreditation 186
  pro-social modelling 73–77, 121,
  147, 151–153, 245
Probation Orders 1, 2, 22, 25
  see Community Rehabilitation
  Order
  as a sentence of the court 5, 28
  breach of 119
  hostels 95–96
  incentives 120
  officers 16
  special conditions 2
Probation Service 3, 28, 33
  accredited programmes 185, 235
  actuarial risk assessment 172–173

aftercare of prisoners 21, 72
and custody 139
and prison service 33, 59–60
coerced supervision programmes 138, 140
cognitive-behavioural programmes 68–70, 97, 121, 153–157, 177, 185
communities 133
community support 135
computerisation 169
Crown Prosecution Service 127
development 245
Drug Action Teams 126
electronic tagging 169–172
group programmes 68
harm minimisation 131–135, 139
in the USA 206–207
legitimate authority 76, 246
management of 5–6
modernity 110–111
monitoring 184
national service 3, 180, 242
national standards 5, 29, 147, 186, 241, 247
partnership arrangements 73, 126–127, 131–134, 139, 140, 244
police, relationship with 134–135
prisons 127
prison welfare 21
reporting 174
risk 188–189
structure 243
technology 168–175
training 33, 178
value of 206
victim support 127, 131
voluntary sector agencies 135
'what works' 117–118, 194
Property offences 29
Public safety
    see community safety
Punishment in the community 1, 34

Racial differences 149
    cognitive-behavioural programmes 157
    ethnic minorities 69
    pro-social modelling 152
    risk assessment 188
Referral Order 10, 11. 97, 113
    Youth Offender Panel 10, 11
Rehabilitation 30, 31, 203
    see also re-offending
    cognitive-behavioural programmes 67–68, 122, 153–157
    community context 122, 184
    criminogenic needs 8
    effectiveness 4
    meta-analytical studies 7, 67, 122, 1554
    methods 8
    non-custodial measures 18
    normative compliance 120
    offenders 137–138
    prisons 233
    Probation Orders 28
    probation service 118
    programmes 9, 67
    programmes in the community 8
    re-offending 118
    reparative justice 196
    response 8
    restorative justice 195
    risk 187
    social environment 80
    treatment 4, 8
    value to the community 195
    victims' interests 32
'Relational damage' 129
Re-offending 2, 6, 7, 69
    cognitive skills programme 153–157
    community penalties 88, 228
    community safety 203
    Community Service 77–78, 245
    custody 78
    drug use 71–72
    employment 71–72, 80
    fair sentencing 78
    harm minimisation 128
    hostels 95–96

money 71
prison 232
pro-social modelling 74–75
reduction of 195, 230, 241
rehabilitation 118
restorative justice 192, 230–231
risk of 71
self-identity 73
social environment 70–71, 75. 81
training 80
Reparation 6
Reparation Order 2, 11
Restorative justice 11, 129, 184, 192,
200–225, 246
community safety 208–211
conferences 229
definition 207–208
in the USA 208
Risk
actuarial risk assessment 172–173
assessment 184, 187
discrimination 188
environments 56
factors 61, 157
management 7, 34
mental disorder 133
offending 243
principle 7
prisoners 234
reduction 5
re-offending 71
sentencing 190

Scientific positivism 98
Sentencing
community justice 191
community safety 218
flexible 190–191
just deserts 190
policy 186
Social differences
pro-social modelling 152
Social enquiry reports 27
Socialisation 91
Social order 59, 90, 243

Social Services Departments 21
Social structure 41
Social theory 56
Special activities 2
Statement of National Objectives and
Priorities (SNOP) 26, 34, 43
'Supervised activity requirement'
25
Supervision orders 25
Suspended sentences 20, 24, 31
supervision order 2, 20

Technology 2, 12, 41, 168–182
see also electronic tagging and
CCTV
assessment 2
changes 56
drug testing 5, 176
supervision 2, 174–175
telephones

Urban regeneration 46

Victims
community safety 216
compliance 91
offender mediation 11
offenders, relationship to 135
Probation Service 127
recovery 136–137
reparation 6
responses 136
restorative justice 6, 137,
214–216
rights of 215
support 32, 127
young offenders 97

'What works' initiative 6–8, 117,
217–218, 244–245
community service 79
justice 184–187
probation 2, 67, 122
restorative justice 217–218
'what works and why' 59

Women
  cognitive-behavioural techniques 70, 154–155
  crime 94
  custody 25
  fear 57
  offenders 21
  non-custodial sentences 28
  prisoners 155
  risk factors 157, 188
  social environment 71
  victimisation 155
Wootten Report 22
Young offenders

  Action Plan Order 2
  crime 26
  custody 9, 25
  electronic tagging 171
  persistent 9
  reparation 6
  referral orders 97
  restorative justice 97
  social circumstances 9
Younger Report 23, 34
Youth Justice Board 10
Youth Offender Panel 10, 244
Youth Offending Teams 10